The World Student Christian Federation, 1895–1925

The World Student Christian Federation, 1895–1925

Motives, Methods, and Influential Women

Johanna M. Selles

PICKWICK *Publications* · Eugene, Oregon

THE WORLD STUDENT CHRISTIAN FEDERATION, 1895–1925
Motives, Methods, and Influential Women

Pickwick Publications
An Imprint of Wipf and Stock Publishers
199 W. 8th Ave., Suite 3
Eugene, OR 97401

www.wipfandstock.com

ISBN 13: 978-1-60899-508-0

Cataloging-in-Publication data:

Selles, Johanna M.

    The World Student Christian Federation, 1895–1925 : motives, methods, and influential women / Johanna M. Selles.

    xviii + 294 p. ; 23 cm. Includes bibliographical references and index.

    ISBN 13: 978-1-60899-508-0

    1. World Student Christian Federation — History. 2. Women missionaries — History. 3. College students in missionary work — History — 19th century. 2. College students in missionary work — History — 20th century. 4. Student Volunteer Movement for Foreign Mission — History. I. Title.

BV2360 S45 2011

Manufactured in the U.S.A.

To Renata

Contents

Photographs

Foreword

IT IS HARD TO think of a more relevant exercise than this splendid critical examination of Christian work on the university campuses of the world between 1895 and 1925. In an increasingly secular and multi-religious world, individuals, institutions, and movements that bear Christian witness on campus today are under fierce scrutiny and review, if not outright opposition. Or, more likely in the West, indifference. All the more reason then that we should be aware of the history and contributions of students on campuses around the world to the ecumenical movement, as we move into a most uncertain future. As George Santayana wrote, "Those who can't remember the past are condemned to repeat it."

The story of the ecumenical movement as expressed in the World Student Christian Federation has usually been told in the past by focusing on the strong *male* leadership that brought it into being: John R Mott, Robert Speer, J. H. Oldham, Nathan Soderblom, Hendrick Kraemer. This book focuses on the significant and central contribution of *women*, as they struggled to make those contributions most scholars have missed.

Further, the story has often been told institutionally, rather than as a movement, with attention first and foremost on the new organizations that arose as expressions of ecumenism: such as The International Missionary Council; Inter-Church Aid; the Churches Commission on International Affairs. These are all important as visible signs of the continuity of ecumenism, but this book adds to those understandings by emphasizing and documenting the work of lay people in the movement that preceded and created such institutions. Intriguing letters are quoted, tensions are acknowledged, and previously little-known ecumenists are introduced into our collective memory.

The book documents the establishment of student relief for refugees; the move from a denominational focus to ecumenism; the raising up of lay and indigenous leadership; the move from evangelization to inter-faith; the emphasis on education and Bible study in a new key; all of which are issues for the contemporary ecumenical movement. The author tells us the ecumenical story of resilience and adaptation by students in Russia, Poland, Germany, Japan, Sweden, and China as they collectively created a worldwide vision of the gospel that the churches could not ignore.

"They had their being once, and left a place to stand on."

—Al Purdy-Robin Mills (Circa 1842)

Lois Wilson, Chair of the WSCF Canada†

---

† The Very Reverend The Honorable Dr. Lois Wilson has served as the SCM President, Manitoba, Canada (1943–1947); the Moderator of the United Church of Canada (1980–1982); the President of the World Council of Churches (1983–1990); an Independent Senator, Canada (1998–2002); and Chair of WSCF Canada (2006–present).

Preface

WHEN I PUBLISHED MY dissertation in 1996, a fruitful era of scholarship in women's studies and in the history of higher education had been underway. My dissertation supervisor, Alison Prentice, as well as other scholars at the Ontario Institute for Studies in Education, University of Toronto, were active participants in an ongoing reinterpretation of North American economic, political, social, and religious history.

My dissertation was a reflection of this drive to recover the "lost" dimension of educational history by looking at women's education sponsored by one Protestant denomination. After graduation, women chose careers including teaching, family, involvement in service work and church, voluntary associations, and missions.

Several Victoria graduates pursued work in international settings. Rose Cullen, who worked in a student foyer in Paris, later joined her husband Rev. E. Wallace as a China missionary. What type of involvement did educated women like Cullen have in regions like China, India, and Africa, and how did their educational experience at university and their own experience of attending university and belonging to student clubs like the YWCA and the Student Volunteer Movement (SVM) affect their work overseas?

The World Student Christian Federation (WSCF), formed in 1895, preceded the Canadian Student Christian Movement (SCM) which formed in 1921. The first two and a half decades of the WSCF established it as an organization with several permanent staff members who provided continuity and contact between faculty, government officials, religious leaders, and business interests in the countries in which the student movement evolved. Staffers such as Mott, Oldham, and Rouse established the policy of the federation and communicated with volunteer secretaries in countries around the world. These early decades were marked by expansion and outreach—attempting to encourage national student movements in countries which had none or to urge those in existence to federate with the WSCF. The early years of the WSCF were focused on extending the Christian faith, evangelizing those who were outside that faith, and building a worldwide movement of students who shared that faith.

Educational connections formed dynamic connections as foreign scholars were sponsored to study in the West and then returned to become leaders in their own countries. New programs, schools, and affiliations were forged between Western universities and other countries. Returning missionaries, teachers, university faculty, and healthcare professionals brought the "foreign" world that they had experienced to the curriculum and encouraged others to follow in their footsteps.

Women WSCF secretaries or Y workers found themselves in situations of world conflict and were not silent. Much to the consternation of head-office officials, women secretaries spoke out when they saw oppression and worked to improve situations for refugee and foreign students. Although not considered key players in the diplomatic and foreign history of the late nineteenth and early twentieth century, women secretaries in the student movement played the role of diplomats in significant ways, before that role was increasingly professionalized and largely reserved for males.

Student secretaries and faculty participants developed expertise in native languages and culture prior to the widespread work of cultural anthropologists, with their claims to scholarship in cross-cultural work less affected by the conversional agenda that had become associated with missions. Some women preferred to work for the student movement and the federation since it did not have the connection with denominational missionary agencies.

Although women graduates of overseas assignments with the student movement in the decades leading up to the post-Second World War generation became leaders in their communities and congregations, they did not achieve leadership in government or university presidencies until many decades later. Unfortunately, their involvement in North American society in a variety of ways has been little understood. Leadership skills and international knowledge gained in the student movement returned to the domestic scene in a variety of ways.

I found unexpected connections and influences from my own childhood. Vaguely remembered stories about my mother's pre-Second World War involvement in the international scout movement; my father's participation as a university student in the Netherlands Student Christian

Movement; my uncle's medical posting to New Guinea after the war; my brother's unforgettable Summer with Crossroads Africa in Kenya in 1965 formed part of a coherent whole when considered in the context of Christian internationalism. Indeed my own visit to Sri Lanka under the auspices of the World University Service of Canada (WUSC) was undoubtedly shaped by the stories and photographs of family volunteerism abroad.

Although I had previously viewed these memories as a bundle of unrelated experiences, I wondered about the formation of global consciousness within families, denominations, communities, and universities. Student voluntary groups of the nineteenth and early twentieth centuries created a culture which valued mission and service and the deepening of personal faith. The student movement created leaders who would empower other individuals to carry forward the vision.

The vision was shaped through educational methods including small groups, mentoring, study materials, and personal outreach. The early ladies' colleges, such as Mount Holyoke, and men's colleges, such as Amherst, had single-sex missionary societies that studied the biographies of missionaries and sought to emulate their lives. The YMCA and YWCA created a college branch that provided men and women with leadership training, educational materials, and possibilities of service at home and abroad. Later, missions and service organizations at coeducational universities brought male and female students together (certainly part of their appeal) to study missions and organize service. The significance of that activity and its influence on later generations of international work, diplomacy, regional and area studies, religious studies, and ecumenism, seems to be underplayed by marginalizing such involvement under the category "missions" or "clubs."

I hope that this work will contribute to a continuing conversation on the significance of student voluntary movements. Studying the contribution of student voluntary societies requires a willingness to examine the work of women within them as individual and influential outside the official and usually male leadership of the federations and associations for which they worked. Such an enterprise will require creative interpretations in the silence and absence of records and "between the lines" readings of polite discourse in the nineteenth and early twentieth century. Second, this understanding will require an interdisciplinary approach that connects the identity of students working for the WSCF with their deepest motivations, as well as with their allegiances to larger forces that shaped their work, including national and imperial motivations.

There are several WSCF member countries whose stories are not included in this book, despite the presence of a thriving student movement. Student movements in the Netherlands, Italy, Romania, Latin America, India, and Mexico have been excluded due to certain limits in creating a narrative with the available materials. In addition, the North American student movement has been intentionally de-emphasized to focus on Europe and Asia. There were, however, active student movements and deeply committed student secretaries in all these countries and current work on women missionaries, teachers, and healthcare workers are expanding our understanding.

The encounter with the "other" that formed the basis of the expansion of the Christian student movement challenged the motivations and values of both colonized and colonizer. In the contemporary university, people from around the world make contact in the learning environment, yet understanding and intercultural exchange cannot occur without a deep commitment to hospitality and fellowship which nurtures something greater than mere tolerance. The extension of that hospitality and fellowship by women secretaries under the auspices of the World Student Christian Federation forms the focus of this book.

Acknowledgments

A RMED WITH BACHELOR'S DEGREES, teaching certificates, nursing and medical qualifications, WSCF secretaries travelled to student fields around the world and in many cases found themselves in the midst of social and political change in countries caught up in revolution and war. Their goal was to extend hospitality and friendship to university students around the world in order to spread the gospel message; they would often graciously admit that they received far more from their hosts than they gave. Their letters home and official reports described optimistic progress, schools opened, camps organized, new leaders trained, and faiths challenged and formed through Bible study, prayer, and lectures. Each context called for different adaptations as they developed their individual styles, negotiating gender, culture, and religious constraints to achieve the intended goal. They were at times homesick, ill, frustrated, even angry, but the majority ultimately expressed gratitude for the privilege of meaningful work and international travel.

Despite the obstacles that slowed and sometimes stalled the completion of this book, the very spirit and sense of adventure of these women demanded that the story be completed. Such a moral obligation to the long deceased objects of one's research seems perhaps excessive; however, the informants themselves exerted a claim that was irresistible. Although much of the attention on the student movement has focused on Mott and other male leaders, the women had a story to tell. Witness, for example, the intrepid Grace Saunders, student secretary who worked in Canada, Britain, and Bulgaria. On one of her trips she travelled steerage from Canada back to Europe. On board she apparently "indulged in public controversy with an Anarchist who was attacking Christianity, and amongst other things, marriage, in his addresses on deck." According to the head of the women's department, Grace ascended the tub to answer him in public. (RR to Winnifred Sedgewick, 12 Feb. 1909, WSCF Archives, Box

210–1600, YDS). Such public engagement in support of justice challenged gender expectations of the time.

Martha Smalley, curator at the Yale Divinity School special collections, invited me to work on a short study of three WSCF secretaries—an invitation that encouraged my thinking on their lives and significance. The opportunity to be research fellow at Yale Divinity School in the early 1990s and again in 2009–2010 provided me with a rich community in which to pursue this project. I am grateful as well to the Yale Interdisciplinary Center for Bioethics for providing me with a sabbatical home in 2009–2010. In addition, I am grateful for the continued friendship of Connecticut friends and colleagues at Connecticut Hospice and Yale New Haven Hospital, Yale School of Medicine and Nursing.

I would like to acknowledge the help of a variety of archivists and librarians who provided answers to questions by phone, mail, email, or in person. The staff of Yale Divinity School Library provided me with a place to begin this research and director Paul Stuehrenberg, Curator Martha Smalley, and Archives Assistant Joan Duffy provided information and hospitality in equal measure. I acknowledge the help of the staff of the following archives: Princeton University Archives; Wilberforce University Archives; Smith College Archives; Miss Porters School, Connecticut; Columbia University Archives; Glasgow University; WSCF Archives, Geneva; Hartford Seminary; Springfield College; Silver Lake YMCA Conference Center; Rockefeller Archives; Mount Holyoke University Archives; Yale University Archives; University of Toronto Archives; United Church of Canada Archives; University of Winnipeg Archives; Bryn Mawr Archives. Scholars generously shared thoughts and information including Michael Gauvreau, McMaster University; Ruth Franzén, University of Helsinki; Ian Welch, Australia National University; Mara Patessio, Cambridge University; Ruth Brouwer, University of Western Ontario; Stuart MacDonald, Knox College, Toronto.

The unexpected invitation to join the faculty at Emmanuel College in Toronto in 2003 opened up a new learning and writing environment. The collegiality and support of colleagues and staff have provided inspiration in this and other projects. Balancing the requirements for tenure with the writing of this book provided a considerable challenge that was eased by the energy and humour of my graduate assistants Robert Brewer, Joni Sancken, and Lori Unger-Brandt. Former Principal Peter Wyatt encouraged this project in a variety of ways and I am deeply grateful.

Two opportunities made possible by the college were helpful in imagining the environment of the WSCF. Through the World Council of Churches I participated in two consultations, one in Dunblane, Scotland (2004) and another at Bossey, Switzerland (2008). The chance to experience these ecumenical events with a small group of women from around the world helped recreate the excitement of WSCF work among women. Second, participation in the Oxford-based conference "Competing Kingdoms" (2005) facilitated contact with a variety of scholars whose aim is to re-integrate missionary history into mainstream history.

Although the errors and omissions remain my responsibility, the manuscript benefited from the careful editing and unflagging support of Kate Merriman. My sister lived with this project from the first day to its completion and her lively interest in the "ladies" of the story kept the vision alive. A story after all needs an audience. I thank my siblings for their interest, vocational counselling, writing assistance, and encouragement. One summer week in 2007 at the Williams family cottage outside Emo captured the very spirit of the student movement. In response to my request to use a small corner of their cottage foyer for my early morning work on the WSCF, my brother-in-law set up a folding table, complete with tablecloth and fresh flower arrangements. Similarly, Celeste Roney and the cabin in the Adirondacks turned the task of transcription into pleasure as the view of the lake brought student camps closer to imagination. Such kindnesses embodied the spirit of the WSCF and its travelling secretaries and no doubt did as much to sustain them in the past as it did me in the pursuit of this project. Writing from the sabbatical cabin on the Long Island Sound in Connecticut, I realize that how powerful the role of nature and creation must have been for overworked students who took a respite at a student movement summer camp.

As one secretary, Ruth Zachariah, wrote from India: "I find great joy here in the work of the Student Department. It is indeed a privilege to do this and I desire to use myself and to be used to my fullest extent in this great and important work." (EZ to RR, 23 January 1919, WSCF Archives, box 238–1924, YDS). I too found great joy in working with these stories and acknowledge the privilege of having travelled the world with them on so many early mornings.

RUTH ROUSE

Introduction

IN 1920, RUTH ROUSE travelled to Austria to assess the needs of students in war-torn Vienna. Despite her years of work as head of the Women's Department of the WSCF and extensive travel, this situation was more severe than any she had encountered: she observed that the suffering she witnessed there "remained burnt in my memory as a yet nearer thing to hell."[1]

Although a variety of agencies rushed to respond to the Austrian situation, the needs of students had clearly been overlooked. As a veteran organizer of student groups, and newly charged with the organization of European student relief, Rouse did not hesitate to invite the presidents of the various women students' societies of Vienna University to a meeting in her hotel room. The women leaders, who had never met together before, represented the German National Student Society, two Jewish associations, the Socialist Union, and the Catholic Student Society. Although they admitted frankly that they were not enthused about the meeting, Rouse won their cooperation in composing a request for help that was broadcast worldwide. While acknowledging their diversity, Rouse worked to mediate a unity of purpose, a strategy that had been developed in the WSCF in two and a half decades of pioneering work with the world's students.

The WSCF, as the only worldwide federation of student Christian movements in existence at the time, was in a good position to send out a successful international SOS to forty countries on behalf of Vienna's students. The mission of the WSCF was fuelled by a global vision known as Christian internationalism. In the case of the WSCF, students were the chosen agents for the proposed dissemination of Christian friendship and for the establishment of the Lord's dominion throughout the earth. Robert Wright's study of Christian internationalism in Canada describes its origin in late nineteenth-century evangelical Protestantism; by the

---

1. Rouse, *Rebuilding Europe*, 17–30.

1920s and 30s it was interpreted by mainline Protestant denominations in Canada as the belief that Christ embodied the ideals required for a new Christian international order.[2]

The WSCF vision was born in evangelical outreach but underwent a transformation that led it to a more ecumenical stance toward other denominations, world religions, and contact with non-Christians. As historian Hans-Ruedi Weber argues, internationalism results in recognition of separation and distinction between member countries; by contrast, ecumenism affirms equality among members and strives to recognize that all have gifts, none are dominant, and together they can achieve a higher purpose. Ecumenism results in a "vision which commits," demanding a transformation or conversion that calls the individual, the church, and all of society to a new way of seeing. Action and work are then directed toward a unity among the whole of humanity.[3] The ecumenism that developed in the WSCF was derived from face-to-face contact with the "other" and recognition of the shared humanity with that other despite differences in language, belief, appearance, or values. In moving toward ecumenism, the WSCF transcended binary oppositions of male/female; East/West and opened the possibility of a third space for human encounter.[4]

As one of the first worldwide organizations to attempt to link national student movements into a federation, the WSCF pioneered in countries where such international relationships had previously been inconceivable. Riding the wave of increased attention to and involvement in higher education, the WSCF took advantage of increased travel and communication possibilities at the end of the nineteenth century, as well as a Western curiosity about other parts of the world. Steamship and rail travel allowed WSCF leaders and student secretaries to visit or work in countries that had previously been much less accessible. Attendance at international meetings or travel home for furloughs allowed secretaries to participate in the creation of a global vision. Telegraphy enabled communication between individuals and between student groups extending participation beyond the moment of a conference or an event.

Instant communication facilitated the creation of a global identity and belonging. Communication between national movements allowed

2. Wright, *World Mission*, 1991.

3. Weber, *Asia,* 44–45.

4. English, "Third-Space," 85–100.

for comparison and challenge, as in the case of the message sent from students in Japan to the Northfield Conference in 1889. When the following telegram was read from Kyoto—"Make Jesus King, Five hundred students, Wishard"—the delegates were galvanized into a fever pitch of enthusiasm for the development of YMCA missionary work in Japan. The enthusiastic response, according to Mott's biographer, was one factor in the eventual establishment of the WSCF.[5]

Technological change and globalization allowed for an increased dynamism in relationships between countries and between individuals. This impetus from the West set in motion complex interactions requiring equally complex negotiations. Presuppositions long unquestioned were challenged by churches in other parts of the world: the meaning of church, denomination, theology; practices such as Bible reading and prayer; the nature of leadership and power. New churches questioned constraints placed on them by Western leaders and administrative structures and challenged the funding and control that left them in a secondary role. Co-operative relationships between countries with histories of domination and colonization required the confrontation of racism, for example, between Chinese and Japanese and between white Americans and African-Americans. A growing recognition that the problem is "us" at the meeting at Oxford in 1909 grew into the realization at Peking in 1922 that repentance and reconciliation were required.[6]

The notion of a global Christian student federation caught the imaginations of students, faculty, and wealthy industrialists such as John D. Rockefeller (1839–1937) and Cyrus McCormick (1809–1884) who provided financial backing to their friend John R. Mott for travel and student movement work, a generosity that was not disconnected from capitalist expansion into missionary fields. Starting with a handful of interested students and organizers in 1896, the WSCF grew to unite national movements representing 2,305 local associations with a total membership of 156,071 students and faculty in forty nations.[7] (See chapter 3 for the history of the WSCF).

Despite the involvement of so many students and faculty at universities and colleges around the world, the Federation has received scant scholarly attention. Ruth Rouse's historical work on the organization

---

5. Hopkins, *Mott*, 70.

6. Weber, *Asia*, 85.

7. Setran, *College Y.*

provides a comprehensive overview by an insider in the movement.[8] Biographical work on John R. Mott reveals the intricate connections between the WSCF and the Y and its supporters.[9] Monographs on the WSCF commemorating anniversaries have also appeared as reminders of the heritage and continuing existence of the WSCF.[10] Because such studies already exist, this book does not seek to provide a complete history of the WSCF or associated organizations.[11]

Early histories and biographies of the federation and national member organizations, such as Tissington Tatlow's history of the British SCM and Ruth Rouse's history of the WSCF, were largely written by insiders who had played significant leadership roles. Biographies of the early founders of these movements, Luther Wishard and Robert Wilder, for example, provide insight but lack a critical or contextual evaluation of the contributions of these men.[12] More recent biographies of leaders such as Richard Morse, John R. Mott, and others provide useful accounts of their multiple commitments to a variety of organizations, their impossibly demanding travel schedules, and the friendships with power elites such as the Rockefellers. Such contacts supported the internationalist agendas of the WSCF and sustained implicit economic agendas to their benefit.[13]

These works tend to obscure the connections between the organization and the context of higher education that fostered its growth. In addition, there is a tendency to view voluntary organizations in isolation from each other, without realizing how the membership and leadership often overlapped. Publication of public lectures, study topics, conference proceedings, and eyewitness accounts created a shared culture of voluntary movements that made the borders permeable. As a federation, the WSCF combined features of the different members affiliated with it. Thus its character is complex and contains a degree of diversity that varies with national context. This flexibility provided resilience to the organization that allowed it to adapt to changing circumstances. Such adaptations, whether planned or unanticipated, are missing from accounts

8. Ruth Rouse, *WSCF*.

9. Mathews, *Mott*; Hopkins, *Mott*.

10. Potter, *Seeking and Serving*.

11. See, for example, Hopkins and Rouse.

12. See, for example, Ober, *Exploring a Continent*; Braisted, *In This Generation*.

13. See Wheeler, *Man Sent From God*.

that document the years of growth and pioneering, followed by years of decline and retreat. The WSCF provided a powerful model to other organizations and international bodies and thus merits further study.

The absence of critical work on the WSCF is a fascinating omission among the proliferation of studies on student groups and activities. Student-focused work has provided a corrective to traditional accounts of higher education that focused on an institution or on the leadership of an institution. Institutional histories were often created by insiders or those who had been close to the project and thus lacked a critical perspective.[14] A narrow focus on one type of schooling or one location, such as elite New England colleges, effectively excluded normal schools, technical schools, and community colleges from the narrative.[15]

Recent academic work provides a more critical understanding of the relationship between institutions of higher education and the social environment in which they operated. Neil Semple, in his study of Victoria University principal Samuel Nelles (1823–1887), describes the intellectual currents and the religious responses to them within the context of Victoria University and the University of Toronto. Similarly, historian William Westfall examines the social, intellectual, and cultural assumptions that inspired the Anglican drive to found Trinity College, Toronto.[16] In his study of the intellectual history of English Canadian culture in the Victorian period, historian Michael Gauvreau portrays the encounter of Methodist and Presbyterian churches in the nineteenth century with modern thought. Rather than dismiss their intellectual traditions as defeated by contact with Darwinism, Gauvreau argues in favour of the resilience of Protestant evangelical traditions until the 1920s.[17] In A. B. McKillop's study of higher education in Ontario, the denominational impulses that gave rise to colleges like Victoria and Trinity are argued to work toward a common purpose, namely, to preserve the Anglo-Canadian social order.

Student life has provided historians with an insight into academic culture and the social and intellectual context within which the academy operated. Early examples of such a focus include J. B. Reynolds' study of

14. See, for example, Burwash, *History of Victoria College*; Sissons, *History of Victoria University*; Eisenmann, "Reclaiming Religion"; Nidiffer, "Poor Historiography," 321–36.

15. Ogren, *American State Normal School*.

16. Semple, *Faithful Intellect*; Westfall, *Founding Moment*.

17. Gauvreau, *Evangelical Century*.

student life at Yale (1901) and Clarence Shedd's study of student movements (1934).[18] In Canada, more recent work edited by Axelrod and Reid brings the world of politics, religion, and social change into the understanding and experience of students and demonstrates how students perceived and expressed the conflicts that were part of the modern university.[19] Student experience, both in the classroom and outside, cannot be artificially separated from culture, but provides an excellent insight into the cultural and social expectations and values of the times.

Studies of specific student groups, such as Diana Pederson's work on the YWCA, highlight the involvement of university women in service work.[20] Cathy James's work on settlement houses and Sara V. Burke's research on social service at the University of Toronto build on that understanding to show how gender, service, and higher education intersect.[21] Women graduates used the experiences gained during higher education to develop careers in teaching, social work, missions, service, church and community work, and health. The connection between higher education and the development of professional identities has recently been explored by Elizabeth Smyth as well as Robert Gidney and Wynn Millar.[22]

The involvement of students in service activities and in voluntary groups thus provided many women with invaluable experience in leadership and co-operation. As historians of women's higher education have indicated, service-oriented club work provided early women graduates an opportunity to practice skills in the field and they often did so as an expression of gratitude for the privilege of their education. Sharon Cook's work on the Women's Christian Temperance Union (WCTU) and Mariana Valverde's work on social reform have increased our understanding of women's role in social reform.[23] By means of their involvement in missionary societies, temperance societies, and social reform groups, women graduates found socially acceptable and morally upright ways to apply their beliefs. Friendship was extended for the redemption of society. The WSCF provided an umbrella for women's reform-

18. See Reynolds, *Two Centuries*. See Shedd, *Two Centuries*, 1934.

19. Axelrod and Reid, *Youth*.

20. Pederson, "YWCA," 20–24.

21. James, "Practical Diversions," 48–66; Burke, *Seeking the Highest Good*.

22. Smyth, *Challenging Professions*. See also Gidney and Millar, *Professional Gentlemen*.

23. Cook, *WCTU*; Valverde, *Age of Light*.

ist work, enabling women to serve and lead in their capacity as student secretaries.

Assumptions about the inevitability of secularization in Protestant higher education have been challenged by George Marsden and others.[24] Building on these histories of higher education and intellectual thought, Catherine Gidney challenges assumptions about the nature of secularization in English Canada by examining the continuing hold of the English Protestant majority in the university from the 1920s to the 1960s. Part of her argument rests on an analysis of student religious organizations on campus.[25] Similarly, David Setran uses the college-based YMCA to demonstrate how students participated in the "construction of a new Christianized world."[26] Student experience in religious organizations has thus proved to be a fruitful source of knowledge in scholarly attempts to understand challenges to the liberal Protestant culture of the university.

As a federation of national student movements, the WSCF in Canada has received little scholarly focus, since scholars have instead studied the organizations that federated with the WSCF. In the late nineteenth century, college Y's attracted many students. Setran estimates that for the United States, the college YMCA had 559 chapters and 31,901 college and university student members. By 1920, YMCA chapters could be found in 764 institutions with a membership of 80,649.[27] In 1914, the Canadian student Y boasted 45 associations with 2500 members.

By creating a Student Christian Movement (SCM) separate from the intercollegiate Y in 1921, Canadian students freed themselves to define an organizational identity separate from the American body and to set an agenda that focused on questions of interest to Canadian students, such as pacifism, industrialization, new immigrants, rural life, the Anglo-French situation, internationalism, and religious matters. The college Y, later the SCM, provided the opportunity to develop national awareness as well as the vision of world citizenship. For countries such as Korea, the Y offered opportunities for national development after annexation by Japan. Korean women leaders such as Helen Kim and Mrs Pilley Kim Choi attended the Peking WSCF conference and successfully argued for

24. Marsden, *Soul of the American University*.

25. Gidney, *Long Eclipse*.

26. Setran, *College Y*, 6.

27. Ibid., 4.

the affiliation of Korea to the World's YWCA as an independent association in 1924.[28]

In exploring the history of the WSCF between its inception in 1895 and the beginning of its decline in the 1920s, this book reflects on the organization's growth, influence, and shifting values through examining the experience of student secretaries in the field. Because the perspective of women secretaries is largely absent from the official record of the WSCF, the narrative will include their stories in order to gain a perspective from "inside." This perspective will be used to understand the vision of Christian internationalism and growing ecumenism that was presented by the WSCF as it shifted from a nineteenth-century evangelical Protestant view to a more modern, twentieth-century understanding of its purpose.

The WSCF saw itself as a *world* organization. From the insider's perspective, was this vision workable in the field or was it flawed as a paradigm that sought to be global and inclusive? During the period described (1895–1925), the WSCF set the stage for international friendship and collaboration in a way that was previously unknown and has not been duplicated since. The organization itself served as a powerful model that was replicated in various ways by student groups who chose a more conservative agenda or who catered to different interest groups, denominations, or ethnic groups. Indeed, the federation may have even provided a negative example for those who organized the League of Nations in 1919 and who decided that the "utopian federation model" was not their preferred choice.[29]

Student outreach sponsored by the WSCF involved a culture of hospitality that sought to meet one's neighbor as an equal. The fellowship that was part of student movement culture included private prayer and public prayer (Universal Day of Prayer); individual and small group Bible study; speakers noted for their evangelical charisma or their academic or practical expertise in an area relevant to the Federation. During student vacation months, summer camps and conferences providing guest speakers, study, sport, and play were organized around the world. Such camps had been popular since the early days of the Haystack movement in Massachusetts, where the influence of evangelists like Dwight Moody helped shape the character of the student movement, and in England,

28. Weber, *Asia,* 99.
29. MacMillan, *Paris 1919,* 87.

where the Keswick camps sparked further development of university-based Christian student voluntary groups.

Lay involvement and leadership opened up opportunities for women and other non-ordained individuals. The YM/YWCA encouraged lay people to use their gifts in Christian service, a service that was not identified with a church or mission organization and thereby provided access to countries where they would otherwise not have been welcome.[30]

Just as historians of higher education have recently started including student experience, historians are rediscovering that the rich resources of missionary history can provide valuable insights into the social, political, and religious context of the host countries. The history of the WSCF might include perspectives from religious studies, diplomatic history, Christian and religious education, church and missions history, as well as political and economic history. A broader approach to missions history creates a more nuanced and critical insight into the discipline; recent scholarship has helped us to understand the enthusiastic and creative response of women and women graduates to the call of mission service. Dana Robert argues that the peak of the women's missionary movement was reached by 1910.[31] Patricia Hill estimates that by 1915, more than three million women were on the rolls of forty denominational missionary societies. Women, blocked from ordination, increasingly sought service possibilities as teachers, doctors, nurses, and social workers in the mission field and flocked to denominational and non-denominational opportunities such as positions as women secretaries.[32] WSCF secretaries and international YWCA secretaries had similar motivations to those described for women missionaries who sought, as Ruth Brower has argued, the chance for adventure mingled with the desire to be of service.[33]

The WSCF extended the same rhetoric of the Victorian sanctification of women that had motivated the movement for higher education for women, i.e., to prepare them for their role as mothers. Gradually the need for specific expertise and training included the growing language of sociology and service that replaced ideologies of the nineteenth

---

30. Weber, *Asia,* 96.

31. Robert, *American Women.*

32. Hill, *World,* 4–5.

33. Brower, *New Women for God.*

century.[34] The professionalization that reshaped missionary methods in the early twentieth century was also extended to the methods and training of Y and WSCF secretaries. Summer schools, training schools, and publications urged student leaders to develop methods in organizing and leading that represented advanced techniques in religious pedagogy. Experts from universities such as Columbia Teachers College were invited to Silver Bay YMCA camp to bring the latest theories combining religion and education. As an alternative to ordination programs, many women bound for international work undertook special training in Bible colleges largely modeled on the Chicago Moody Bible College (1887), for example, the Toronto Bible Training College (founded 1894, renamed Ontario Bible College), and schools such as the Hartford School of Missions.[35]

Historians of women missionaries and teachers are thus attempting to move the subject of missionary women from the margins to the centre of historical scholarship.[36] The resources continue to present challenges, though, to the researcher who would seek to fill out the account of white missionaries with the experience of those being missionized.[37] Mara Patessio's work on Japan reminds us that Japanese women were already engaged in educational activities decades before the missionary women arrived, and missionary influence on Japanese women was partly effected by providing a living example of women who were single and engaged in professions outside the home.[38] Although records that provide insight into how missionary teachers and WSCF secretaries were received are scarce, the perspective of those in the host countries must continue to

34. Hill, *World Their Household*, 5.

35. The Hartford School originated with the Springfield, Mass. School for Christian Workers, which admitted female students in 1889. This Bible Normal School moved to Hartford to affiliate with the Seminary in 1902 and renamed the Hartford School of Religious Pedagogy, and later the Hartford School of Religious Education. In 1911, in response to the Edinburgh World Missionary Conference, Hartford established the Hartford School of Missions with specific training in Arabic and Islam as well as other traditions and religions. Online: http://www.hartsem.edu/about/history.htm.

36. See, for example, the website that accompanied the recent Competing Kingdoms conference at Oxford in April 2006 http://womenandmission.binghamton.edu.

37. Bowie, et. al., *Women and Missions*; Hill, *World*; Graham, *Gender, Culture, Christianity*; and Hunter, *Gospel of Gentility*.

38. The question of impact is a challenge, as the women secretaries and missionaries reports cannot be taken as literal truth of the effect of their work, since these reports were written for a specific readership that expected to hear of success overseas.

challenge all official and unofficial accounts by visitors and workers in such countries. Despite the constraints imposed by the larger political and social context, women found in such work a variety of opportunities for leadership.[39] Yet the story continues to challenge historians to provide a more complete account that does not separate religious motivations from the history of globalization and the various economic and political interest groups that carried their agendas into foreign fields. To an audience accustomed to the careful separation of church from state, or academic inquiry from personal religious belief, this era of federation crossed boundaries where religious leaders were public figures whose presence on diplomatic missions was sanctioned by presidents and recognized by world leaders. As Kinley Brauer indicates, women of the era were ignored by historians of diplomatic history because they could not serve as diplomats or commercial agents, held no elective office, could not vote, and never presented themselves as a self-defined group with a foreign policy agenda. Thus, because scholars considered women only as a group, they missed the significant role women played as individuals.[40]

The goals of the WSCF were packaged in North American and British methods of organization and leadership. How those methods were received in the contexts to which they were important is one subject of this study. As recent work based in postcolonial understandings of gender, race, and missions reminds us, the reception of methods and message is difficult to imagine in the absence of records that clarify the experience of the colonized and missionized individuals. Even in the absence of such records, the historian must be aware of the temptation to view the records of white women colonizers as literal truth, disregarding that such records were narratives that were written to satisfy readers back home, bureaucracies, mission agencies, and male leaders. [41] For example, women WSCF secretaries wrote letters to Ruth Rouse and she selected relevant parts of the text to circulate among members of the Women's Department. Historian Renate Howe notes that for Australian women, the movement was still associated with imperial colonialism.

The founding goal of the WSCF was to evangelize and reach out to students around the world through a global federation. That mission,

39. Howe, "Australian SCM," 311–23.

40. Brauer, " Great American Desert Revisited," 44–78.

41. Haggis, "White Women and Colonialism, 161–89. On the complications of measuring methods and reception, see Hare and Barman, *Good Intentions*.

however, was transformed in the process of reaching around the world. Different strategies were employed that promised the highest rate of success in winning students' confidence in the organization. Aggressive evangelism in the early years in China contrasted to the cautious incursions into Russian student politics in the early twentieth century. Students were targeted as being future world leaders. Experiments in conversation between denominations led to the recognition that dialogue with non-Christians and other faiths was also essential. As new conversations opened, new obstacles also appeared in the forms of sexism, racism, anti-Western feelings, and obstacles related to caste or class structures. If the enemy originally appeared to be clothed in heathenism and lack of faith, in the twentieth century the enemy was clothed in garments of nationalism and materialism.

By the 1920s, the gradual decline of interest in organizations such as the WSCF and the YMCA can be attributed to a variety of factors including changing attitudes toward missions, decline of the Christian-based service motive, disillusionment following the war, and multiplication of other voluntary organizations. Disenchanted conservative students eventually found new homes in such organizations as the Inter Varsity Christian Fellowship, Navigators, and Campus Crusade. In addition, the college voluntary movement was further subdivided by new organizations that formed around specific tasks, sports, or interests, rather than voluntary international service. The increased diversification of professional services in the university environment left organizations like the YMCA excluded from providing services that had traditionally been within their mandate.[42] Generations of students had various foci—local contexts, professional success, and personal gratification—as opposed to a vision of service to the world. The climate of such commitment reflected the values of the culture as a whole; indeed, missionary and international commitments are often enculturated by home, school, and faith groups.

A visit to a club day on today's campus reveals that universities and colleges now offer a myriad of voluntary and extracurricular groups representing the diversity of race, ethnicity, gender, religious affiliation, and identity-based affiliation of the student population. And then there are groups organized around sports, hobbies, service, or academic discipline. It is easy to forget that during the period in question, leaders in a

42. See Setran, *College Y,* ch. 3.

student generation were likely to have been formed through the Y and/ or the WSCF and to have been present at the same events or to have heard the same speakers. This cohort of Y and WSCF members presumably created a lifelong network of involvement in politics, international work, and faith communities.

New light is shed on the history of the WSCF through the focus on the work of the student secretaries, mostly but not exclusively women. Women secretaries in the field gained expertise in local conditions, languages, and organizational skills, and operated quite independently at times as diplomats, teachers, and professionals in bringing the notion of Christian internationalism to a variety of contexts. Their work was sometimes at odds with official positions and created conflict and disillusionment. Their experiences help one to understand the WSCF as an organization and its adaptation over time to different challenges and changes in the local and national contexts. In addition, women secretaries developed new methods in the field that pushed the organization away from more traditional missionary work to a pattern of working ecumenically.[43]

The re-examination of the experience of student movement secretaries is not merely an attempt to add their voices to the official record, but also to re-engage with the questions of the overall significance of the organization and the creative contributions it made despite a decline in growth and expansion after the First World War. It would be a mistake to equate success only with growth and development, and underestimate the influence, both productive and destructive, of the well-intended efforts of women working for the WSCF. The narratives of women secretaries that form the primary sources for this work are often interrupted as their career with the federation ends, or their health deteriorates, or war interrupts their correspondence. Although attempts have been made to follow the narrative thread of individual lives after their posting as student secretary, such accounts are often left frustratingly incomplete. Furthermore, the records, though fragmentary, provide evidence that tensions existed between individuals and the organization for which they worked, and these will be explored. The strategy of focusing on the experience of secretaries, however, excludes many individuals whose contributions were no less important, but whose narrative proved difficult to construct on the basis of available records. Thus the stories of

43. See also Robert, *American Women in Mission,* xix.

student movement work in Italy, Romania, United States, Latin America, and India are not included here but deserve further research. It is my hope that this work will contribute to the ongoing telling and re-telling of the story of the WSCF and will encourage others to pursue different aspects, retrieve new papers, and draw different conclusions.

Chapter 1 presents the history of student voluntary movements in higher education during the period when such groups and universities were restricted to males. Chapter 2 looks at the formation of women's missionary organizations and voluntary organizations such as the YWCA and SVM that contributed to the establishment of the WSCF, even though the contributions of women have largely been ignored in favour of the male contributions to the federation. In chapter 3 the founding and the structure of the WSCF including its mission and methods is described. Chapter 4 focuses on the pioneering work of Ruth Rouse and her colleagues in Russia in the early 1900s. Contact with Jewish and radical student groups, as well as Orthodox students and authorities, provided an early training ground for Rouse and others that served her well as the WSCF expanded into European universities. Chapter 5 studies the effects of the First World War on student life in Switzerland through the work of American student secretary Elizabeth Clark. Chapter 6 highlights the effect of war on the methods of the WSCF in Poland through the work of Canadian William Rose and his wife Emily. In chapter 7 the WSCF in France is seen through the experiences of French student secretaries Suzanne Bidgrain and Suzanne de Dietrich. Chapter 8 explores the federation in Japan and the experience of Michi Kawai, who served as a leader in the Japanese Y and the WSCF and eventually opened her own girls' school. Chapter 9 focuses on the work of the WSCF in Sweden. Finally, chapter 10 examines the role of student movements in China.

Many women students viewed their education as a privilege that motivated them to take part in global support for the expansion of higher education and the fostering of an international Christian vision of friendship and understanding. According to Ruth Rouse, the service motive was present from the beginning in the belief that to be redeemed meant that one became the agent of redemption in the nation and in the world.[44] It was not merely gratitude, but a religiously inspired vision, that motivated WSCF secretaries to work for women in other countries who, they believed, deserved to taste all the advantages of higher education.

44. Rouse, *WSCF*, 84.

Rouse, meeting with students that night in Vienna, urged student leaders to organize around a global vision of service. Although that vision served the purpose of generating assistance for students in postwar Europe, its fundamental basis shifted in the decades since the founding at Vadstena Castle. Through the stories of women secretaries, this book will examine how the WSCF shifted and adapted to changing social, political, and religious contexts in the pre- and post-World War I world.

PART ONE

Student Christian Movements

1

Sowing the Seeds

Precursors to the World Student Christian Federation

MALE STUDENT SOCIETIES ON UNIVERSITY CAMPUSES

IN AN EDITORIAL WRITTEN in 1831 promoting the Methodist Upper Canada Academy, future principal Egerton Ryerson (1803–1882) explained that the academy would be a Christian but non-sectarian institute of higher education. Ryerson claimed that the school would produce habits of intellectual labor and activity, skills in time management, physical health, virtuous principles, and Christian morals.[1] A spectator at the exhibition in 1841, where students delivered essays on various subjects, attested to the truth of Ryerson's claim: the college, he observed, cultivated true intellect; refined the tastes and feelings of its students; induced habits of industry, order, and diligence; and "imbued their minds with true religion and sound morality."[2]

Another promoter of higher education, Noah Porter (1811–1898), Yale's president from 1871 to 1886, argued that college was a place to learn habits that would foster growth in later life.[3] The administration of colleges and universities, in both Canada and the United States, acknowledged that in addition to a solid liberal arts curriculum and good teaching, the overall purposes of education could be complemented

---

1. Ryerson, quoted in Putman, *Ryerson,* 70. Education was also tied to the stability and support for good government, since "an educated people are always a loyal people to good government."

2. Burwash, *History of Victoria College,* 88.

3. Marsden, *Soul of the American University,* 125.

by extracurricular activities in pursuit of the development of manly Christian character.[4]

This manly character would be shaped in the matrix that was college life. Teachers and staff served as exemplars. Extracurricular clubs often employed faculty advisors who modeled leadership and lent authority to the proceedings. Ryerson's Upper Canada Academy, for example, had a Philatelic Society by 1838, which seems to have been a literary club in which professors were made honorary members and the president was one of the school's masters.[5] Students normally lived within the confines of the college buildings. Attendance at worship services and other pious practices were compulsory.

However, a growing sense of student autonomy in the mid to late nineteenth century resulted in students having more control over their clubs. In fact, although the extracurricular activity was intended to fully complement the work of the curriculum, it also provided opportunities for resistance and creative subversion of the norms imposed by higher education. In male colleges, such creative subversion was often tolerated as expected masculine behavior.

College life, then, provided rich soil for the planting and growth of early student religious societies. They developed along three lines: theological societies; those emphasizing devotional life and practical evangelistic activity (or gathered in opposition to gambling and intemperance); and missionary societies, including both foreign and home missions.[6] Such religious student clubs formed a pre-organizational matrix or network that facilitated the eventual establishment of a student movement that would transcend local contexts.[7] Local college clubs were thus an

4. Ibid., 5.

5. Burwash, *History of Victoria College*, 47.

6. Although the concerns of the societies were quite similar, one exception was Gettysburg College, where the Society of Inquiry on Missions voted in 1835 to educate a pious young black man to educate free blacks in the country. They chose Daniel Alexander Payne who became Bishop of the African Methodist Episcopal Church and President of Wilberforce University (founded 1856).

7. See McFadden, *Golden Cables*. McFadden argues that the origins of nineteenth century feminism lie in the existence of a pre-organizational matrix or network of international experiences and relationships which then served as the basis upon which an autonomous movement and explicit feminist consciousness could later develop. I have applied the notion of a matrix to the men's clubs that preceded the network of women's relationships but functioned in a similar way to create conditions conducive to the organization of a worldwide university movement that became coeducational.

important step in creating later inter-university, national, and world student organizations.

Historian Clarence Shedd attributes the formation of religious clubs in the United States to the influence of Cotton Mather (1663–1728), Harvard graduate, Puritan minister, and influential writer. Several student clubs existed at Yale between 1706 and 1716; indeed, student religious societies existed in sixteen out of twenty-two colleges founded prior to 1800.[8] Yale boasted one of the earliest clubs, the Yale Moral Society, founded in 1789; Harvard had a similar society founded even earlier in 1785.[9]

At the beginning of the nineteenth century, the influence of materialistic and atheistic philosophies on higher education led students to reject traditional moral and religious standards. Student participation in religious clubs decreased radically. Revivals, such as the Second Great Awakening that began in 1798 and carried on into the first decades of the nineteenth century, re-engaged many students in Christian religion with a corresponding increase in participation in student religious societies in schools such as Andover, Harvard, Dartmouth, Brown, Williams, Bowdoin, and Middlebury.[10] The return to Christian piety was not received hospitably by all, of course; clubs met in private to escape the derision of the less spiritually minded.[11] Although the Dartmouth society met openly, a smaller group called the College Praying Society met weekly in a private room for fear of being disturbed by the "unpenitent."[12] Some clubs resulted in fragmentation of the student body on the basis of faith or common interests such as missions that excluded students without religious interest.

8. Shedd, *Two Centuries,* 5.

9. Distinguished members of this Yale society included Richard C. Morse, 1809; Theodore Dwight, 1813; Theodore Woolsey, 1817; William Bushnell, 1824, and Samuel Porter, 1826. See Shedd, *Two Centuries,* 25. Members had to promise secrecy and its meetings involved discussion of a moral or religious subject. The Moral Society participated in the revival at Yale in 1802 and again in 1812–1813. The last recorded meetings were held in 1861.

10. Van Die notes that some historians consider this movement to have originated in Yale College under the preaching of President Timothy Dwight. See Van Die, *Evangelical Mind.*

11. Shedd, *Two Centuries,* 53.

12. Ibid., 41.

Revivalism resulted as well in renewed social activism on university campuses. From the 1830s until the 1850s, some American student societies focused on such social issues as slavery, temperance, and the "menace" of Unitarianism; Yale, for example, had a temperance society in 1826. At Andover in New Hampshire, discussion of slavery was so intense among students that the trustees and faculty tried to suppress the debate.[13] Conflict between administration and students increased when student clubs grew in number or appeared to undermine the administration's expectations of the seriousness of academic life.

Student clubs were sometimes initiated by a student or a group of students; Williams College student Samuel Mills (1783–1818), for example, led weekly prayer groups in the outdoors away from the college. Mills had experienced a conversion through revivals that were part of the Great Awakening, leading him to perceive a call to missions.[14] During a rainstorm in 1806 his prayer group, including students James Richards, Luther Rice, Gordon Hall, and Adoniram Judson, took shelter under a haystack, a location that inspired their organizational name—the Haystack Group. On that day they focused on prayer for the awakening of missionary interest among students. Influenced by their reading of India missionary William Carey (1761–1834) and his book *An Inquiry into the Obligation of Christians to use means for the Conversion of Heathen*, the group claimed as their watchword the phrase "We can do this if we will." The Haystack group created a more formal organization known as the Society of Brethren in 1810 to focus exclusively on missionary matters.[15] They met regularly for prayer and were bound by an oath of secrecy as they prepared to dedicate their lives to missionary service.

In 1791 the Society of Inquiry on the Subject of Missions at Andover College was formed. Of the 372 students who were members of

---

13. Ibid., 89.

14. Walhstrom, *Creation of a Student Movement*, 24. After an outdoor event called the Haystack Prayer Meeting, this band officially organized in 1808 as the Society of the Brethren. The Society of Brethren transferred to Andover Theological Seminary in 1810 and held its last meeting in 1870. The society never became intercollegiate. The Andover Society of Inquiry on the Subject of Missions was founded in 1811. Wahlstrom notes that from 1811 until the Civil War, scores of religious societies were formed in the colleges. The Philadelphian Society at Princeton, founded in 1825, was one of those groups. None of these societies were able to transcend the boundaries of their colleges and become intercollegiate.

15. Shedd, *Two Centuries*, 49–50.

the Society during the sixty years of its existence, 217 became missionaries. Royal Gould Wilder, Andover alumnus and member of the society, married Mount Holyoke graduate Eliza Smith and under the auspices of the American Board of Commissioners and Foreign Missions left for missionary work in India in 1846.[16] After his retirement he returned to Princeton and provided leadership for a Princeton-based student missions group. Wilder also began a journal called the *Missionary Review* that informed readers about the missionary movement.[17]

By transferring to or continuing studies at other colleges, students were able to spread missionary clubs to other locations; the missionary society at Middlebury College, for example, was founded in this way. Samuel Mills continued his studies in 1809 at Yale with the implicit purpose of organizing a student missionary group. And, while at Yale he was himself influenced by a Hawaiian student, Henry Obookiah (1792–1818), who created a flurry of interest in missionaries to the Pacific.[18]

While a student at Andover Theological Seminary, the intrepid Mills led a small group of students to petition the General Association of Congregational Churches in 1810 to form a sending agency for students who wanted to serve as missionaries. The student group included Adoniram Judson of Brown, Samuel Newell of Harvard, and Samuel Nott, Jr. of Union College. Persuaded by the student appeal, the Association of Congregational Churches formed a Board of Commissioners for

16. Wahlstrom explains that the ABCFM was originally an interdenominational association of mission benefactors. Mainline denominations formed their own mission boards. For example, between 1810 and 1817, Baptist, Methodist, and Episcopalian mission societies were formed. By 1860 the ABCFM became the missionary organization for the Congregational church alone. See Wahlstrom, *Creation of a Student Movement*, 27.

17. When Royal Wilder died suddenly, his wife decided to follow through with their plans to return to the mission field. She sailed for India with her daughter Grace in 1887 and worked there until she died at the age of eighty-eight. See Braisted, *In this Generation*, 40.

18. Obookiah's memoir was a best seller that inspired a great deal of interest in missions to Hawaii. He died of typhus in 1819 while studying at a mission school in Cornwall, Connecticut that had been established by the American Board of Foreign Missions in 1817 to educate youths of "heathen nations." By the second year of the school's existence, attendance had increased from twelve to twenty-four including four Cherokee, two Chocataw, one Abenaki, two Chinese, two Malays, on Bengali, one Hindu, two Marquesans, and three Americans. Online: http://www.cornwallhistoricalsociety .org/foreign_mission_school.htm and http://digital.library.okstate.edu/Chronicles/v00 7p242.html.

Foreign Missions in 1812 that immediately began sending missionaries, including Judson and Newell and their wives, to India and Burma to join William Carey who had been working there since 1793.[19] The difficulties faced by this early group and their heroic response formed part of missionary lore. By 1821 the board of commissioners had sent out seventy-six more missionaries.

These early missionaries faced unending trials and disappointments, but the stories of their lives provided examples of courage and faith for all who read them and for those who continue to read them. The compelling nature of their triumph over all difficulties, even when death was the imminent result, provided powerful narratives of courage and challenged others to a missionary vocation. Both Ann Judson (1789–1826) who died in Burma and Harriet Newell (1793–1812) who died before arriving at a missionary destination after childbirth on board ship, continue to be remembered through their writings. Newell is celebrated as the first martyr to the cause of missions and her memoir, published in 1915, was reprinted almost every year in the twenty-five years following her death.[20] Judson's writings reached an appreciative audience who triumphed in the example of her courage in caring for her husband while he was imprisoned.

Student clubs promoted creative change and pushed the church to develop structures and to help finance the enthusiastic and growing numbers of those who desired to serve as missionaries. The formation of mission boards allowed students to focus on recruitment and preparation, whereas boards took responsibility for the sending.

Because these early colleges were often extremely isolated, with no telegraph, no railroad service, and very slow and infrequent mail, contact between university clubs was limited.[21] Nevertheless, college clubs still managed to keep in touch; a missionary interest group at Princeton, for example, communicated common interests with a similar group at Andover. Participation in an inter-college network of clubs would eventually require a willingness to join student movements that

---

19. See Voelkel, "Great Cloud of Witnesses." No pages. Online: http://www.urbana.org/_articles.cfm?RecordId=899.

20. Porterfield notes that Harriet Newell became a major religious figure in death and no other women in the second decade was so widely eulogized or emulated. Porterfield, *Mary Lyon*, 5.

21. Henkin, *Postal Age*. See also McFadden, *Golden Cables*.

were intercollegiate or trans-denominational; a belonging that would demand recognition of common purpose beyond individual difference. The ability to set aside local and individual differences would eventually contribute to the formation of an inter-denominational and international student Christian movement. Missionary societies, even at this early stage, focused more on the goal of missionary service than on doctrinal differences; this allowed for interdenominational co-operation among students, colleges, missionary boards, and even across gender. In the later decades of the nineteenth century, increased communication would shape student identity and enable affiliation with student movements from a variety of colleges for shared purposes and involvement in a federation.

The travels of individuals in search of advanced education helped disseminate ideas about campus clubs and student life across universities and national borders. The history of Victoria College bears the stamp of such influence. Victoria College's future principal Nathanael Burwash (1839–1918) completed a period of postgraduate studies at both Yale and Garret Biblical Institute in Evanston, Illinois. Another future Victoria principal Samuel Nelles (1823–1887) attended Genessee Wesleyan Academy (1841) in upstate New York and Wesleyan University in Middletown, Connecticut in 1845. Nelles deeply enjoyed the extracurricular and residence life at Wesleyan where he engaged with his fellow-students who called themselves "the Mystics." The group gave each other nicknames and discussed philosophy and literature as well as their personal hopes for the future. The bonds formed during college through extracurricular adventures and social life persisted into their adult life and shaped for Nelles an ideal of college fellowship formed outside of the classroom through student participation.

The geographical isolation presumably also contributed to the religious fever that would sometimes grip these institutions. Nathanael Burwash had been a student at Victoria in 1853–1854 while it was still located in Cobourg. (Victoria federated with the University of Toronto and moved to Toronto in 1892). While there, he observed that in response to the conversion of some students at a local revival, students held prayer meetings, classes were suspended, faculty held meetings for "deeply distressed inquirers," and prayer could be heard day and night from student rooms where two or three had gathered. Burwash noted that every undergraduate was converted through this process;

presumably it would have been difficult under the circumstances to resist such pressure.[22]

Victoria College gradually added extracurricular clubs to its college life. John Campbell, a tutor in Classics who served as its president, formed the Literary Association in 1856. Members held weekly meetings to discuss a designated topic. In 1862 the Association held a *conversazione* that served refreshments to about 400 of Cobourg's elite.

During the 1870s, Victoria College witnessed the formation of diverse student societies with a variety of purposes including social (the "Bob"), student newspaper (*Acta Victoriana*), a science association (Victoria Pyramid Society), and a theological society (Jackson Society). In addition, while the college was located in Cobourg, a college prayer night was held on Saturday nights. Nelles saw clubs as an extension of the overall purpose of the college and of the liberal arts curriculum, namely, the balanced development of all the faculties. As principal, Nelles encouraged the formation of new clubs on the Victoria campus. He urged students to be committed to running them because, in his opinion, leadership was as valuable as classroom learning.[23] By the 1890s, the transmission of culture in both curricular and extracurricular activities promoted the use of human rationality in the development of the whole being; knowledge acquired in college could be applied to all walks of life.[24] College administrators viewed college clubs as an acceptable adjunct to the aims of university life and a worthwhile focus for student enthusiasm.

FOUNDING OF THE YMCA

Another organization that played an important role in the formation of the student volunteer movement was the Intercollegiate YMCA. The YMCA had been founded in England in 1844 by George Williams and transported to Boston and Montreal in the early 1850s. In 1854 delegates met at a convention in Buffalo and affiliated in a confederation of the YMCA of the United States and British Provinces. Although the YMCA was a new organization, it built on the traditions of clubs established in previous decades; in fact some pre-existing student societies were re-

---

22. Burwash, *History of Victoria College*, 179–81.

23. Neil Semple, *Faithful Intellect,* 212.

24. McKillop, *Matters of Mind,* 230.

placed or absorbed. In 1858, YMCAs were formed at the University of Virginia and University of Michigan, as well as in 1862 at the University of Rochester, where the Judson Society for Missionary Inquiry was absorbed by the student Y.[25] Prior to the formation of the YMCA at the University of Virginia, campus clubs included the Society of Missionary Inquiry, a temperance society, and a club that ran a Sunday school for slaves. Still, revivals were held in a Baptist church where parishioners revolted against the "dissipated habits of collegians."[26]

The Princeton Y in 1876 absorbed a continuity of clubs that dated from the earliest decades of the college. The first religious societies at the College of New Jersey (renamed Princeton in 1896) date to the late 1770s. There were two Bible clubs, the Nassau Hall Bible Society instituted in 1813 and the Nassau Tract Society founded in 1817. The Chi Phi, established in 1824 as a secret fraternity, was dedicated to spiritual life and holiness and changed its name in 1825 to the Philadelphian Society. To belong to the society one had to testify to a conversion experience and be unanimously elected by the group. Students were attracted to this exclusive club because it was student-run and offered a spiritual alternative to the required chapels and Bible classes of the university.

Clubs such as the Philadelphian at Princeton developed in a religiously saturated atmosphere that included Sunday sermons, guest speakers, revivals, and weekday religious observances. In addition, Episcopalian students began their own campus club and students organized a Temperance Society in the 1870s. Revivals by the visiting Moody and Sankey team led to the conversion of 100 students in 1876.

In later years members of the Philadelphian/YMCA society became prominent in national and international student Christian movements. When faculty, in the late nineteenth century, had become less interested in organized general campus religious life, the work was turned over to students who organized events, Bible study, and volunteer work. According to historian Paul Kemeny, Princeton retained the discipline and piety curriculum well into the nineteenth century. The college administration hoped that such religious clubs and evangelical piety would balance the secular side of the curriculum and provide a unifying centre.[27]

---

25. Hopkins, *History of the YMCA*, 125; 37–39.

26. Ober, *Exploring a Continent*, 3–12.

27. Kemeny, *Princeton in the Nation's Service*, 56.

One student movement leader, Luther DeLoraine Wishard (1854–1925), had faced considerable challenges in his pursuit of education due to visual impairment at a young age. Although his parents took him to an "asylum" for the blind when he was seven, he was convinced that he could overcome this disability and "win the battle of life on the conditions imposed on other men."[28] He asserted his right to follow a "normal" path for education. Luther's father was self-taught in science and pharmacy and gained practical experience in hospital wards during the Civil War. The contact with soldiers led him to establish homes for disabled soldiers and soldiers' orphans—one of which became home for Luther and his widowed father for a number of years.

His father's return from the 1870 convention of the YMCA "charged with spiritual electricity" had a profound influence on Luther. [29] Although his involvement with the student movement was interrupted when he left school for financial reasons, the resumption of his studies at Hanover College allowed him to join the Y. He was appointed to represent the College Association in Massachusetts in 1872. After graduation from Hanover, Wishard attended Princeton (1875–1877) and joined the campus Philadelphian Society. Initially disappointed that this society was not affiliated with the YMCA, he rectified that situation when he became president. (Wishard's roommate at Princeton was Cleveland H. Dodge, future president of the New York YMCA movement.)

While at Princeton, Wishard not only helped the Princeton society broaden its platform by affiliating with the Y, but he also supported the growth of the Intercollegiate YMCA by sending circulars to over 200 colleges urging representatives to attend the Louisville Convention.[30] At that 1877 convention, the college movement of the YMCA was successfully established with Wishard as head. He combined a dedication to missions with college work for the remainder of his career with the Y.[31] Although he had originally planned to become a missionary in China,

28. Ober, *Exploring a Continent,* 12.

29. Ibid.,14.

30. Wishard entered Princeton in his junior year and most of his courses were required including Logic, Metaphysics, Psychology, Mechanics, Physics, Science, Religion, History, Physical Geography, English Literature. In addition to these courses, he took electives in German (or Greek) and also perhaps Latin.

31. Wahlstrom, *Creation of a Student Movement,* 32.

he found his life's challenge in his YMCA work. In his position as secretary he provided leadership and continuity to the organization.[32]

Another important figure in the formation of the student work of the YMCA was Charles Kellogg Ober (1856–1948). In his book *Out of the Fog* (1929) he describes his conversion as a young man on a ship that became lost in the fog off the coast of Newfoundland. After his rescue, he decided to become a missionary. He enrolled in a one-year course at Williams College that would prepare him to enter seminary. In order to pay for his education, he served as manager of a boarding club for students. While presenting a paper at a YMCA convention, he gained the attention of notable leaders including Mr. Richard C. Morse, General Secretary of the International Committee, who suggested his name as a candidate for association secretary. Ober gave up his plans to be a foreign missionary and instead served the YMCA for forty years.[33]

As secretary of college work of the International Y committee for five and a half years, Ober worked as a junior associate of Luther Wishard and as senior college secretary with John R. Mott as his assistant.[34] The practice of mentoring provided continuity to the organization while supporting new secretaries during the first stages of learning the job. In the early years of student organizations, there were no training courses for those who pioneered and planted new student movements; they learned in the field and mentored those who followed them.

James Bronson Reynolds (1861–1924) was another pioneer who expanded the international borders of the collegiate YMCA. A Yale graduate, Reynolds undertook post-graduate studies in Berlin and started a student club affiliated with the Berlin YMCA in the late 1880s. He travelled to Paris as a representative of the American Student Christian Associations.[35] His mission was to promote the organization of Christian students in the universities of Europe and the formation of national and

---

32. Ober, *Exploring a Continent,* 15.

33. Ibid., 16. His experience managing the boarding house served Ober well in the summer of 1885 when he was part of the International Committee that spent six weeks in Northfield, Massachusetts at the home of Dwight L. Moody. The goal of the summer meeting was to prepare a course of Bible study for use in the college associations. When the accommodations for the 400 conference guests fell through, Moody asked Ober if he could oversee the logistics and he obliged.

34. Ibid., 42.

35. Rouse, *WSCF.* Apparently a Scottish woman named Jane Howard had started student work in the Latin quarter of Paris.

international union between the Christian students in the universities of Europe and America. He was met with enthusiastic welcome by academics and students at Oxford, Cambridge, Stockholm, Paris, Bonn, Berlin, and Amsterdam. During one period of three years of continuous travel, he visited forty-four universities with 87,527 students, spoke at many student conferences, and helped establish the Paris Students' Association. This pioneering work helped create a student movement that would be ready to participate in federation with the World Student Christian Federation when it was founded less than a decade later.

FOUNDING OF THE STUDENT VOLUNTEER MOVEMENT

While a student at Cornell University in 1886, John R. Mott (1865–1955) travelled by rail, rowboat, and on foot to attend a student conference at the home of evangelist Dwight Moody (1837–1899). As president of his college Y, he had received an invitation to attend this summer school and had been invited to bring several students with him. Although conferences had been held at Northfield and Mount Hebron since the early 1880s, this particular conference was the first to target members of the Young Men's Christian Association on campus.

The program included Bible study and training in Y methods. Ninety different associations sent a total of 250 students who spent their days listening to guest speakers and engaging in discussion groups. An informal missionary agenda galvanized the participants so that a large number signed pledges expressing their intention to become missionaries. The event marked the largest gathering of college students that had ever been held. Their presence was largely due to the social networks and contacts that had slowly been built up through individuals like Luther Wishard who spread the word through the YMCA's; Robert Wilder, son of India missionary Royal Wilder, who contacted Princeton students; and Mott at Cornell. The meeting represented eighty-nine colleges in the United States and Canada. Clearly the era of isolated colleges had passed and in its place a student movement with a vision for the world emerged. Students were not merely intellectually engaged; they were considering life service in foreign countries or domestic missions.

Mott described the spiritually charged atmosphere of the conference: "Up to this noon over 80 of the students have consecrated themselves to the foreign missionary work and ere Sunday night I know they will number 100. It thrills me through and through to record the fact.

I have received a far richer anointing of the Spirit than I had dared to ask for before I came here."[36] Mott signed a missionary pledge but left his anticipated field of service blank; he could not have known that part of his field was serving the organization that emerged from this gathering, namely the Student Volunteer Movement, for the next thirty years.

The power of visiting preachers, such as Philadelphia Presbyterian pastor and future editor of a missionary review Rev. A. T. Pierson and Boston Presbyterian pastor Rev. William Ashmore, generated much interest among students, but the presence of Moody with his "fervency of spirit" had a powerful effect on Mott and convicted participants of the urgency of the cause.[37]

A year later, in 1887, Robert Speer, future secretary of Presbyterian missions, attended a Northfield conference for the first time. The leaders quickly noted his leadership abilities. Four years after his first conference, Speer was asked to lead Bible studies at the conference. During this visit he also met his future wife, Emma D. Bailey, who would herself become a leader in the YWCA.[38]

The organizers of the Northfield conferences and the student movement that emerged from them represented several strands in American Protestant religious history including evangelical religion, revivalism, the holiness movement, and the growing missionary impulse.[39] Dwight Moody had been a member of the Boston YMCA in 1854, three years after the organization took hold in the United States from its origins in England. Moody worked among Chicago's poor as a lay pastor and president of the YMCA. He was an heir to the tradition of revivals of the 1820s and 1830s led by George Whitfield and Charles G. Finney. Moody continued the non-denominational tradition of Whitfield with a call to personal piety and moral living.[40] Moody's emphasis on the role of the laity created possibilities for training and education for service that did not require seminary education. In addition, by emphasizing piety over doctrine, Moody shifted the focus away from doctrinal divisions to what the movement could share in interdenominational work.

---

36. John R. Mott to parents, July 30, 1892, in Hopkins, *Mott*, 27.

37. Ibid., 28.

38. Piper, *Speer*.

39. Parker, *Kingdom of Character*, 3–5.

40. Ibid.

Wishard's experience in student clubs at Princeton proved valuable when he was asked to help Moody organize the summer conference. The YMCA missionary department that he had established in 1879 organized missions education events on campus and published the *College Bulletin* to promote missionary news. Wishard was involved in the Inter-Seminary Missionary Alliance (1880–1898), an organization dedicated to generating missions interest among seminary students. Wishard's leadership skills led to growing responsibilities in the student work.

Students responded with enthusiasm to conferences: at the Inter-Seminary Missionary Alliance (ISMA) Convention in 1886, there were 235 delegates representing thirty-three seminaries. The ISMA had also engaged the imagination of Princeton student Robert Wilder. Along with two other students, Wilder attended the ISMA meeting in Hartford, Connecticut. Enthused by the experience and the preaching of A. J. Gordon in 1883, the students returned to Princeton to form the Princeton Foreign Missionary Society (PFMS). This new group was a missionary band in which members signed a declaration of their willingness to serve the unevangelized parts of the world.

The ISMA published proceedings that disseminated missionary knowledge throughout the United States and Canada. Colleges that were unable to send representatives sent their greetings to the assembly; Noah Porter sent a message from Yale to the group assembled in Chicago in 1882. At the ISMA meeting in 1886, participants representing a variety of Protestant denominations—Presbyterian, Reformed Church in the U.S., Evangelical Lutheran, Protestant Episcopal, Baptist, and Congregational—listened to an address entitled, "Why Should I Go to the Foreign Mission Field?"[41] The ISMA offered an important educational function on the subject of missions that was broadly interdenominational within a number of Protestant seminaries.

To maintain the momentum gained at the Northfield conference, Wishard and Ober toured colleges in the 1886–1887 academic year with John Forman, son of India missionaries. They enrolled 2,106 volunteers that year, of which one quarter were women.[42] The women's participation was further fuelled by the work of the YWCA which also supported missionary engagement. Students signed pledge cards and formed missionary bands on campus.

41. Proceedings of the ISMA, 1882 and 1886. Online: http://hdlhandle.net/10118/6.

42. Parker, *Kingdom of Character,* 11.

Although Robert Wilder's college tours were restricted by his enrolment in studies at Union Theological Seminary in 1887, he continued as much as possible to visit schools and churches. In 1887 Wishard was instrumental in sending missionaries to Japan and India. Japan had requested English teachers so Wishard founded a Foreign Education Commission and at Northfield enlisted John Swift and five others to go to Japan. A year later he went to Britain and to Germany before heading on his world tour. In addition to the pioneering work, establishing and encouraging new city and student YMCAs around the world, Wishard published letters of his travels in several journals. His reports contributed to a growing excitement and awareness of the expansion of student work into a worldwide effort.[43]

By the end of the second year of SVM work, 600 additional volunteers had signed. However, these small college SVM bands tended to develop locally without oversight or accountability to an overall leadership structure. To provide a governance structure for the movement, the student leaders at Northfield in 1888 decided that a committee should be formed to organize these student volunteer bands under the name Student Volunteer Movement for Foreign Missions.

An executive committee represented the four student organizations that were involved with missionary work and student recruitment—the Intercollegiate YMCA and YWCA and the Inter-Seminary Missionary Alliances, both American and Canadian. Mott had been recognized as someone with leadership potential and he was chosen as college secretary and then as head of the SVM. The subsequent executive was appointed in December 1888 and included Mott for the YMCA; Nettie Dunn for the YWCA; and Wilder representing the two inter-seminary alliances. The bands that had been formed on the campuses agreed to be the missionary departments of the college Y associations, thus creating a division of labor which persisted in the subsequent decades. The SVM adopted the watchword "The Evangelization of the World in this Generation." Robert Speer (1867–1947) became a travelling secretary for the SVM in 1889.[44] Mott was appointed the international

---

43. Ibid., 83–95.

44. Speer was educated at Andover and Princeton. He became involved in missions after hearing Wilder and Forman speak at Princeton in 1886. Speer and his wife Emma, a Bryn Mawr graduate, traveled to England in 1894, where he spoke to the British Student Movement conference at Keswick. He served as Secretary of the Board of Foreign Missions of the Presbyterian Church for forty-six years. See Reginald Wheeler, *Man Sent from God.*

student secretary to the SVM Executive Committee, a position he held for thirty-one years.[45]

As historian Nathan Showalter observes, the SVM was never intended as a separate, fully independent organization, but rather as a complementary part of the larger Protestant Christian student movement. The result was that in different countries, the movement developed different characteristics. In New York, the SVM had an office in New York City (50 East 70th St.) and functioned as a missionary department of the YM and YWCA. In England the Student Volunteer Missionary Union (SVMU) became the missionary arm of the Student Christian Movement (SCM). In countries with weaker Protestant student movements, such as France and Italy, the student volunteer movement was less vigorous. The SVM was particularly robust in countries where it was supported by the larger Christian student movement as in the United States, Canada, and Britain.[46] Despite national variations, by 1898, the SVM had been established in 839 institutions of higher education with commitments from about 4,000 volunteers and 1,173 missionaries sent out.[47]

The notion of well-trained students, disciplined in spiritual practices and committed to action in the world, developed over several decades through a variety of student organizations that were precursors to the World Student Christian Federation.[48] The pre-organizational matrix of student clubs on early campuses, as well as the formation of the SVM and the college YMCA, were multiple threads in the student movements that eventually formed the national movements that affiliated with the WSCF. The entrance of women into higher education would soon challenge the exclusivity of these male organizations by pushing them to become coeducational or by developing single-sex voluntary movements of their own, but that story will be examined in the next chapter. In many cases the shift to gender-integrated participation was less a progressive plan than a grudging acceptance in the face of the hundreds of educated, enthusiastic women graduates.

45. Ober, *Exploring a Continent*, 87.

46. Showalter, *End of a Crusade*, 3.

47. Parker, *Kingdom of Character*, 13.

48. Founded in 1895 as the World's Student Christian Federation, the WSCF formally changed its name in 1960 to the World Student Christian Federation, the form of the name followed here.

SVMU Britain

Robert Wilder travelled to Britain in 1891 and a year later organized the Student Volunteer Missionary Union (SVMU) comprising a committee of four representing England, Scotland, Wales, and Ireland. Membership in the SVMU was open to both women and men who signed a declaration proclaiming their intention to become a foreign missionary. In previous travels, Wishard had built support for such an initiative when he spoke to university students in England and Scotland in 1888 and personally enlisted ten British students and one Dutch student to attend evangelist Dwight Moody's Northfield Conference.

The increasing number of missionary recruits posed the problem of raising the necessary financial support. A new plan was worked out to make up this deficit whereby the candidate would be sent out by the board of their denomination, but the colleges and churches would help support the missionary.[49]

The SVMU struck a chord among students; by the first Quadrennial Student Conference in Liverpool in January 1896, 1,038 students signed and 212 had already left for mission fields. The success of the movement led to the formation of another British student movement with a broader scope called the Inter-University Christian Union (IUCU) in 1893 (six women were present). The IUCU became the British College Christian Union (BCCU) in 1894 (with fifty women and 143 men). The new name was intended to invite non-university students into the movement including those in teacher training, art institute, and technical training programs.[50]

Wilder prepared thoroughly before speaking with British students. Apparently his words were well received; Donald Fraser, later missionary to Africa, heard Wilder speak at a conference in Keswick and said that the address moved him deeply and caused him to dedicate himself from that moment to the mission field. J. H. Maclean, later missionary to India, participated in the meetings in Edinburgh where the SVMU was constituted. He described Wilder's humor and spiritual earnestness: "To this day I remember the glow of it, and the willingness of the early volunteers to undertake whatever toil was involved in their new propa-

---

49. Braisted, 46.
50. Tatlow, *Story of the SCM*, 59.

ganda. The women were as keen as the men."[51] In Scandinavia, Wilder had the same effect on students. His quiet manner contrasted with the "typical American revivalism which was familiar and much disliked by Scandinavian students."[52] Although Wilder was forced in 1892 to rest, he subsequently had a nervous breakdown in 1902 that required a more intensive rest cure in Switzerland. This pattern of intense involvement and travel followed by a breakdown in health persisted throughout his career, but he presumably forged ahead despite these difficulties.

Membership in the SVM depended on two things—possession of the appropriate educational status and a willingness to make a sacrificial commitment. The sacrificial commitment called for by the SVM was epitomized by the watchword that it adopted in 1888: "the evangelization of the world in this generation." The slogan was the subject of increasing debate as the WSCF carried it into the twentieth century to a student population growing more skeptical.[53] Individuals could be members of a denomination and of the SVM at the same time—a fact that was important to those churches who feared that the SVM was an attempt to undermine traditional church membership.

Student Volunteer Movement Conferences

From their inception in the later decades of the 1800s, conferences were highlights of both the American college YMCA/YWCA and the British student Christian movements. Published proceedings and eyewitness accounts in student journals effectively communicated the essence of such gatherings. In the United States, the success of Dwight Moody's first student summer conference for Bible study and religious work at Mount Hermon in 1886 led to its relocation to a site in Northfield, Massachusetts. These conferences attracted Canadian, American, and international delegates. Attendees included future leaders in the missions and ecumenical movement—Karl Fries and Nathan Söderblom, Sweden; Fritz Mockert, Germany; Wilfred Monod, France; Henry Drummond, Alexander Simpson, J. H. Maclean, and Rutter Williamson, Scotland; Vernon Bartlett and Frank Anderson, Oxford University. In Canada, China missionary James Endicott heard John Mott speak at a

---

51. Maclean, quoted in Braisted, *In This Generation*, 58.

52. Braisted, *In This Generation*, 60.

53. Clements, *Faith on the Frontier*, 65. See Porter, *Religion Versus Empire?* 30–36.

student conference in Minneapolis and decided to offer himself for missionary service. Endicott wrote that "there is an awful significance in the figures presented concerning the great millions dying in darkness, and there seems to be great explicitness in the command, 'Go ye into all the world.'"[54]

In the United States, the success of these conferences led to the formation of the Student Volunteer Movement. Between 1890 and 1920, the SVM comprised the missionary department of the college YMCA/YWCA.

In England, the Holiness revival movement inspired the Keswick conferences first held in the 1870s. These camps provided a place where students could gather until they organized their own student conferences. Conferences thus multiplied on both sides of the Atlantic and generated retreats, regional conferences, and training schools.[55]

The SVM encouraged students to declare their intention to serve as missionaries by signing the following pledge: "It is my purpose, if God permit, to become a foreign missionary." The watchword, which declared the goal to be "the evangelization of the world in this generation," summarized the purpose of their work. These two sentences provided the motivation not only for individuals but also for student movements. Students, inspired by this commitment, put pressure on their churches to provide the necessary support. While the WSCF never officially adopted the watchword, it supported students in demanding that churches sponsor their commitment to missions.

Conferences challenged each student generation to consider God's purpose for them in mission work. Quadrennial Student Volunteer Conferences were held in Cleveland, 1891; Detroit, 1894; Liverpool, 1896; London, 1900; Toronto, 1902; Edinburgh, 1904; Liverpool, 1908 and 1912; Halle, Germany, 1897, 1901, 1905, and 1909; Kansas City, 1914; Des Moines, 1920; and Indianapolis, 1924. Before the war, the quadrennial convention of the SVM had become the largest gathering of students in North America; there were 680 delegates at the first convention at Cleveland in 1891 and five thousand at Kansas City just before the war.[56]

The Liverpool SV Conference (1896) welcomed 2,093 delegates including 151 international participants and 400 guests (professors,

54. Endicott, *Endicott*, 8.

55. Rouse, *WSCF*, 70.

56. Showalter, *End of a Crusade*, 28.

clergy, and visitors).[57] The conference was organized around two distinct themes, one devotional and the other missions-related. At this conference, the British SCM launched a financial appeal on behalf of John Mott. The leadership wired the surplus money to Mott in India to cover his expenses for travel to Australia and New Zealand. His trip ultimately resulted in the founding of thirty unions in the universities of Australia and New Zealand. Through increased travel and telegraphy, a global student consciousness was raised.

Student conferences were not isolated events. Newspapers and journals provided eyewitness accounts. In Japan, Luther Wishard organized the country's first student convention in 1889 in response to the urgent request by Japanese students for a conference "just like Northfield." He gave the keynote address entitled "Christian students united for World-Conquest." Five hundred students attended, of whom ninety-six were women.[58]

Concerns raised about social issues at the Liverpool Conference encouraged the organization of a smaller conference at Matlock, England focused on the relation of the SCM to social issues in Great Britain. The conference put pressure on the SVMU, which had previously organized all conferences on a missionary theme, to include the SCM and to expand the theme to the unity of the Christian task at home and abroad. Similarly, the WSCF also attempted to maintain the tension between domestic social problems and foreign missions in their planning and programs.

The Edinburgh Quadrennial SV Conference of 1912, organized on the theme "Christ and Human Need," combined an interest in missionary work with concern for poverty at home. International tensions pervaded the conference; the German SCM sent a message expressing their hopes that the conference would be blessed and that the Holy Spirit would "give peace between Christian people as a testimony for non-Christians. *Ut omnes unum sint.*"[59]

---

57. *"Make Jesus King."*

58. Fenn, *Learning Wisdom*, 4.

59. Ibid., 57.

YMCA WORK WITH BLACKS

Although the work of the college YMCA was largely segregated, there are some indications that African-American and aboriginal students were encouraged to take a limited role in the emerging student Christian movement. Although existing student movements among Blacks functioned within segregated associations, the success of the leadership in building the African-American Y created a parallel movement that grew steadily on college campuses. The strength and success of this movement would eventually demand recognition that the SVM was reluctant to provide; one of many factors that led to its decline as a movement representing Christian student concerns.[60]

A handful of African-American leaders worked tirelessly to develop a student movement on campuses throughout the United States. One Black student worker, William Hunton, was born in 1863 in Chatham, Ontario, the son of a freed slave who had migrated north from Virginia. In 1858 the abolitionist John Brown, originally from Torrington, Connecticut, visited Chatham and decided to use the town as base for his fight against slavery. William Hunton's father, Stanton Hunton, was a supporter of the Harper's Ferry attack.[61] Because of its strategic location on the Underground Railroad, Chatham became home to a number of African Americans. Another member of this Black community in Chatham was the physician and editor Martin Delaney (1812–1885). Delaney had worked with Frederick Douglas on his paper *The North Star.*[62]

William taught Sunday school at an early age. After finishing high school, he graduated from the Wilberforce Institute of Ontario. The Wilberforce Institute had opened in 1873 in Chatham, a product of a merger of the Nazrey Institute (founded 1869) and the British American Institute (founded 1842). The purpose of the Wilberforce Institute was to educate youth, regardless of race, not just at the primary and second-

60. Michael Parker, *Kingdom of Character*, 160–61.

61. In July 1858, John Brown held the Chatham convention, a planning and fundraising meeting for the insurrection at Harper's Ferry. The attack took place in October 1859. The only Canadian in the raid out of twenty-one men is Osborne Perry Anderson, a freed Black from Chatham as well. Anderson escaped and wrote about the attack in the *Provincial Freeman*, a newspaper published by Mary Ann Shadd of North Buxton, Ontario.

62. Delaney's biography was written by an African-American writer named Whipper (1845–1910) and was entitled *Life and Public Services of Martin R. Delaney.*

ary levels, but also for entrance into law, art, medicine, teaching, and commerce at the university level. William's father was a member of the board of the Institute.[63]

Although Hunton accepted a teaching post at a Dresden, Ontario high school, he privately hoped to find a job that would allow him to study for the ministry. He took an examination for a government position in Ottawa and was appointed clerk in the Department of Indian Affairs. While in Ottawa, he joined the Ottawa YMCA. He was very interested in the work being done in the United States to organize a YMCA for "colored" men. Appeals were made before the International Convention in Montreal; the International Convention in Richmond, Virginia in 1875; and in Toronto in 1876. Henry E. Brown was appointed secretary of the International Committee for work among "colored" men. In 1886, members of the YMCA noted the quality of Hunton's work and supported a motion to hire him for the American branch. Thus, in 1888, Hunton became the first Black YMCA secretary in Norfolk, Virginia.[64] The leadership of the Y was aware that the appointment of a Canadian to a very different racial context would present some difficulties. Mr. Brown asked, "Does he realize the very different relation he must in the South bear to the white folk from that which he now bears? Is he sufficiently consecrated to bear the change?"[65]

Hunton's hard work and constant travel throughout the historically Black colleges and universities of the United States showed results: by 1896 there were sixty African-American associations, of which forty-nine were in colleges. There were many problems facing the black YMCA, including increasing racial tensions and a lack of money. The YMCA

63. The other members of the board of the Wilberforce Institute included a Rev. Disney, Morris Potter, Issac Holden, Nelson Robinson, Nathaniel Murray, and Perry Chase. There were 100 pupils in the early years with thirty-six in preparatory levels, and twenty in primary. The school existed due to the philanthropy of Charles Avery of Allegheny County, Pennsylvania. The teachers of the school included Lillian Shreve, Dolly Scott, Vera Bently, Emma Fox, and Mollie Lewis. The school was erected in 1887 and demolished in 1952. Another school in Chatham was the Woodstock Institute that opened in 1908. The principal was Rev. James Richards and the teachers included Helena Lynn (music), Jeff Lucas (blacksmith), Laura Butler (dressmaking) and another teacher for wireless telegraphy. Online: http://www.ckblackhistoricalsociety.org/.

64. Hunton, *Hunton*. In 1907, Hunton's wife was called to serve the YWCA with Eva D. Bowles. They were to work for cooperation between black and white groups. See Rice, *History*, 138.

65. Brown to Kuhring, cited in Hunton, *Hutton*, 15.

movement continued to support segregated Y's but left decisions up to the local association. Prior to Hunton, there were very few independent Black YMCAs.[66] When Henry E. Brown began his work in 1879, there were approximately five YMCA's in black colleges. Until 1933, student YMCA work in black colleges was administered by a colored work department of the YMCA.[67] In 1914 an African-American student convention at Clark University brought together 512 African-American men and women and sixty whites with John Mott in attendance.[68] Speakers included Booker T. Washington, William Hunton, and a group of southern white speakers. At Mott's invitation, Hunton attended and addressed WSCF conferences at Tokyo in 1907 and Lake Mohonk in 1913 where he shared a vision for an all-inclusive "brotherhood" of man.[69]

Willis Duke Weatherford's (1875–1970) *Negro Life in the South*, published in 1909, was widely read on campuses; Hopkins estimates that 30,000 students studied this book during the next five or six years.[70] Weatherford was a pioneer in interracial relations and initiated interracial conferences in the aftermath of the Atlanta race riots of 1906. His book documented racial inequality. There were limits to his perspective, however, as his approach was conservative in envisioning actual equality.

An interracial conference in Atlanta provided support for student work in 1914; however, conflict threatened to destroy even this initiative. A call for special seating for black students led to an emergency meeting of the Black students including representatives of the Colored Men's Department of the YMCA and Addie Hunton and Josephine Pinyon of the National Board of the YWCA. They gathered with William Alphaeus Hunton at the home of Dr. John Hope, the president of Morehouse College.[71]

His wife, Addie Waite Hunton, has recorded the story of Hunton's work with the YMCA. She studied sociology at the College of the City of New York and at Kaiser Wilhelm University in Strasbourg, Germany.

66. Hopkins, *History of the YMCA*, 219.

67. Ibid., 290.

68. Wilson, *Fifty Years*, 272.

69. Black delegates at Mohonk included the following men: Hope, Moton, Aggrey, Tobias, Jones and Hunton. Black women included Merriman, Bond, and Pinyon. See "African Share in the WSCF," RG 46, Box 6-54, YDS Archives.

70. Weatherford, *Negro Life*.

71. Hunton, *Hutton*, 128–29.

She taught at Alabama Agricultural & Mechanical University and helped to found the National Association of Colored Women.[72] The Huntons settled in Atlanta in order to facilitate his travels to the colleges in the south, but after the riots in Atlanta in 1906, they moved to Brooklyn with their two children. Hunton died of tuberculosis in 1916 leaving his wife to raise the two children and continue her work of advocacy and community development.[73]

CAMPS, CONFERENCES, AND TRAINING PROGRAMS

During the time that Y work was thriving among African-American college students, Wishard was forced to take leave from his Y work to recuperate from a nervous breakdown. However, by 1897–1898, he was again involved in student association work, a task that involved fundraising, education, and organization. He was responsible for the administrative budget, the secretaries in the field, and for raising his own salary. These pressures, combined with constant travel under less than desirable conditions, continually tested the emotional and physical health of student leaders. For Wishard, the financial burden caused him the "most anxious period of his public life."[74] In December 1898, he resigned permanently from the YWCA to pioneer a missionary project for the Presbyterian Church for a year. When he resigned from the International Committee work, Mott took over the Student Department and Charles Kellogg Ober assumed leadership of the home field. Wishard wanted to develop an interdenominational effort that would provide education and support for the student missionary movement. He established a connection with the American Board of Foreign Missions.

In 1902 Wishard was instrumental in securing a property at Silver Bay, Lake George, New York, which became a permanent summer headquarters for the missionary education movement, as well as a training ground for workers of the YMCA and YWCA. While Wishard was in

---

72. See "Addie D. Waites Hunton." See also Weisenfeld, *African American Women*.

73. See "Inventory of the William Alphaeus Hunton Papers, 1926–1970." Hunton's son Alphaeus graduated with a PhD in English literature and became very involved in the National Negro Congress and the Council on African Affairs. He worked in Africa until he was expelled in the 1960s. He returned to Zambia but left uncompleted a historical project when he died there of cancer at the age of sixty-three in 1970. Three generations of African-American and African-Canadian social activism can be traced in the remarkable history of the Hunton family.

74. Hopkins, *History of the YMCA*, 358.

hospital in Chicago recovering from an appendectomy, a friend came to see him. Their discussion concerned the need for religious training for young people. Wishard expressed his longing for a training place similar to Northfield, Massachusetts and Lake Geneva, Wisconsin. The visitor mentioned that his uncle, Silas Paine, owned a hotel near Lake George. The conversation was forgotten until 1900, when Wishard happened to be looking for a house for his family in Lake George. As he boarded the steamer he looked at the view and was struck with a powerful image: "I had a vision of another City of God coming down from God out of Heaven, peopled with young men and maidens, their brows shining with the dew of morning, their ears anointed to hear the Captain's marching orders, their lips touched with live coals from God's altar, with which they would kindle fires which shall shine around the world."[75]

The hotel fitted the need for a training camp. Wishard convinced Paine to allow a portion of the hotel to be used to train students, initially all men, for missions both at home and abroad. By 1906, Silver Bay hosted a conference sponsored by the Young People's Missionary Movement[76] with eighty-four representatives of seventeen denominations, as well as representatives from the Sunday School Editorial Association, the Executive Committee of the International Sunday School Association, and the Religious Education Association (REA). Experts in pedagogy included George Dawson,[77] Professor of Psychology at the Hartford School of Religious Pedagogy (1902); Dr. Lawrence K. Doggett (President of Springfield College from 1896–1936) and Dr. Goodman of Springfield College; Walter Rauschenbusch, Rochester Theological School; and Dr. H. H. Horne of the School of Pedagogy at New York University. Pedagogical experts were employed to combine science and education in a way that would increase the efficacy of missionaries in home and foreign fields. Silver Bay hosted YWCA conferences; in 1905 one such conference drew 734 students from 111 educational institutions in the U.S. and Canada. Students who gathered in this idyllic setting were absorbed in sports, games, music, sermons, and lectures and experienced a fellowship that was not easily forgotten.

75. Wishard quoted in Workman, *Silver Bay*.

76. The Young People's Missionary Movement changed its name to the Missionary Education Movement and it provided formal training for missionary leaders in both home and foreign missions.

77. Prior to his appointment to Hartford, Dawson had been a professor at Mt. Holyoke from 1903–1904 and later at the YMCA college in Springfield.

The need for mission workers schooled in the latest educational theory and biblical knowledge created a demand for new academic programs and postgraduate training. The Springfield School for Christian Workers was founded in 1885 with a YMCA department to provide physical training. This school was renamed the Bible Normal College in 1902 as it moved to Hartford and affiliated with Hartford Seminary as the Hartford School of Religious Pedagogy and later the Hartford School of Religious Education. [78]

At the Bible Normal College, students were trained to be Sunday School superintendants, missionaries for city, home, and foreign fields, and superintendants in reformatories and social agencies. Between 1904 and 1910, the enrolment increased from fifty-four to 130 students. The mostly male faculty covered studies in Old Testament, New Testament, psychology, and pedagogy. Miss Orissa Baxter, who taught home economics, was also on the faculty. Supported by gifts, the school eventually merged into Hartford Seminary.

CONCLUSION

Future WSCF leader John R. Mott was optimistic about the potential power of student volunteers to take the gospel message around the world: "Each volunteer should be an educational force. In the college or seminary, in the association or the missionary society, in the church, and in the young people's organization he should have the reputation of being well informed on missions; and, more than that, of being able to present the subject in an interesting and forcible manner." A student volunteer required a wide set of skills and qualities—the ability to communicate the principles of missions and to raise money for missions, prayerfulness, and the flexibility to work effectively in foreign and domestic mission fields. Mott challenged students with the question, "If you cannot win souls in your own college or your own town, how can you expect to win souls in Africa and India?"[79]

The SVM enjoyed impressive initial success. The organization was simple—local bands, regional unions, and travelling secretaries. There was a high level of student participation and total commitment

78. Four years later the Seminary's Board of Trustees voted unanimously to admit female students, and in so doing, became the first seminary in America to open its doors to women. Online: http://www.hartsem.edu/about/about.htm.

79. Mott, "The Volunteer as a Force."

to missions. The conventions and quadrennials renewed and inspired the members. The ever-increasing opportunities for travel on rail and steamship meant that students could attend conventions and conferences, events that were crucial in disseminating the ideal of a Christian student movement around the world.

The value placed on education is evident in the appointment of D. Willard Lyon as education secretary for the YMCA in 1894. He was followed by Harlan P. Beach who served for ten years from 1896–1906. Beach organized a four-year curriculum for colleges and secretaries that covered theory, biblical studies, history, comparative religions, missionary biographies, and regional studies.

In 1894, John Mott explained the power of the movement: "The secret of the power of the Movement is found in its six-fold purpose: to unite the Christian college men of the world; to win to Christ the students who are not His followers; to guard college men against the many temptations which assail them—not only in the body but also in the realm of the intellect; to deepen the spiritual life of the Christian men; to increase their efficiency in Christian work; and to lead them, as they go from college, to place their lives where they will count most in advancing the Kingdom of Christ." [80]

Thus, the Christian student movement grew from early missionary clubs established on college campuses from the late eighteenth century to the early decades of the nineteenth century in North America. The movement included the Intercollegiate YMCA, Student Volunteer Movement for Foreign Missions, Inter-Seminary Missionary Alliance—all of which functioned in both the U.S. and Canada. Eventually a structure emerged that would unify the local organizations in the universities and seminaries and clarify the purposes of the movement.

The theology that guided the movement was clearly situated in nineteenth-century evangelical Protestantism. Historian Marguerite Van Die notes that in the Victorian era, evangelical referred to mainline denominations such as Methodists and Baptists and to some degree Presbyterians, Congregationalists, and members of the Church of England. The main tenets of evangelicalism included a conviction of the importance of individual salvation through repentance and conversion and the acceptance of a disciplined life that reflected a spiritual

---

80. Online: http://www.cacmboston.org/index.php?option=com_content&task=vi ew&id=109&Itemid=233.

transformation. The Scriptures were considered the ultimate authority as a record of God's saving work.[81] Historian George Marsden observes that the American university system was built on a foundation of evangelical Protestant colleges, and most of the major universities evolved directly from such colleges. Until the 1920s, the vast majority was evangelical in character.[82] The Protestant and evangelical character of many institutions of higher education created a hospitable climate for student religious voluntary associations.

At the same time, historian Timothy Wahlstrom reminds us that in the early nineteenth century, the concept of mission opportunities for college students was largely unknown. The college environment in general neither offered such opportunities, nor did it provide an intellectual environment where such choices would be encouraged. American higher education was shaped by the rationalism and materialism associated with the French Enlightenment.[83] The intellectual climate at North American women's colleges, on the other hand, had stronger links to evangelical theology. For male students, the commitment to overseas service often required a conversion experience and a shift in expectations and beliefs, whereas for women students, the call to serve was a logical extension of the spiritual commitment within which their educational privilege was situated and offered an outlet for the skills and training which they had acquired.[84]

Education both shaped the movement and provided momentum for its growth. While developing and co-operating with national student movements around the world, student secretaries, many of whom were women, were extending the practice of international relations before that field became professionalized and generally limited to men. In their work the women simply extended the practice of hospitality over tea, established recreational opportunities and summer camps, distributed readings on biblical, social, and even feminist subjects, and provided hope and relief for hundreds of foreign or displaced student refugees in the process. To understand their contribution, the next chapter will explore the involvement of women in the student movement.

---

81. Marguerite Van Die, *An Evangelical Mind,* 9–10.

82. Marsden, *Soul of the American University,* 5.

83. Walstrom, *Creation of a Student Movement,* 10.

84. Marsden, *Soul of the American University,* 7.

2

Male and Female

Women in Student Christian Movements[1]

A PICTURE TAKEN OF the founders of the World Student Christian
Federation—all males—might suggest that women were absent
from the movement at its founding in 1895 until they were formally admitted several years later.[2] Official histories of the movement and of its
leaders would support this assumption.[3] The formal entrance of women
into the WSCF is generally marked by the appointment of Cambridge-
educated Ruth Rouse (1872–1956) as women's secretary in 1905.

This interpretation neglects an important part of the heritage of the
WSCF, namely, the culture that blossomed from within women's higher
education and women's involvement in Protestant churches, service, and
missionary clubs. The interest and involvement of female students in
missionary studies and clubs in nineteenth-century higher education for
women formed an important stream that fed directly into the student
movement. This chapter examines two such organizational streams—the
pre-organizational network of college clubs and participation in national
organizations such as the Young Women's Christian Association and the
Student Volunteer Movement. Biographies of the period indicate women
were involved in numerous philanthropic and service organizations that
were often founded, led, and staffed by women.

The organizational culture and methods that women brought to the
milieu of student movements and that led ultimately to their inclusion
in the WSCF have received insufficient acknowledgment. Exclusive at-

---

1. An earlier version of this chapter was published in the *IBMR,* 189–93.

2. Founders included Luther Wishard, John R. Mott, Karl Fries, Rutter Williamson,
Johannes Siemsen, and Martin Eckhoff.

3. See, for example, Hopkins, *Mott.*

tention to male leadership in the founding of the WSCF neglects the active role played by women in the formation of wider student organizations, such as the Student Volunteer Movement, that were immediate antecedents to and components of the WSCF. Biographical interest tends to focus on the leaders of the student movements, especially John Mott, Robert Speer, Robert Wilder, and Luther Wishard. Recent work on women missionaries and teachers is moving toward balancing the historical record with a critical appraisal of their many contributions.[4]

Many of the individual women participants in student voluntary movements had multiple overlapping commitments that can be discerned only by reading from inside the individual lives as much as the records allow. The women's missionary and service organizations of the second half of the nineteenth century can rightly be spoken of, along with the SVM and YWCA, as precursors to the WSCF.

WOMEN'S ENTRY INTO HIGHER EDUCATION

Emma Douse (1849–1926) arrived at the Wesleyan Female College in Hamilton, Ontario (also known as the Wesleyan Ladies' College) in 1866 to begin her studies for the academically demanding Mistress in Liberal Arts (MLA) degree. She studied Latin, French, English, Mathematics, Astronomy, and Chemistry. After graduation, she was employed for two years as a teacher before she joined the faculty of the WLC to teach a variety of courses in the academic stream.

Missionary zeal was an inherent part of the learning community at the WLC. An accepted alternative to direct missionary service was service as a missionary wife. As the previous chapter indicates, missionary wives such as Ann Judson and Helen Newell made a lasting mark on missionary lore through their writings. These revealed women who drew on deep spiritual resources and faced overwhelming suffering with heroism. In the mission field, missionary wives "were considered essential to modeling appropriate behaviour to their indigenous counterparts."[5] Their presence also served to curtail the allegations of impropriety that threatened single male missionaries in the field.

---

4. Two excellent contributions include Dana Robert, *Gospel Bearers, Gender Barriers*, and Porterfield, *Mary Lyon*.

5. Jan Hare and Jean Barman, *Good Intentions*, 6.

When Emma met single missionary Thomas Crosby on a speaking tour that brought him to her college, it took her only a week to perceive a call to marry and accompany him to his missionary post in British Columbia a few months later. Douse's affections for Crosby were no doubt sincere, as was her sense of call. She attempted to articulate both in letters to her mother who did not share her daughter's enthusiasm for this radical change in plans. Emma assured her mother that she was not carried away by the romance of the thing; she believed "that a blessing will rest upon my life."[6] Like many women in Canada and the United States, her expectations for marriage and for career as a missionary wife were formed and sanctioned by the educational environment of the ladies' college learning community.

The religious revivals that had galvanized religious life in the Maritimes and Ontario in the 1850s and 60s and again later in the 1880s were based on an egalitarian notion of sin and salvation that ultimately sanctioned women's right to participate in extended lay opportunities for service.[7] In Canada, the involvement of women in such work did not gain momentum until the post-Confederation era, partly due to the frontier nature of much of the country and partly due to the lack of educated women to provide leadership in such work.[8] Although the church became the primary agency for women's public involvement, education shaped the models of organizing, teaching, communicating, and leadership appropriate to women. Women embraced the challenge; before the turn of the century, Canadian women outnumbered men in many overseas posts.[9]

In the United States, the participation of women in service and missions work had been accelerated by their experience of service work in the Civil War. Women's education was justified on the basis of building mothers for the nation. In an earlier era, as Porterfield explains, educator Mary Lyon's (1797–1849) educational drive was rooted in New England

6. Emma Douse to her mother, Feb 18, 1874 and Feb 27, 1874, quoted in Hare and Barman, *Good Intentions*, 13–14.

7. Gagan, *Sensitive Independence*, 14.

8. Ibid., 12. Some missionary efforts were initiated by the Methodist Episcopal Church in 1824 and work was concentrated on converting native peoples of British Columbia. Minimal success in evangelistic efforts in Quebec among Roman Catholics presumably made the goal of foreign missions an attractive challenge. Missionaries were sent to Tokyo in 1873.

9. Brower, *New Women*.

Puritanism that attracted women through its "egalitarian spirituality." Joseph Emerson, a New Divinity teacher, influenced Lyon to join the Congregational Church and shaped her education. Central to her life and educational mission was the New Divinity notion of self-sacrifice as the central element of Christian virtue.[10]

The late nineteenth century witnessed an unprecedented growth in women's participation in female seminaries, ladies' colleges, and universities.[11] In the United States, women's colleges such as Mount Holyoke Female Seminary (founded 1837) in South Hadley, Massachusetts established traditions of service, self-sacrifice, and missionary involvement under the leadership of Principal Mary Lyon. In the Protestant and non-denominational college, habits of piety were encouraged through attendance at communal chapel services and talks, prayer, and Bible study, as well as private devotions twice a day. The spiritual formation embedded in college life and experience tied education closely to piety in a way that made missionary service a logical outcome of one's education.

Since women students were not considered fully formed adults, a schedule of rules and duties was implemented to provide a parental structure. This structure persisted from the early Mount Holyoke days into early twentieth-century universities and women's residences.[12] Historian Helen Lefkowitz Horowitz argues that Mary Lyon transformed women's lives into ones that could be planned: in every element of the building, the curriculum, schedules for tasks, exercise, and spiritual devotions, she created a form of discipline that "propelled students out into the world." Although Holyoke shared many aspects with Amherst, its brother college, Holyoke was designed on a house model that allowed for strict control and oversight of student lives. By contrast, students at Andover enjoyed a realm of freedom in dormitories with multiple exits that allowed unsupervised involvement in secret societies and traditions. The curriculum at Mount Holyoke bore some resemblance to that at Andover, but lacked Greek and upper-level work in Latin and mathematics. Holyoke's mis-

10. Porterfield, *Mary Lyon*, 16.

11. This increase has been documented in a variety of educational histories. For Australia, see Marjorie Theobald, *Knowing Women*; for England see, Hunt, *Lessons for Life*; for Canada, see Heap and Prentice, *Gender and Education*; and for the United States, see Barbara Solomon, *Company of Educated Women*.

12. Gidney, *Long Eclipse*, 37.

sion to educate teachers met with great success; of graduates between 1838 and 1850, 82.5 percent taught school.[13]

Bonds of friendship between alumnae continued after college graduation when women gathered at events related to missionary fellowship, read missionary narratives, attended lectures by missionaries on furlough, and participated in alumnae associations. The story of Harriet Newell, wife of Andover graduate Samuel Newell, was widely read and very influential. On her way to the mission field with her husband, she died on board ship off the coast of India at the age of nineteen.[14]

Lyon was instrumental in establishing several New England schools for women including Ipswich, Hartford, and Wheaton Female Seminaries. These schools followed the lead of Sarah Pierce's Female Seminary in Litchfield (1792) and Catharine Beecher's Seminary in Hartford, Connecticut (1823). The ninety women accepted in the first year of the Mount Holyoke seminary's existence were subject to a strict routine of religious observance, physical work, outdoor exercise, and academic rigor. Education and self-sacrifice were part of Lyon's educational philosophy: education was a means of "facilitating women's role in the process of global redemption."[15] The effectiveness of her teaching is evident in the contributions of Mount Holyoke to the missionary endeavor; in the first fifty years of its existence, the college provided one-fifth of all missionaries sent out by the United States.[16] In addition, many other women's seminaries and academies were modeled on Lyon's school, including Vassar and Wellesley.

In the religious climate of women's colleges and female seminaries, missions became the focus of clubs and academic culture. Missionary service was an accepted expression of student piety and spiritual formation. The Mount Holyoke Missionary Association (MHMA) formed a club around the subject of missions led by Mariana (MaryAnn) Holbrook in 1878. This small group met in secret, reticent about letting people know they were considering foreign missionary service. Each member

13. Horowitz, *Alma Mater*, 17–27.

14. Porterfield, *Mary Lyon*, 6. Another notable missionary heroine was Nancy Hasseltine who was connected to Mary Lyon through their common teacher Joseph Emerson. Hasseltine married Adoniram Judson, another member of the missionary group at Andover run by Samuel Mills.

15. Ibid., 17.

16. Ibid., 6.

signed a pledge card and secured the signature of all other members on her copy. The pledge read, "We hold ourselves willing and desirous to do the Lord's work wherever he may call us, even if it be in a foreign land." By 1884, thirty-four students had signed a declaration of their missionary purpose. In 1888, the MHMA ceased to be a secret society and accepted new members who shared their purpose.[17] The group included daughters of missionary families, as well as others with an interest in missions.[18] Grace Wilder, class of 1883, was a member of the MHMA. Wilder, daughter of India missionary Royal Wilder, presumably influenced her brother Robert's decision in 1883 to begin a Student Volunteer Movement at Princeton.[19]

Mariana Holbrook, founder of the MHMA, was the daughter of Richard Holbrook and Ruth Ford Holbrook from Rockland, Massachusetts. At the age of fifteen, she experienced a conversion and joined a church led by Rev. J. Cook in East Abington, Massachusetts. Although she began her studies in 1871, she was forced to work as a teacher from 1872–1874 for financial reasons and subsequently returned to Mount Holyoke for the academic year 1874–1875. At Mount Holyoke, she initially found the subject of missionary purpose very dull. However in 1875, she became "haunted" by the idea of becoming a missionary but felt she had no qualifications. During a college Fast Day, she told her roommate she had attended every prayer meeting that day and suddenly she felt that "I could endure the rebellion no longer. The prayers of

17. Mary L. Matthews to Ruth Rouse, 29 March, 1943, WSCF Papers, RG 46, box 71–576, Special Collections, Yale Divinity School Library, New Haven, Connecticut (subsequent references will be to the WSCF papers unless indicated and the location will be abbreviated as YDS).

18. Thirty four girls signed the pledge in the graduating classes from 1880–1885, including Grace Wilder, who served in India; Elizabeth Post, South Africa; Mary Preston, '85 South Africa; Anna Cummings, Principal of Huguenot Seminary, Wellington, South Africa; Mattie Fixley, '86, East Africa; Carrier Keerner, '85, China; Mary Hall, '83, teacher Constantinople College; Helen Flint, Constantinople College; Emily Bissell, '83, India; Marie Oldham, India; Ellen Peet, China; and Mary Matthews, Near East. In addition, some were called to home missions, such as Mary Pease, '82, Utah; Sarah Guernsey, '83, taught among the Indians in Michigan and in Utah among the Mormons; Euphemia Corwin, '85 who became librarian to Berea College; Helen Haines, '83 taught Indians at Santee Agency, Nebraska; Katherine Marvin, '85, librarian at Fisk University; Lillie Sherman, '80, taught at Northfield Seminary, served as General Secretary of the Cleveland YWCA and Secretary of the Women's Home Missionary Society of Massachusetts and Rhode Island.

19. Ruth Rouse, WSCF, 104.

that day melted my stubborn will, and in my room I told my Heavenly Father I was willing to go if *He* would make the duty so plain I could not doubt."[20] She surrendered to the call and experienced a peace and a love she had never known before, with a hearty interest in mission work at home and abroad.

She left the college in the spring due to illness. During that summer she joined the Missionary Association of the Women's Board of Missions in Rockland and began teaching again in the fall of 1875. Then in 1877, a Mrs. Lord of East Braintree asked her to consider the mission field. She decided to go as a physician and returned to the seminary to finish the necessary courses, taking a private course with Dr. Kelsey, the physician at the college.

In the fall of 1877, a committee of the church met with her and asked her to consider an alternative placement in the South as a teacher. She prayerfully considered it but decided it was not for her. At this point there was no prospect of another teaching post because the public school semester had already started. With no funds left, she asked her father for a loan: "At last at my request he told me I might give him my note for what I would need that year and I might pay it back, or in case of inability to do so, the amount would be deducted from my share of the property when divided."[21] With her studies thus financed, she returned to Mount Holyoke for the 1877–1878 academic year. When no teaching opportunity emerged, she increased the amount owed to her father and entered medical school in 1878 at the University of Michigan.

Holbrook maintained an interest in events at Mount Holyoke and noted in 1879 that there were twenty-seven in the Missionary Association, many of whom were interested in studying medicine.[22] She was initially very interested in the possibility presented to her of working in the Kyoto Home School in Japan but, by 1880, she had shifted her interest to the North China Mission. She interned in Boston at the New England Hospital for Women and Children and then went to Tung-cho, North China in 1881. In ill health, she returned to the

20. "Mary A. Holbrook, M.D.," copy of clipping file, Mount Holyoke Library Association, box 71–576, YDS.

21. Enoch Bell to Ruth Rouse, 20 May 1942, box 71–576, YDS.

22. Mary A. Holbrook to N. G. Clark, 10 May 1879, quoted by Enoch Bell to Ruth Rouse, 20 May, 1942, box 71–576, YDS.

United States in 1887 but recuperated sufficiently to return, this time to Japan, two years later.

In 1889, Dr. Holbrook and three Mount Holyoke alumnae—Cora Stone, Caroline Telford, and Lizzie Wilkenson—wrote to the American Board for Foreign Missions, offering themselves for service in Japan. Holbrook and her three friends offered to help establish a "Mt. Holyoke College" in Japan so that Japanese women could be trained to their "sphere of usefulness" and that the college might do what the American Mount Holyoke had done for the world, namely, elevate the status of women. The proposal was rejected, and the possibility of cloning the Western educational model for women in the form of Mount Holyoke was never realized.

The women instead found employment on the faculty of Japan's Kobe College, where Dr. Holbrook established the science department. Tuberculosis forced Stone to return to the United States in 1894, but she later served as a home missionary in North Carolina.[23] In 1907, Holbrook also resigned due to ill health; she died in 1910 in East Haven, Connecticut. Her achievements included two books in Chinese, one a science book.[24]

Prior to the formation of the MHMA, an earlier society, *Stella Vigiles* (Watchers for the Star), existed at Mount Holyoke from 1865. Primarily daughters of missionaries, the members called themselves SVs. They used "Watchman, what of the night?" as a motto and held monthly Sunday prayer meetings as well as social evenings with refreshments and guests.[25] Grace Wilder was secretary of the SVs during part of 1882–1883 and also for 1883–1884. The *Stella Vigiles* society may have overlapped with the MHMA. The MHMA itself continued until 1898, when it was incorporated into the Mount Holyoke Young Women's Christian Association (organized in 1893), as the Missionary Literature Committee.[26] During the same period, the YWCA absorbed the pre-existing Christian Endeavour Society that had begun in 1881 as a way to train young people to become leaders in their local churches. Mission

23. Enoch Bell to Ruth Rouse, 20 May 1942, RG 46, box 71–57, YDS.

24. Clipping file in the Mount Holyoke Library Archives, copied in, box 71–576, YDS.

25. Bertha Blakely to Ruth Rouse, 19 March 1942, box 71–576, YDS.

26. Blakely to Rouse, 16 May 1942, box 71–576, YDS.

study classes under the auspices of the YWCA were formed in 1897 and flourished for about twenty-five years.

Meetings of the MHMA were held once a month on Sunday afternoons. Members, who were recruited by personal invitation, signed a pledge committing themselves to missionary service even in "a foreign land." Members of the association subsequently worked in India, South Africa, East Africa, China, Constantinople, and India. Other members worked in the United States in various academic and social service positions.[27]

The women's colleges and female seminaries fostered a desire to learn about the foreign field as well as domestic problems, and planted the idea that mission work was an appropriate vocational goal for women. Students at Mount Holyoke pursued this goal well before the founding of the MHMA: Charlotte Bailey left in 1838 to work in Africa; Fidelia Fiske, in 1843, went to Persia to start Fiske Seminary for girls; and two nieces of Mary Lyon, the founder of Mount Holyoke Female Seminary, graduates of 1838 and 1840, both taught at Mount Holyoke before marrying and departing for India and China.[28] In 1897, the Mount Holyoke YWCA voted to adopt a missionary who was a recent graduate of the college. In 1907, Olive Sawyer Hoyt, class of 1897, was sent to Japan to teach at Kobe College (1902–1913) and later to serve as a principal of a girl's school in Matsuyama, Japan (1913–1940). Alice Seymour Brown, class of 1900, was adopted as Mount Holyoke missionary and sent to China in 1905. The pattern of club life and commitment to overseas service demonstrated by Mount Holyoke in the late nineteenth century was replicated in many of the women's colleges of the time.

Missionary ideals spread with the growth of nineteenth-century women's education in North America. In some cases, ideas were disseminated by teachers and lady principals who taught in more than one school. At the Methodist Ontario Ladies' College in Whitby, Ontario, for example, a missionary society was organized in 1889 by the lady

27. Typescript by Mary Mathews, 1937, box 71–574, YDS.

28. YWCA file, box 71–570, YDS, show that there were mission study classes at Mt. Holyoke as follows: in 1902, two classes, with twenty-one enrolled; in 1903, six classes with eighty-seven enrolled; in 1904, five classes, with ninety-one enrolled; in 1905, twelve classes with 181 enrolled. The figures for subsequent years are similar. In 1919/20 when study classes were called World Fellowship classes; that year there were fifteen classes with 229 enrolled. The numbers reflect a growing interest in missionary concerns among students.

principal Mary Electa Adams. Adams was an experienced educator who had studied at Montpelier Academy in Vermont (originally Newbury Seminary and renamed Vermont Female College) and worked as a teacher and lady principal at a number of schools in Ontario, including Dundas Female Seminary, Hamilton Ladies' College, Ontario Ladies' College, Picton Ladies' Seminary, and at the Albion Female Seminary in Michigan in the 1850s.

Adams' experience in a variety of institutions, combined with her travels—sometimes with her sister—to visit schools in the United States, Canada, and Britain meant that she could create a school that combined the best features of all that she had seen. Although the schools with which she was associated generally had a missionary society or club, the emphasis on mission and piety seems to have been more muted than at Mount Holyoke. Historian Alison Prentice notes that Adams saw herself as a mentor and guide to her students but was no republican and valued a "solid" education for women that "encompassed moral principles." According to Prentice, Adam's working life extended across the romantic period of early female seminaries into the reformist period of establishment of women's colleges like Wellesley, Smith, and Vassar.[29]

Adams opened a school in Cobourg, Ontario in the 1870s, Brookhurst, which she had hoped to develop into a women's university parallel to Victoria University. However, various difficulties including financial led to the closure of Brookhurst and the absorption of women into Victoria.

Other Methodist ladies' colleges in Ontario, such as Alma College in St Thomas and Albert College in Belleville also had a Missionary Society.[30] Ella Gardiner taught at the Methodist Alexandra College, also in Belleville, from 1884 to 1928. A graduate of the University of Toronto, Gardiner was supportive of the development of a Student Missionary Society at the college. The mission movement had begun in June 1876 when a group of women organized the Women's Missionary Society of the Methodist Episcopal Church. In 1887 a mission band was formed and one member, Minnie Wilson, went to Shanghai, China. Other missionaries from the college included Kate Curtis, who taught music in India; Annie Lake, missionary to Africa; Marion Lambly, teacher and evangelist to Tokyo Girls' School; Rose Swayze, 1890, teacher in a Native

---

29. Prentice, "Scholarly Passion," 258–84.

30. Selles, *Methodists*, ch. 3.

mission school at Norway House, Manitoba; Mary Doyle, who attended between 1892–1893 and served as a teacher at a mission college in South Africa; and her sister Martha Doyle, who matriculated 1897 and studied medicine at Trinity Medical School to prepare for the mission field.[31]

Educational institutions that fostered ideals of women in service and leadership led to the expansion of education opportunities around the world. Graduates of ladies' colleges, seminaries, and academies saw service as a direct expression of a spiritual call. Not only did the graduates themselves spread the word of a larger world; missionary narratives formed a popular account that provided vicarious experiences for those at home.[32]

Travel began to open up as a possibility, and the stories of intrepid early women travelers created precedents for women travelling alone. These women adventurers, who published accounts of their heroic quests, brought the exotic attractions of the world into the public imagination.[33] Rail and steamship travel provided leisure opportunities for women who could afford adventure, rest, or respite from domestic duties. Publication of missionary observations and travel books, and visits of missionaries on furlough generated a great deal of interest in foreign lands and cultures.

The increased numbers of women in higher education also affected the numbers who enrolled in mission societies, churches, or mission service. Several factors led to this increase: the greater availability of primary and secondary schooling that provided the necessary preparation for higher education; the public acceptance of coeducation, preparing many girls to follow their brothers to university; and the creation of the ideal of the middle-class woman who would use her educational gifts to provide moral guidance to the domestic sphere and society.

31. Ella Gardiner, "Missionary Movement in Albert College, Christian Guardian, 4 July 1900; "Missionary Conference of Albert College," *Christian Guardian,* 23 May 1900.

32. See Austin, *Canadian Missionaries.*

33. Some early women travelers who defied Victorian conventions included Harriet Martineau, Isabella Bird, Gertrude Bell, and Mary Henrietta Kingsley. Part of their relative safety in travelling was a result of European imperialism. Their impressions were recorded in travel diaries that recorded observations from a woman's point of view and gained an avid readership. On women travelers see, Lapierre, *Women Travellers* and Birkett, *Spinsters Abroad.* Missionary writings also provided an insight into little travelled areas of the world. See Romero, ed., *Women's Voices on Africa.*

Historians Gidney and Millar have identified the rural or middle-class small town Ontario origins of those who entered medical and other professions. The forces of economic change, rural depopulation, and urbanization combined to push both girls and boys off the farms. In addition, from the 1860s onward, high school was accessible to women who could therefore achieve the same qualifications as boys for white-collar work, as well as the matriculation certificate required by universities and the professions.[34] Women were motivated by both the need to support themselves and the desire to pursue adventure. Missionary work provided a socially acceptable rationale for professional education for nurses, teachers, and doctors.

The first generation of women university students experienced their education as a privilege. Their first-hand experience of the forces of social change that resulted in the educated woman as a middle-class ideal made them optimistic that this change could be extended around the world with college graduates as ambassadors.

The momentum gained in the nineteenth century with the opening up of educational possibilities, the growth of clubs and women's movements, the increased numbers of women participating in teaching, nursing, medicine, and missionary work, found an outlet in work for the Y, SVM, and eventually the WSCF in the late nineteenth and twentieth centuries.

With the entry of women into coeducational universities, change was required: previously male mission groups had to consider whether to include women. Or should there be separate women's missionary clubs? Societies and clubs that flourished in the United States made their way north to Canadian universities. A branch of the Young Women's Christian Association was established at Victoria in the 1870s at its original Cobourg campus and continued once the college moved to Toronto in 1892. Other missionary organizations included Inter-Collegiate Missionary Alliance (ISMA) in 1885. From the 1870s until the First World War, a variety of clubs and organizations emerged to engage students' commitment to missionary work, including social and moral reform. These included the Methodist Missionary and Women's Missionary Society, the denominational Epworth League and Young People's Forward Movement for Missions, and the non-denominational Student Volunteer Movement, and in 1921 the Student Christian Movement.

34. Gidney and Millar, *Professional Gentlemen*, 323.

A Ladies' Missionary Society was formed at the coeducational Victoria in 1891, but previous to this women were generally welcome also in the nominally male missionary societies. [35]

YWCA

Forerunners to the YWCA, founded in England in 1855, include an array of efforts by individual women and endeavors by women's organizations to meet the needs of women industrial workers as well as displaced or immigrant women in the cities. Though these early efforts were limited in scope, over time they coalesced to inspire the international organizational vision of the YWCA. Most directly two individual efforts in England gave rise to what eventually became the YWCA—one was a prayer union founded in 1855 by Emma Roberts, and the other was a London hostel established by a Mrs. Arthur Kincaid. The vision of the YWCA that emerged was based on a commitment to serve those in need, including the displaced, the marginalized, and the working poor, as well as the high school or college girl.

The American YWCA, inaugurated in 1858, began with a commitment to personal piety and social service and grew to incorporate educational methods and leadership training, traditions that were also part of the English and Continental YWCAs. Y associations offered a structure that transcended denominational lines and allowed for the building of local organizations with the help of voluntary, unsalaried leadership. Emphasis on Bible study and special evangelistic work was common to the YWCA work in various countries. In addition, programs such as summer camps and courses promoted the health of body, mind, and spirit.[36]

The trans-denominational approach of the YWCA provided an opening to work in new fields where a church- or missions-based strategy might have been denied access. Such ecumenical work characterized the student branches of the YWCA as well; indeed, the YWCA was more ecumenical than even the interdenominational church boards.

35. Semple, *Faithful Intellect,* 216.

36. At Silver Bay Conference Center on Lake George, New York, YWCA conferences drew enthusiastic participants. In 1904, there were 810 delegates to a YWCA conference, of whom 550 were college students and fifty were preparatory students. In 1905, there were 734 students from 111 institutions in twelve states and Canada. See E. Clark Workman, *Contribution of Silver Bay.*

By 1920 it had dropped the condition of membership in a Protestant evangelical church[37] By 1894, the vision of an international movement led to a debate among YWCA members, who argued the merits of the title "International" versus "World." They finally settled on the name "World's Young Women's Christian Association" because it emphasized unity, whereas for them "International" would signify only co-operation between separate entities.[38] The constitution provided YWCA members with active membership in the worldwide association but this was limited to those who had a national organization. At the first World's Conference in 1898, representatives of national organizations were present from Great Britain, United States, Norway, Sweden, Canada, Italy, and India.[39]

The rapid diffusion of the YWCA opened up worldwide employment possibilities for young women.[40] Women university graduates who sought meaningful employment were attracted to the possibility of service work with organizations like the YWCA or the WSCF that offered local, national, and international opportunities. Such involvement continued the interests that had already been established in college years.

The rapid growth of the YWCA led to problems organizationally since there were multiple organizations now working in the same international field. Some countries resisted what they saw as an aggressive takeover of work by British or American leaders. At the World's YWCA meeting in 1902, the decision was made to approve and sponsor the development of the association in countries then regarded as "mission fields," with the proviso that the association intended only to supplement, not to take over, the work of missionary societies.[41]

The YWCA in America developed as a separate women's movement, even though one of the early organizers, Luther Wishard, had originally supported the college Y's that had developed organically at coeducational Midwestern universities. When this development was reported to the executive of the American YMCA, they adamantly insisted on separate YMCA and YWCA organizations and thus ordered Wishard to undo this coeducational work. Women were told that they were best served by

---

37. Rice, *YWCA*, 50. See also Boyd, *Emissaries*, 92.

38. Seymour-Jones, *Journey of Faith*.

39. Ibid., 13.

40. Rice, *History*, 4.

41. Seymour-Jones, *Journey*, 15.

having their own movement.[42] Women graduates, especially those who left other jobs to work for the organization, provided the YWCA with a skilled workforce. For example, Corabel Tarr left teaching in 1889 to become the second General Secretary of the International Committee and served until her marriage in 1892.[43]

Nineteenth-century activists belonged to a variety of organizations concerned with social betterment, and they brought an ethos of social service, outreach, and leadership that in many cases eventually carried over into the WSCF. Helen Barrett Montgomery (1861–1934) illustrates the multiple social service commitments that were common to many women in this period.[44] After graduating from Wellesley in 1884, she taught high school in Rochester and then worked for two years at a school in Philadelphia. She married a widower and moved back to Rochester where she was active in women's clubs and the Baptist church. She worked to open the University of Rochester to women, and she served on the Rochester Women's Education and Industrial Union.[45] Her book, *Western Women in Eastern Lands*, sold 50,000 copies in the first six weeks.[46] In addition to playing on the irresistible appeal of Eastern women to the mind and heart of women in the West, the book described the wrongs experienced by women in the East and offered a social gospel rationale for missions, arguing that women had to intervene to end the degradation of women in heathen lands.[47]

Among her many activities, Montgomery was president of the Women's American Baptist Foreign Mission Society from 1914–1924. She helped organize the Worldwide Guild of Northern Baptist Young Women. Her views on the importance of women's education and the need for mission work provided a strong impetus for missions. In her

---

42. For example, Luther Wishard who was urged to reverse the gender-integrated policy he had started in the United States arranged for Fanny Beale, YWCA delegate, to speak at an Ohio state convention in 1883 to advocate for a separate association for women. Beale argued that only a girl could reach the heart of a girl. See Ober, *Association Secretaryship*, 69.

43. Rice, *History*, 50.

44. See Brackney, "The Legacy," 174–78. See also Marshall, *Peabody Sisters*.

45. Montgomery, *Western Women*.

46. Ibid., 56.

47. Parker, *Kingdom of Character*, 58.

own words, missions were shown to be "great social settlements suffused with the religious motive."[48]

Annie Marie Reynolds (1858–1892), born in Kiantone, New York, and the daughter of a clergyman, was another influential nineteenth-century activist. She was a sister of J. B. Reynolds who played a leading role in the pioneering work of the International YMCA in Berlin and Paris. After attending a private school in New Haven, Connecticut, she studied at Wellesley for two years and then left for France and Germany, where she studied French, German, possibly Spanish, and later learned Swedish. She taught school in Nyack, New York, and became secretary of the YWCA in Brooklyn; State Secretary for the YWCA of Iowa 1889–1892; secretary of the YWCA in London. For nine years she travelled through Europe, Asia, and South Africa and realized in the process that the World YWCA must serve a common ideal despite regional varia-tions. In her first annual report as Secretary of the World YWCA, she claimed that "the aim of the world's Association must be to encourage unity of purpose while recognizing liberally great diversity of method."[49]

In 1899, during a tour of India, Reynolds attended the opening of the new YWCA building in Bombay. She tried to work out a plan for co-operation between the National YWCA movement and the student movement established in 1897 by British university women. Ruth Rouse, who also arrived in 1899 to work with the Bombay Settlement and to be a Student Secretary for the YWCA, helped facilitate a plan for co-operation between the Y and the Missionary Settlement for University Women (see chapter 3). The plan assigned workers to specific regions: Agnes de Sélincourt of the Missionary Settlement for University Women was appointed Student Secretary for North India; Laura Radford of the YWCA for Bengal; and Ruth Rouse served as general student worker for India and Ceylon.[50]

Reynolds sailed to China and Japan in 1900 to investigate condi-tions there. She found some possibilities for pioneering association work among missionaries who were familiar with the movement from home. Two student YMCAs were established in the 1880s in China after the visit of Mr. and Mrs. Wishard (Eva Fancher of Mount Vernon, Iowa). Willard Lyon, education secretary for the Y, went to China to continue this work

48. Peabody, cited in Montgomery, *Western Women*, 121.

49. Reynolds, "First Annual Report," 1895, cited in Rice, *History*, 69.

50. Rice, *History*, 85.

in 1894. The YMCA helped start a movement for women. Both the YM and YWCA in China recognized the importance of developing indigenous leadership. China sent a special appeal to the World Committee of the YWCA, inspired by the need to help the thousands of women employed in industrial and factory work. Japan had similar concerns about women working in industries and living away from home. In addition, Japan was seeing a growing number of women graduates who had no opportunity to apply their education or to engage in social service. The appeals from China and Japan led to discussions at the Second World Conference in Geneva in 1902 as to the proper function of the work of the YWCA and the extent and character of the missionary program of the YWCA.

Annie Reynolds resigned from the YWCA in 1904 and wrote a brief history of the World's YWCA. In 1904 she settled in the family home in North Haven, Connecticut. She was an active member of the North Haven Congregational Church and a member of the Daughters of the American Revolution and the Wellesley Club.

Clarissa Hale Spencer was appointed to succeed Miss Reynolds. Her father was a Methodist clergyman who became Secretary to the Board of Extension of the Methodist Church and moved to Philadelphia. Spencer attended Wellesley for one year and returned home for a year due to ill health. She resumed her studies and graduated from Goucher College, Baltimore, Maryland with a BA in 1895. Spencer was the organizer and first president of the college YWCA at Goucher. She became a student volunteer and travelled for two years, particularly among the Southern colleges. Between 1896 and 1901 she spent five years in Japan under the auspices of the Methodist Church, returning home when her father died. Back in the United States she became involved in the YWCA and attended the summer training course in 1902 sponsored by the American committee. She was appointed the State Secretary for Ohio and then the General Secretary of the World's Committee.

Work in these voluntary student movements was often a family affair; brother and sister teams included Annie Reynolds and James Bronson Reynolds and Robert and Grace Wilder. Married teams included Luther Wishard and his wife, Eva Fancher, who was a founding member of the YWCA and accompanied her husband on his tours abroad from 1889–1893. John Mott's wife, Leila White Mott, a graduate of Worcester College, Massachusetts, travelled with her husband overseas and represented the women's interests while he worked on behalf of the WSCF. Douglas Fraser, eventual missionary to Africa, travelled and worked with his wife, Agnes Fraser, a medical doctor. Emma Bailey Speer, who became president of the American YWCA after the death of Grace Dodge in 1914, apparently drew heavily on the field experience of her husband Robert Speer who served as Secretary of the Board of Foreign Missions of the Presbyterian Church (1891–1937).[51]

GRACE DODGE (1856–1914)

Nineteenth-century activists belonged to a variety of organizations concerned with social betterment and they brought an ethos of social service, outreach, and leadership that in many cases was carried over into the student movement. One activist whose influence and leadership was felt in organizations around the world was Grace Hoadley Dodge, the granddaughter of William Dodge, a metals business executive. Her leadership and philanthropic work supported an array of charities and dispensed more than a million dollars of funding. In 1880 she founded the Kitchen Garden Association (later renamed the Industrial Education Association) to foster manual and domestic training and industrial arts in the public schools. She funded the New York College for the Training of Teachers in 1886, which was absorbed by Teachers College in 1892. In 1884 she organized a club for working women that became the Working Girls' Societies and served as its president until she helped to merge the group into the YWCA in 1905. She served as president of the YWCA board until her death in 1914.[52]

Dodge travelled to Vassar, Bryn Mawr, and Smith College to speak about the cause of working girls. While a student at Bryn Mawr Emma Speer heard Dodge speak—not realizing that someday she would succeed Dodge as the head of the YWCA (1915–1932). Another person in her audience was Vida Scudder (1861–1954) who became a leader in the college settlement movement and an educator. Scudder differed from Dodge on her interpretation of the roots of change. Dodge emphasized change at the level of individual character, whereas Scudder emphasized the need to analyze root causes of economic conditions and their effect

51. Boyd, *Emissaries*, 15–18.

52. For a biography of Dodge, see Graham, *Dodge*. For a reprint edition of Dodge's writings, see *Grace H. Dodge, 1974*.

on the workers.[53] After hearing theologian and Baptist minister Walter Rauschenbusch (1861–1918) in 1914, Dodge was disturbed by the economics of his gospel of the social order. She believed that the wealthy should hold their goods in trust for all.[54]

Dodge entertained many prominent women educators and social activists, including Bryn Mawr alumna Ume Tsuda who was a guest at Riverdale in 1913 and who began her own school in Japan. Another visitor was Mary Mills Patrick who had a PhD from Berne in Greek and philosophy and who began a school that became Constantinople Women's College.[55] Established in 1871 in Istanbul, the school went through a succession of names: the American High School for Girls, the Istanbul Girls' School, and the Constantinople Women's College. Mission staff had targeted educational opportunities for girls early on, including the need to move from primary to collegiate to higher education.

This educational mission in Constantinople was supported by a Mrs. Henry Bowker of Boston, who worked for soldiers in the Civil War, headed the Union Maternal Association, and was president of the Women's Board of Missions for twenty-two years starting in 1867. When Grace Dodge was originally approached for support for the Constantinople Women's College, she was too preoccupied with establishing Teachers College to assist, but later became involved. The realization that Mary Mills Patrick, principal of the school, functioned without a budget, convinced Dodge to become president of the board and to provide not only cash but also administrative training for the leaders of the school.[56] (Other financial donors included Mrs. Russell Sage, Mrs. Henry Woods, and Mrs. Rockefeller.) Dodge pursued an interfaith stance in her support of Constantinople and she did not expect all students to be

53. Graham, *Merchant,* 114.

54. Ibid., 263.

55. Mary Mills Patrick (1850–1940) was an American missionary to Turkey, Greece, and Armenia. In 1871 she was sent by the American Board of Commissioners for Foreign Missions to teach in an eastern Turkey mission school. In 1875 she began teaching at the Constantinople Women's College. Her leadership kept the school open through the Balkan Wars, the Turkish Revolution, and World War I. She retired as president of the school in 1924 and wrote a history in 1934.

56. See Curti, *American Philanthropy,* 164–68. Some of these missionary efforts in education were notable because, as in the case of an American sponsored school for poor children in Agora, they made no attempt to convert children away from the Orthodox Church. See also Patrick, *Bosphorous Adventure.*

Christian. Such interfaith understanding was part of Dodge's approach; in New York, she had been a friend of Rebecca Kohut (1864–1951) who was a social worker and educator and became president of the World Council of Jewish Women.

At her family estate, Greyston, in Riverdale-on-Hudson, New York, Dodge used her resources to entertain and to run training programs from home, including the first YWCA training course in 1908. She established the Riverdale Library Association in 1883 out of her greenhouse, which merged with Riverdale Neighborhood House in 1937. In addition to these commitments, she managed to care for her invalid mother and run the household.

John Mott appealed to Dodge for support for a women's secretary devoted to women's work. As he explained to Dodge, "The world field is too large for me to cover properly. Moreover there are certain problems and opportunities in work for women students which a woman can treat far better than a man. The woman's student field is enormous. Such a worker can serve all the Christian organizations at work in this field."[57] Dodge was concerned that the prospective candidate have a "broad" Christian sympathy and be able to appreciate the "broad" Christian thoughts and work that was being undertaken, work that she assumed many would not consider evangelical. Mott replied that Ruth Rouse was a person with broad sympathies who had won support in the New England women's colleges, as well as among women students in Britain, and showed adaptability in Scandinavia, Germany, Holland, Russia, and India. The challenge for Rouse, explained Mott, would be to develop self-directing and self-supporting national student movements and to work largely through their leaders. By contrast, in the first decade of student work, Mott had to devote himself entirely to planting national student movements and doing pioneer work.[58]

Dodge met with Rouse and found her a satisfactory choice for a women's secretary for the student movement. The non-sectarian goals of the service organizations such as the YWCA were a comfortable fit for Dodge. Her instincts for ecumenism led her to attend the Edinburgh Conference in 1910 where she served on an educational commission.

Dodge's involvement in voluntary movements allowed for an extension of the values that she held and promoted from her New York

57. Mott to Dodge, 18 July 1904, RG 45, Series I, 23/433, YDS.

58. Mott to Dodge, 25 July 1904, RG 45, Series I, 24/433, YDS.

base. She supported a movement based on education that would extend knowledge to areas of the world that had been disadvantaged, and provide skills training appropriate to one's social level.

Dodge was one of the first women appointed to the New York Board of Education in the late 1880s. She also served as a member of the Educational Commission for the Ecumenical Missionary Conference, which she attended. Dodge worked for a united effort among Jewish, Roman Catholic, and Protestant women to greet incoming girls at the stations and docks. The National Vigilance Committee, which later became the American Social Hygiene Association, was formed at her house in 1905. This organization involved itself in the development of laws against the trade in women.

Influenced by the writings of Johann Pestalozzi (1746–1827) and Friedrich Froebel (1782–1852), Dodge had a talent for organization and creativity and was deeply dedicated to providing education and training.[59] Ruth Rouse, who became the Women's Secretary for the WSCF, spoke about the opportunities in student work to a group in Dodge's home. Dodge apparently left a bequest for women's work in the WSCF, one that by the 1940s had been redirected into the general funds of the organization.[60] When she died at the age of fifty-eight in 1914, she had bequeathed a million and a half dollars to a variety of causes including the WSCF.[61]

Dodge's varied interests and wide involvement provide an excellent example of the overlapping engagements of those involved in Christian social service, student work, and YWCA-sponsored activities. Her broad philanthropic and mission participation arose not merely from her inheritance, but even more from her commitment to provide practical help to those in need in order that they might have the skills necessary

59. Johan H. Pestalozzi (1746–1827) was a Swiss-born educator who attempted to apply Rousseau's ideas to education by encouraging children to learn through activities and to draw their own conclusions. Froebbel was a German-born educator influenced by Pestalozzi who is credited with the introduction of the kindergarten movement with its emphasis on activity and play.

60. Mackie to Rouse, 29 June 1942, RG 46, box 1, file 2, YDS. Mackie wrote: "I did not know that this money was still supposed to be set against women's work, but I have no qualms of conscience on the subject. The only two members of staff being paid directly from our central funds are Suzanne and myself, and quite obviously a very high percentage of the students in the movements we are seeking to help are women students."

61. "Dodge," *Notable American Women*, 489–92.

for survival. Many of the early supporters and leaders in the WSCF carried forward this commitment to multiple constituencies. Dodge did not live to see the demise in 1928 of one of her projects, the National YWCA Training School.[62]

Educated women were inspired to take up careers in student voluntary movements such as the YWCA. YWCA leader Annie Reynolds observed the following on the connection between education and the growth of the YWCA movement: "It is the best education, the best brain, the strongest constitution and the deepest consecration that must stand in the breach of this advanced stage of the world's civilization. There is work for all, but now, when everywhere the standard of education has been so much raised, there is an especial need for those who have the higher advantages of any land to make their influence felt for Christian womanhood."[63]

Education made it possible for women to bring skills to the job but education in the late nineteenth century was not automatically linked to employment possibilities that offered sufficient challenge. Women had a limited range of occupations to choose from, including teaching and secretarial work. Organizations like the YWCA and the WSCF offered the opportunity for both travel and meaningful work at a time when choices at home were limited.

Nettie Dunn Clarke, first national secretary of the YWCA in the United States, who went to India in 1893, commented on the cooperation between the WSCF and the YWCA. Looking back in 1940 on her career with the Y, she observed in a letter to Rouse,

> You may remember how I really hunted for something to do in YWCA lines. In our first Station, Ludhiana [India], we had a YWCA mostly made up of young medical students and nurses of the Medical School there. But it was only after five years, when we moved to Ambala and had that camp that I felt that this was YWCA work that counted. By that time I had been hearing about the Federation and was rejoiced to have its help from you and Miss Cooke and to feel that here was an organization made to really help our student associations in a sympathetic way. It was something that the Federation has its own financial budget and paid workers who could give time to college groups in India, as we knew it was doing in various parts of Europe and other lands.

62. Boyd, *Emissaries*, 92.

63. Reynolds, "Annual Report for 1899," quoted in Rice, *History*, 85.

And I judge that one great advantage was that the Federation gathered up a great number of Associations with various names, not always YMCA or YWCA and these needed to be helped and coordinated. In those days it was therefore a much needed unifying influence in Europe and America as well as a spiritual stimulus to real Christian work in the Colleges. As to the World's YWCA, that was started several years before the Federation and in those years it was a great help to both city and college Associations, though at first it seemed far away from our American Associations, and we rather felt that the English organizations were getting most of the help . . . So perhaps the World's Federation was more warmly welcomed by the students.[64]

Women students reached eagerly for opportunities to serve through student movements and voluntary associations. The coordination of efforts in overseas missions required the type of oversight that the international federation could bring. The work of the women's student secretary and the women's coordinating committee was essential in creating communication links between workers in the field and policy makers at home.

ROLE OF WOMEN AND THE SVM

The notion of women's work for women inspired women at SVM conferences and bands to make commitments to serve abroad. Parker notes that women were seldom keynote speakers at SVM conferences; specific themes on women were gathered within smaller venues within the conferences. In 1891 the SVM convention included a session by Nettie Dunn on "Women's Work for Women." This was also the case at the 1898 convention, but after that women's issues were generally handled in sessions related to specific countries. Women also addressed themes outside specific women's issues. Several women attained prominence in the SVM including Abbie Child, Lucy Peabody, Geraldine Guiness, Dr. Pauline Root, and Una M. Saunders and Bertha Conde. After 1898, women held two places on the American SVM executive.[65]

An interest in social reform became a major force in student culture between 1890 and World War I. The reform impulse was supported by the emergence of the theology of the social gospel and a consequent

64. Dunn Clarke to Rouse, 22 April 1940, box 84–689, WSCF Archives, YDS.

65. Parker, *Kingdom of Character*, 59–60.

liberalization of Protestantism. Social gospel beliefs emphasized the establishment of the kingdom of God on earth through social reform. Women members of nineteenth-century Protestant churches found that the social gospel validated the efforts of laywomen working together to bring forth the kingdom.[66] Although women did not occupy a large place in national Canadian political parties, their influence was felt through pressure groups. After forty years of organizing in the Women's Christian Temperance Union, the National Council of Women, and various farm organizations, women were able to push for social reforms.[67] Methods of social investigation developed gradually from settlement house work to social research.[68] Canada's first school of social work was established in 1914 in an attempt to professionalize the investigations of the social conditions of the poor and immigrant classes and the services to them.[69]

Women's missionary work also aimed at social reform through industrial and vocational instruction, orphanages, and relief efforts. Medical and public health missions included training of health care workers, dispensaries, and direct assistance.[70]

CONCLUSION

Women joined organizations like the YWCA and the Student Volunteer Movement that allowed them to find or support meaningful work at home and overseas. Many women's colleges had helped socialize women to the notion of service and missions. Although a desire for adventure and a fascination with exotic cultures around the world contributed to such missionary service, missionary engagement was also celebrated as the ultimate expression of piety. Such service was supported by those at home through financial donations, prayer, and publicity through written and spoken word.

According to Austin and Scott, Canadians sponsored more missionaries than any nation in Christendom. In the absence of formal diplomatic relations in the 1880s, the missionary movement was Canada's foreign policy and provided the main source of information about the

---

66. McKillop, *Matters of Mind,* 206.

67. Christie and Gauvreau, *Full-Orbed Christianity,* 117.

68. James, "Reforming Reform," 55–90.

69. For a study of the origins of social research and the relationship between settlement house work and investigation, see Shore, *Science of Social Redemption.*

70. Curti, *Philanthropy,* 164.

larger world.[71] The connection between foreign policy and student movements is more than symbolic. As Catharine Gidney indicates in her study of university student culture, experience in the student movement was linked to leadership in the university in the roles of president, dean, don, and tutor.[72] Thus, for women, involvement in student movements could result in positions as deans of women and lecturers.

Women who worked in the field served as informal diplomats. They developed expertise in local culture, language, and religion and adapted their programs in crisis situations with a high degree of autonomy. In these decades, Western women working for voluntary organizations claimed for themselves freedoms that were greater than they would have achieved at home. A vision of Christian internationalism and ecumenism would attempt to consolidate diverse student movements in various countries into a vision for the future. The ultimate failure of that vision to encompass the diversity of the world does not undermine the contributions of individual women and of the organizations they represented in furthering intercultural and interfaith dialogue. As a vision, Christian internationalism recognized that religion could not be separated from politics and that diplomacy began with understanding and friendship.[73] Such a simple approach proved effective time and again in countries around the world where students gathered for meals, fellowship, study, sport, prayer, and music. A world where hospitality, trust, and friendship found central place was a world where the experiences and traditions of the colleges and universities were expanded to a world stage.

Arguments against women's education which resounded loudly throughout the nineteenth century were gradually reduced to a persistent whine in the twentieth—dismantled by the apparent academic success and physical stamina of women students in seminaries, academies, colleges, and universities in Canada, the United States, England, Australia, and parts of Europe.

Graduates were eager to apply their new learning and leadership skills to a vocation that called for a life of service.[74] This eagerness was inspired partly by a spiritual call to vocation and partly by an adventur-

71. Austin and Scott, *Canadian Missionaries*, 5.

72. Gidney, *Long Eclipse*.

73. For a study of Christian internationalism, see Wright, *World Mission*.

74. See for example, Brouwer, *New Women For God*; Robert, *American Women*; Reeves-Ellington, *Competing Kingdoms*.

ous curiosity that quietly defied middle-class expectations for marriage and home and made the world home to educated women. Missionary service was carefully cultivated by the socialization of women in the early academies and seminaries and provided a normative example of the type of service one was expected to give. Such service was freighted with expectations and assumptions that provided women graduates with the moral authority that was felt to reside particularly in those who were Western, white, middle class, and Protestant.[75] The extension of middle-class domesticity to a realm outside the home provided a realm for action and involvement that opened up the world at a time when travel also made such experience feasible.

Women for whom the university years had been formative hoped to share the experience with their less fortunate sisters in various parts of the world. Western-educated Protestant women, whose role in terms of moral superiority was already exalted, were duty bound to extend this moral influence within their families and charged with extending this mothering role to the world. They provided models of the elevated womanhood whose education provided them with skills that others would need to be recreated in their image. Values implicit in this transfer included middle-class ideals for relationship, family life, hygiene, industry, hard work, and honesty—values that were consistent with the liberal arts and character-building education they had experienced. Having been formed in women's educational settings, graduates were prepared to repeat the process—teaching by example and assuming that the lessons were as appropriate in the new context as they had been at home.

75. Garner, "Global Feminism." Online: http://www.historycooperative.org/journals /jwh/15.2/garner.html. See also McClintock, *Imperial Leather*.

3

The Lord's Dominion

The Formation of the World Student Christian Federation

DURING A YMCA SPEAKING engagement in the Swedish town of Vadstena, Karl Fries, student leader in charge of the logistics for an upcoming Scandinavian student conference in 1895, decided that a deserted local castle would make a perfect location for the conference. He obtained permission to use the building, unoccupied for two hundred years, and arranged to furnish it with hospital beds intended for a hospital still under construction. Undaunted by the refusal of the state to allow the installation of lighting inside, Fries arranged for an electrician, who was a member of the YMCA, to suspend lights outside the windows.

In addition to the two hundred student delegates who arrived from Norway, Sweden, and Finland, the invitees included representatives of Christian student movements from North America, Britain, Germany, and the Movement for Students in Mission Lands and the Far East.[1] As they gathered in the old Council Hall, Fries described the moment: "To help our imagination, we had before our eyes colossal pictures of armed knights and the robust construction of the hall, now decorated with garlands of green and with the flags of various nations, helped to inspire us with a feeling of solemnity and responsibility. It would become a historic gathering, although few of us realized then what was to follow."[2]

When Karl Fries matriculated in 1879 from Uppsala University in Semitic languages, his goal had been a missionary career. Instead, he

1. The North American student movement consisted of the Intercollegiate YMCA, the Student Volunteer Movement for Foreign Missions, and the Inter-seminary Missionary Alliance. All three of these movements functioned in both the United States and Canada.

2. Fries, quoted in Adler, *Memoirs*, 13.

served the WSCF as chair for twenty-five years. His student experiences in organizing were a useful training for this position. While he was a student, the membership in the university student club that met for Bible study and prayer had dwindled to ten. However, a revival at Uppsala during the 1880s inspired Fries to found a missions study group. Under his leadership they published a missionary review, pamphlets, and a missionary hymnbook.[3]

In addition to Fries, organizers of the Vadstena conference included John Rutter Williamson, a twenty-three year old medical student from Edinburgh; Johannes Siemsen, a twenty-three year old recent law graduate from Germany; two Americans, John R. Mott, thirty-year old graduate of Cornell and Luther Wishard, graduate of Princeton who was at that time thirty-nine years old; and Pastor Eckhoff who was between forty and fifty years of age from Norway.[4] These delegates represented the British, German, North American, Mission Lands,[5] and Norwegian student Christian movements.[6] The religious affiliations of this group included Lutheran, Presbyterian, and Methodist. Four were volunteers (they had signed a pledge to become missionaries) for the mission field.

Gathered in the attic of the castle, these six men created an administrative structure for the proposed WSCF including a General Committee composed of two members of each national student movement. Appointed to executive positions were Karl Fries, chair; John Mott, general secretary; Johannes Siemsen, vice-chair; Rutter Williamson, corresponding secretary; and Luther Wishard, treasurer.

A provisional constitution gave direction to the WSCF until the first General Committee meeting could assemble in the United States in 1897. The purpose of the Federation was to unite student Christian

3. Founded in 1895 as the World's Student Christian Federation, the WSCF formally changed its name in 1960 to the World Student Christian Federation (WSCF), the form of the name used in this book.

4. Eckhoff was the president of the Norwegian Students' Missionary Union that had been founded in Christiania in 1881.

5. At Vadstena, the Student Christian Movements in Mission Lands entered the Federation and included college associations in Asia, later joined by Africa, and Latin America. Their name was changed to "The SCM in Lands without National Organization." Rouse claimed that it had been an odd affair: "a sort of Federation crèche: little could be done for the College Associations in it except through correspondence, and occasional visitation. But from there it hived into an independent existence in the Federation the national movements in India, China and Japan." Rouse, *WSCF*, 47.

6. Rouse, *WSCF*, 63.

movements or organizations throughout the world, to collect information regarding the religious conditions of students in all lands, and to promote the following lines of activity: to lead students to become disciples of Jesus Christ as only Savior and as God; to deepen the spiritual life of students and "to enlist students in the work of extending the Kingdom of Christ throughout the whole world."[7]

Prior to the Vadstena event, pioneering YMCA secretaries J. B. Reynolds and Luther Wishard had worked toward the formation of a world student organization under the auspices of the YMCA.[8] Wishard's strategy was to plant new YMCAs around the world that would then unite into national YMCAs and ultimately into a world movement. In the global strategy of conquest, students could be converted and made into "strongholds and distributing centers of Christianity." Colleges would turn into "academies of the Church Militant to train leaders for the present crusade of evangelization."[9]

In his travels around the world and in consultation with student leaders, Mott had concluded by 1894 that the ideal organizational structure for a world federation should allow countries to develop their own style of national student movements linked to the Federation. This was a departure from Wishard's proposal to unite movements through a world YMCA. Mott's plan allowed for regional variations in student organizations and did not force them to conform to a North American YMCA model.[10] As Mott observed, "It would be better to encourage the Christian students in each country to develop national Christian movements on their own: adapted in name, organization and activity to their own particular genius and character and then link these together."[11]

According to Mott, the federation model offered several advantages including the potential to survey the religious experience of students around the world. The Federation would allow strong and established

---

7. Ibid.

8. Wishard argued in 1884 that Christian movements among students should not be limited to any one country or continent and that students were to unite with American students to create a world movement whose purpose would be "Christ for the students of the World and the Students of the World for Christ." Reynolds proposed joining together the agencies in Europe in order that they could benefit from each other's experience and help each other. Rouse, *WSCF*, 53.

9. Wishard, *New Program*, 15–16.

10. de Dietrich, *50 Years of History*, 24.

11. Mott quoted in Weber, *Asia*, 67.

student movements to support weaker ones, and would distribute best practices and new policies to all members. Finally, the Federation would be able to provide a unifying force to student movements through conferences, publications, and speakers; a force that, according to Mott, would hasten the answer to the Lord's prayer in John 17:21, "that they all may be one."[12]

In reality, however, by 1896, many countries simply did not have an organized student movement that was eligible to join the federation. Scandinavian students, for example, before the founding of the WSCF, had a committee that arranged conferences. However, by the end of the Vadstena conference, they had formed the Scandinavian Student Christian Movement—a new member in the federation. The Federation thus not only provided a valuable framework for existing student movements, but also helped non-existent or fledgling movements to aspire to a national structure that would be eligible to join the WSCF.

Not all countries responded with enthusiasm to the idea of a world organization; some resisted perceived American or British control. In other countries, political circumstances inhibited participation; restrictions imposed by Russian control meant that twelve Finnish delegates travelled secretly to Vadstena because the Russian government would not have approved of their participation.[13]

The Federation thus brought together national student Christian movements with very different histories and traditions. In Germany, the evangelical revival of the 1870s and 1880s provided the impetus for the creation of the German Student Christian Movement. The leadership of the German student movement had been influenced by their

---

12. Rouse, *WSCF,* 63–64. Mott, after meeting the British students at Northfield in 1888, felt that the time was coming for an intercollegiate organization in Britain and elsewhere but not under the name of the Y. Thus the idea of a world federation began to shape itself in his mind and the minds of some of his fellow workers. As early as the World's YMCA Conference in Amsterdam, 1891, Mott's first visit to Europe, Raoul Allier of the Sorbonne recorded that he and Mott had talked of common concerns. He wrote that "it seemed to us as clear as day that student Christian associations in all lands should combine their forces to glorify Christ. We parted full of this ambition" (quoted in Rouse, *WSCF,* 52). At the Jubilee Conference of the YMCA in London (1894), he consulted with Dr. Karl Fries of Sweden and Count J. Moltke of Denmark on a possible federation and earlier that same year with Donald Fraser of Glasgow when he was a delegate to the SVM Convention in Detroit. He also discussed the matter with an international group at the British student summer conference in Keswick.

13. Rouse, *WSCF,* 60.

participation in American conferences; in 1885 Graf Pückler attended the World's YMCA Convention in Atlanta and in 1889 a Freiherr von Starck attended the Northfield Student Conference. Challenged by the success of the American student movement, the two men began to organize student conferences. These in turn led to the formation of Christian unions in the universities culminating in 1895 in the formation of the German Student Christian Alliance just two weeks before the WSCF was founded.[14]

The component student movements in North America (YMCA/YWCA) and the Student Christian Movement (SCM) in Britain that participated in the WSCF brought to the federation a similar evangelical Victorian culture with a strong missionary emphasis. Continuity in methods and organizational culture from the constituent student movements eased the process of federation. The Federation employed organizational methods that had proved successful in the student voluntary movements that preceded it, such as the use of student secretaries, invited international speakers, summer conferences, and special events. In the Student Volunteer Movement, local bands were affiliated with regional unions who met regularly at national conventions. The SVM quadrennial conference provided an occasion for every student generation to meet for education and celebration. Such methods ensured involvement of students at a variety of levels and brought local movements into contact with international representatives. Similarly, the WSCF encouraged participation at local and national levels and organized conferences for international co-operation.

Mott, as a leader in the SVM, the Y, and the WSCF, was well positioned to transmit a common core of values and successful practices to the new federation. Of the three organizations, the SVM proved the least resilient to the changes in student culture after the war and eventual disillusionment with the missionary enterprise that had formed its unitary focus for decades. However, in the late nineteenth and early twentieth centuries, the membership in organizations such as the SVM continued to increase. By 1891, missionary bands were present in 350 higher education institutions in Canada and the United States in 1891 and this number increased to 839 institutions by 1898.[15] Mott's leadership of the

---

14. Ibid., 48.

15. Parker, *Kingdom*, 13. By 1906, there were 19,000 Protestant missionaries in the world and about 6,000 of them were student volunteers.

SVM coincided with a rapid expansion of enrolment in higher education, another factor that contributed to the increased attendance in voluntary organizations.[16] For the college Y, that explosion of membership meant that by 1912, there were 800 chapters of the American college YMCA with 65,000 members. Also experiencing a rapid growth, the WSCF by 1913 had united national movements representing 2,305 local associations and an individual membership of 156,071 members.[17]

Activities central to the college Y could be found in the new federation. College Y secretaries disseminated curricula on topics such as Bible, missions, and social questions. Other college Y activities included an annual day of prayer, missionary meetings, intercollegiate correspondence, and the organization of club space in designated rooms or buildings. Training in Bible study methods was provided at summer conferences and training events and Bible study publications were translated into relevant languages and distributed to a variety of countries.[18] In both organizations, Bible study was encouraged for personal spiritual formation and for apologetic training. There were differences in practice, however. Ruth Rouse felt that the Bible was more central to the British student movement than to the American one.[19]

In the early twentieth century, students were increasingly preoccupied with social change rather than personal formation and evangelism. To this end, deputations of student Christian groups and voluntary organizations from England and Scotland, as well as students at Yale and Harvard, visited jails, Sunday schools, hospitals, and rural churches. Similar activities took place at the University of Toronto, as university students participated in downtown settlements such as Evangelia House (est. 1902), Fred Victor Mission (est. 1894), and the University Settlement (est. 1910). Arthur Burnett and George Bryce, two theological students from Victoria University, founded Central Neighbourhood House in the heart of downtown Toronto in 1911.[20]

Missions continued to share the agenda with social questions, but this tension could not be held together indefinitely. Historian Michael

16. Undergraduate enrollments grew from 62,839 in 1870 to 355,430 in 1910. See Setran, *College Y,* 63.

17. Setran, *College Y,* 73–77.

18. Rouse, *WSCF,* 87.

19. Setran, *College Y,* 47.

20. See James, "Reforming Reform," 55–99.

Parker suggests that the social gospel critique of Western institutions and nations began undermining the confidence of the missionary enterprise even before World War I.[21] Although evangelism still remained a goal during the time of Mott's leadership of the college Y, goals and methods changed to reflect an emphasis on the new character and service ideals of the college movement, as opposed to emphasis on personal conversion.[22]

In the early decades of student conferences, invited speakers addressed college meetings and conferences provided evangelical addresses. These speakers included the American evangelist Dwight Moody, who visited Britain in 1873 and 1882; Glasgow's Free Church Theological College lecturer Henry Drummond who visited North America, as did cricketer J. E. K. Studd. That such events proved to be life changing for participants is evident in Mott's claim that a meeting with Studd during his tour at Cornell resulted in a personal transformation that resulted in his lifelong career in missions and ecumenism.[23]

Gradually this personal evangelical approach through lectures and small group meetings shifted to an early twentieth-century focus on speakers who understood social investigation and could respond to students' questions about race, religion, immigration, and labor reform. Victorian rhetoric of conversion and personal change was slowly replaced by the language of social inquiry and social change. This emphasis on improving current conditions resonated with women who for decades had learned to organize for social improvement. Unlike the theological language of ordained clergy, the language of social investigation challenged women as workers and later as professionals. One such investigator was Mary Van Kleeck, an Anglican graduate of Smith College (1904) who investigated various trades that involved women and children and worked for the Russell Sage Foundation. Van Kleeck had been associated with the College Settlement Association and taught in Smith's School for Social Work.

21. Parker, *Kingdom,* 126.

22. Setran, *College Y,* 135–37.

23. Rouse, *WSCF,* 48.

WOMEN AND THE WSCF

Ruth Rouse (1872–1956), student volunteer, missionary, and women's travelling secretary for the World Student Christian Federation, was tall and commanding and in possession of an lively intellect. Undergraduate university women were reportedly completely awed by her. Beatrice Glass of Newnham College described Rouse in the following:

> As a traveling secretary I think she was extremely valuable in Britain through her quiet massiveness, good looks, good clothes (as compared to women missionaries of those days), good introductions, good degree from Girton. Most heads of women's colleges then were definitely extremely afraid of religious enthusiasm and outwardly at any rate did not seem in any way to identify themselves with religious at all and they had at least to respect Ruth and listen to what she had to stay. She was good at finding openings into women's colleges and picking out people to follow up her work.[24]

Rouse had been confronted by fellow students in her early university studies who were self-proclaimed atheists; her interest in apologetics proved to be a useful tool in discussions with students. Rouse visited countries where women's education was just beginning, as well as others where such education was well established. There were undoubtedly few women of her era who had such first-hand knowledge of the conditions of women students around the world. Her information-gathering visits to various countries was one of the pioneering strategies used by the Federation to determine the potential for establishing student Christian movement work.

Speaking to hostile and non-Christian students, Rouse observed that there were psychological barriers to overcome as her hosts tried to imagine what her motives might be: "I have been suspected of being an agent of Protestant propaganda, or, again, of clerical Catholicism; of being employed by some political party—pan-Germanism in Austria, Czarism, or Social Democracy in Russia; of belonging to the Salvation Army; of desiring to spread Christian Science, theosophy, Tolstoi-ism or free love; of leading an attack on the higher education of women, or on the Jews."[25] Public speaking on matters of faith by a woman was

24. Mrs. Alek G. Fraser to Wilmina Rowland, 25 January, 1957, quoted in Rowland, "Contribution of Women," 73.

25. Rouse, *WSCF.*

unprecedented in many countries. Annie Reynolds had visited some of these areas on her world tour for the YWCA in the late 1890s, but Rouse openly represented an organization and spoke confidently to mixed audiences.

Rouse's preparation for this work had been gained in the field, since there were at that time no training schools for women preparing for international work and no mentors to supervise a role that emerged in response to the growing numbers of women students eager to participate in student movement work. In the latter nineteenth century a variety of educational options engaged women who sought to prepare for foreign and domestic mission. Such training included missionary training programs, Bible programs, and deaconess programs. In Rouse's case, her training was accomplished in a variety of positions she held after her graduation from university.

Born in England, Rouse was the oldest child of an upper middle class London family.[26] Her father was a cotton broker from a Plymouth Brethren background, with some Evangelical Anglican roots, and her mother was Scottish Baptist (the result of English Radcliffe revival in Aberdeen in the 1860s).[27] She attended Notting Hill High School and then studied science for a year at Bedford College, London. Her university studies were completed at Girton College, Cambridge, in 1894, a time when women were still not formally given a degree.[28] The norms that governed behaviour of the first generation of women students were concerned with both respectability and political conservatism.[29] A famil-

26. Rouse presents the story of her federation work in a chapter entitled "An Autobiographical Interlude," *WSCF*, 111–23. Rowland's thesis on the WSCF provides biographical information about Rouse. I would like to acknowledge the generous assistance of Ruth Franzén in sharing her work on Rouse. Franzén's recent book on Rouse provides an insightful study of this women's leader. For information on the WSCF and women, see Balan-Sycip, *Towards a Women's History*. See also Potter and Wieser, *Seeking and Serving the Truth*.

27. Reginald Radcliffe was a mid-century revivalist who believed that conversion was a change in a particular moment, as opposed to something gradual or unconscious. See Bebbington, *Evangelicalism*, 8.

28. The first university level colleges for women in England were Girton College in 1869 and Newnham College in 1872. The first Cambridge women students were examined in 1882 but attempts to make them full members did not succeed until 1947, twenty years later than Oxford. Other educational ventures for women included a teacher's institute founded in 1879. See Williams, "Pioneer Women Students at Cambridge," in Hunt, *Lessons for Life*, 171–91.

29. Vicinus, *Independent Women*. Oxbridge colleges were apparently more actively

iarity with higher education served her well in her eventual work with the gender integrated British student movement. In addition, her commitment to the needs of women students was shaped by her own experience and extended into her work with students in different countries.[30]

Rouse attended her first student conference at Keswick with fifty women and 143 men in 1894. Keswick had been the focus of holiness gatherings since the mid-1870s, where the Americans Hannah and Robert Pearsall Smith helped shape the pattern of evangelical piety for much of the twentieth century. Transatlantic influences included holiness camp meetings in the 1860s—which provided a model for its British equivalent.[31]

At this meeting, she met the Americans John R. Mott and Robert Speer who became, respectively, the first and second travelling secretaries of the SVM. In 1896 Rouse attended the Student Volunteer Convention in Liverpool with 700 other students. As noted in chapter 1, the Student Volunteer Missionary Union (SVMU) had been formed in Britain in 1891 when Robert Wilder visited Britain to work among students.

Rouse had experienced a personal conversion at the age of eighteen while on vacation with her family at the seaside resort of Bournemouth. A layman who was leading the children's Special Service Mission on the sands asked her to undertake the swimming classes for the younger children. Watching the activity on the beach, she had a sudden insight that conversion involved something in which God took the initiative and not something she had to do for herself. This insight was consistent with the holiness teaching that rejected effort and conflict as the path to sanctification in favour of salvation as gift in which one could rest. She submitted to baptism despite some resistance to the notion of baptism, and especially baptism in the Charles Spurgeon church of her youth. At the age of twenty-two, she became a member of the Church of England.

---

involved in settlements whereas Girton and Somerville sent volunteers and made donations, but their involvement remained more perfunctory.

30. Rouse was an author in her own right and served as historian of the WSCF and the ecumenical movement. She wrote three histories in addition to the one on the WSCF. The other two included *Rebuilding Europe* and another edited with Neill, *History of the Ecumenical Movement.* She was interested in psychology and co-authored with H. Crichton Miller, M.D. a book entitled *Christian Experience.* She wrote not only these monographs but also penned pamphlets, published addresses, articles, and letters. See Franzén, 1993 for a full bibliography of her work.

31. Bebbington, *Evangelicalism*, 151.

The Church of England was influenced by Keswick ideas and may have attracted Rouse for its many missions including foreign missions, home missions, orphanages, and the work of deaconesses. The Church of England held annual conferences for Christian workers at Mildmay Park in London that were nondenominational but welcoming to those in sympathy with the various missions and the pursuit of a holy life. Women preachers and nondenominational work were part of Mildmay work and created a precedent that may have benefited Rouse.

In England, as historian David Bebbington notes, the church offered respectability to both the bourgeoisie and the artisan classes. Both Methodist and Congregational churches also offered community at a time when industrial and urban development created dislocation. Church work was an outlet for women and thus missionary support work, the YWCA, Christian Endeavour, and the Student Volunteer Movement contributed to the "Epiphany of Women."[32] Despite the idealization of a domestic role for women, evangelical religion, some have argued, was more important than feminism in enlarging the opportunities for women in the nineteenth century. Involvement in church sponsored activities offered an outlet to women of all classes and was an important arena for the training and development of leadership, speech, community development, and adult education. [33]

Rouse passed her tripos in classics and then studied Sanskrit for one year at the British Museum in London in order to prepare for missionary work. Rouse's best friend from her high school days at Notting Hill High School, Agnes de Sélincourt (1872–1917), had been converted through the mission of a Rev. E. A. Stuart, inspiring her decision to become a missionary. After Robert Wilder's visit to Cambridge, Agnes signed the SVMU card that formalized her intent to become a missionary, a requirement for membership in the organization. Rouse took a card but struggled for two years before signing her commitment to be a missionary.[34]

After Agnes de Sélincourt and Ruth Rouse left college, they helped to bring several independent organizations in the women's colleges into affiliation with the British College Christian Union (BCCU). Cambridge in the 1890s sponsored university missions, open-air meetings with

32. A. T. Pierson, quoted in ibid., 129.
33. Ibid., 129.
34. Franzén, *Legacy of Rouse*, 154.

prominent evangelists of the day, including Sir Arthur Blackwood, Wilson Carlisle, Lord Radstock, E. A. Stuart, Douglas Hooper, and cricketer J. E. K. Studd. Personal piety was central to the campaign as students were encouraged to follow a routine called the Morning Watch characterized by Bible study and prayer. Rouse and de Sélincourt were leaders of the daily Girton prayer meeting.[35] A number of women students from Oxford were also present at Keswick in 1893, when the SVMU held a conference there. Founded in England in 1892 as a coeducational student association, the SVMU met in conjunction with the Keswick Convention and proposed to create an intercollegiate Christian organization to deepen the spiritual life of students.

Among the Oxford women attending in 1893 was the sister of Alexander Fraser (CMS missionary educator in Africa and Sri Lanka), Mary, who was a student at Somerville College. The founders of the recently rechristened British College Christian Union hoped that the new name would also help establish Christian unions in colleges not of university standing, such as teachers training colleges, where presumably the students were largely women. Of women students at Keswick in 1894, the majority were Student Volunteers and medical students, largely from the London School of Medicine for Women.[36] By 1898, thirty-two women's unions were affiliated with the BCCU, which in 1900 included 1,300 women students.[37]

In 1894, Rouse and de Sélincourt, who had been teaching at Sheffield High School, had planned the outlines of what would become the Missionary Settlement for University Women in Bombay (MSUW). Historian Martha Vicinus notes that college women brought to the English settlement movement traditions of community life and professionalism.[38] They managed to transfer the ideals of social settlement work—which involved serving a community by living among them—

---

35. Ibid., 158. After missionary work in India, De Sélincourt became the principal of Westfield College. She died tragically in a car accident in 1917.

36. Tatlow, *Story of SCM*, 59.

37. Rowland, "Contribution," 51.

38. See Vicinus, *Independent Women,* especially chapter 6. Oxbridge colleges were apparently more actively involved in settlements whereas Girton and Somerville sent volunteers and made donations, but their involvement remained more perfunctory.

from college life into missions. Based in Bombay, the MSUW developed work among Parsee women.[39]

The settlement idea both detached their work from the control of traditional denominational sending agencies and empowered women student leaders to make their own arrangements. While de Sélincourt and another woman student, Una Saunders, travelled to India to found the Missionary Settlement for University Women, Rouse stayed behind to support the organization at home. The MSUW objective was to place Christian educated women from English universities in the educational centers of India to reach Indian women doctors, lawyers, and teachers in training.[40]

Rouse's ideas about women students continued to develop as she read a book by a German lawyer about women students at the University of Zurich. Rouse in 1895 became the editor of the journal *Student Volunteer*, a role that automatically ensured a position on the executive of both the SVMU and the BCCU.[41] Her appointment in 1896 as travelling secretary meant that she served the SVMU, the BCCU, and the MSUW—evidence of the interconnected relationships among the organizations.

When Rouse made her first visit to Scandinavia in 1897, she created a stir. She met almost complete ignorance of missions and a general apathy about student involvement in such matters. In Finland, at the University of Helsinki, there were about 215 women students in 1897, and from this group she formed the women's student Christian union with about twenty members.[42]

Rouse travelled to North America in 1897–1899. She served as Student Volunteer Secretary and then as the YWCA College Association secretary for the U.S. and Canada, stepping in to relieve the College Secretary Effie Price who had become ill. While in North America, Rouse experienced the power of summer conferences as well as the quadrennial SVMU conference at Cleveland in 1898. She visited at least

---

39. Tatlow, *Story of SCM*, 57–58. By 1898, there were thirty-two women's unions affiliated with the BCCU, which in 1900, included 1300 women students. See Rowland, 51.

40. Lindsay, "History of the Missionary Settlement for University Women," *The Student Movement*.

41. Rowland, "Contribution," 65.

42. Ibid., 76–89.

100 universities and colleges, women's colleges and coeducational, denominational and state or provincial institutions in both Canada and the United States. Her own student years at Girton College, Cambridge gave her ground for comparison as she was exposed to different models of women's education and met the leaders of this movement throughout North America. In Canada she visited ladies' colleges; McGill University; University of Toronto, including the Anglican Trinity College and the Methodist Victoria College; and the Baptist McMaster University.

She confessed that she had initially despised the small colleges that she felt were generally doing a low grade of academic work, but later she realized that they had an enormous influence on the lives of men and women who passed through them who would never have gone to the larger universities.[43] The North American tour also offered a different perspective on the place of religion in the lives of the students because Rouse was more accustomed to the strenuous opposition to Christianity among European students. In Canada, she found that the YWCA was less widespread than the YMCA. Both in the U.S. and Canada, the weakest point of Y work was the missionary work.[44]

She urged the college Y to pursue students not currently served by them such as medical, art, and music students. Because many of the women's colleges of the Eastern United States did not have a college movement, Rouse made links between these schools and the Y movement and urged their graduates to work in college Association work. Both Canadian and American Y members needed to expand their work beyond city work to include Student Department work. Graduates, she felt, should be sent to the Orient thereby "influencing nascent movements for women's education in the East."[45] Her time in America helped her to win the confidence of wealthy women such as Nettie Fowler McCormick of Chicago and Grace Dodge, and enlisting their support for the women's work strengthened the missionary work within the colleges.

After the Cleveland SV conference in 1898, Rouse was offered a Y position as international student secretary among women students. According to historian Wilmina Rowland, it was significant that such a position was imagined seven years before such a post became a reality under the Federation. Rouse agreed in 1898 to serve for one more

43. Ibid., 93.

44. Ibid., 94. See also *The Student Volunteer,* 19 (June 1898).

45. Rouse, *WSCF,* 117–19.

year and then she returned to spend the summer and fall of 1899 in England, followed by a vacation in Switzerland with Una Saunders. [46] Rouse continued to visit North America frequently; over the course of her career, she estimated that she spent the equivalent of nine years in North America, usually as a consultant with a specific mission or in a region that needed her expertise.

When Rouse finally reached Bombay in December 1899, she joined old friends Mary Dobson and May Cooke. Her friend Agnes was in northern India. Rouse worked on language studies of the Gujerat language, and spent part of her time in settlement work and the rest in student work. In the settlement work in Bombay, Rouse accompanied Mary Dobson on her visits to the Parsee women.

Rouse had experienced student work in the British joint work model, but had also been exposed to the American gender separated work. In India, social relations between men and women made a gender segregated movement necessary. However, the British "settlers" there planned to institute women's work in such a way that it could develop into joint work when the time was right.

Rouse visited schools and colleges in areas not covered by other workers or organizations. There were approximately 200 women in higher education at that time. Many women students were enrolled in secondary schools that were missionary boarding schools—a field that had been developed by the Christian Endeavor Society or the Epworth League. The student work attempted to not duplicate or complete with the already existing work of these organizations. Having witnessed the success of camps and conferences in America, Rouse began to organize similar efforts in India. A summer camp was held in the Punjab in 1900 with seventy girls representing thirteen schools and colleges. Unfortunately, Rouse was absent due to illness.

Rouse never lost sight of the need to train indigenous workers in order that she and her colleagues could eventually retire from the field.[47] She spent some months in Calcutta followed by a tour of South India. Sickness forced her return to England in December of 1901 as well as her retirement from the MSUW work. There were, however, other challenges awaiting her.

---

46. For a summary of her contributions see *The Intercollegian*, 21, 9 (June 1899).

47. Rowland, "Contribution," 109.

On her return, John Mott asked her in 1903 to visit Holland, Germany, France, and Russia to study the religious conditions of women students. By 1905, this work was recognized and funded under the auspices of the Women's Secretary for the WSCF. Mott had successfully negotiated with Grace Dodge to provide salary and expenses for the position of travelling secretary for women students.[48]

The introduction of women into the WSCF was a rather complicated affair. There was a great deal of ambivalence about women's place in the federation. In Britain, the Christian student movement had been established from the beginning as gender-integrated. In this context, Rouse had worked in the British student movement at Cambridge and then at the national level. She never presumed the work to be just women's work; in fact, she was very careful to work for joint work and not just hold teas or jeopardize women's position in joint unions.[49]

The issue of women's membership in the WSCF had been officially raised in Williamstown in 1897 but at that time the committee was apparently not prepared to allow women full membership. While the debate continued, Rouse successfully worked with women students in Scandinavia in 1897 with the result that in 1899 the Federation received an application for affiliation from the Women's Student Christian Union of Finland, an application that preceded the formation of a Finnish men's movement by several years. Research committees continued to investigate how women might fit with the movement. The Eisenach committee suggested in 1898 that the Intercollegiate YWCA of North America become temporarily federated with the American movements already recognized by the Federation (namely the American and Canadian intercollegiate YMCA).[50]

New members of the WSCF, such as Australia, New Zealand, and South Africa, all had women students in their national student Christian movements. In 1900, the subcommittee on women's membership wanted to move forward on the issue, but realized the need to suggest change tactfully in order not to provoke conservative members. They recommended that national movements should receive women students into their movements "when practical."[51] It was decided at the Versailles

48. J. Mott to Grace Dodge, 25 July 1904, RG 45, Series I, 24/433, YDS.

49. Rowland, "Contribution," 75.

50. Rouse, *WSCF*, 102.

51. "Minutes of Versailles, 1900, quoted in Franzén, "Ruth Rouse," 66.

conference in 1900 that women correspondents be appointed and that leaders in women student work make occasional visits to women student centers. At the Federation conference in Soro, Denmark, the General Secretary of the WSCF argued in 1902 for the hiring of a woman secretary. During this time Rouse continued her exploratory visits to Scandinavia, Holland, Germany, Italy, and North America. This experience turned out to be a further training ground for an expanded role in the WSCF, a role which was finally formalized at the Zeist conference in the Netherlands in 1905.

A total of thirty-two women from fifteen countries attended the Zeist conference in 1905.[52] Professor Lilavati Singh of Lucknow College was appointed vice-chair of the women's department and Ruth Rouse General Secretary. The conference proclaimed the WSCF mission: "to lead students to become disciples of Jesus Christ as Saviour and as God." This reaffirmation of their aim followed a long and careful discussion as to the meaning of "conversion"—a discussion that resulted in agreement on all the essential points.

The conference was organized in a way that kept the presence of women carefully curtailed—the women had a parallel conference in a nearby town and attended only four of the main meetings of the whole conference. One of the women delegates to the Zeist conference described how women were constrained by gender expectations:

> We tried to behave very well and prove ourselves worthy; we lived submissively in a village a mile away from the men. We attended only such meetings as were open to us, and trooped out again obediently when they were over. We tried to win implacable enemies of women students, by being very discrete and 'womanly' and keeping silence as to any ideas that might be seething in our brains, and the result is that now we are allowed to have a special woman's co-operating committee under the Federation and that as its secretary we have Miss Rouse, whose experience of the colleges of so many lands makes her so suitable as the connecting link to bind together the women students scattered throughout the world.[53]

52. R. Rouse, "Draft of Means and Methods of the WSCF," Typescript, 1912, RG 46, 2–22, YDS Archives.

53. Saunders, "Women in the WSCF," *Evangel*, 18, 179 (Jan 1906), quoted in Rowland, "Contribution," 76.

While provision was made for the appointment of corresponding members of the Federation, "both men and women," the minutes of the next meeting show no women's names in the list of corresponding members.[54]

The Federation modeled its structure on a patriarchal family organization with Mott as a father locating financial support and distributing it throughout the organization to develop the overall direction. Rouse served as mother, communicating, leading, and encouraging, and at times acting as intermediary between the women secretaries and John Mott. Rouse was not a radical feminist.[55]

According to historian Keith Clements, "What Mott and his generation were seeking was a form of organization which would be capable of generating its own loyalty and resources through the commitment of those who shared its aims and values. This would put a very high premium on corporate strategy and planning, and likewise on the leadership and organizational qualities at a national level."[56] The place of women in this strategy would eventually be formulated by the willingness of many women members willing to serve overseas.

Rouse stayed in Japan three months after the Tokyo conference in 1907. Compared to China, where the women's education movement was just about to take hold, Japan's education of women was "in full swing." Because parents were keen to have their daughters educated they sent them to the cities where they might have a chance at schooling or work. Rouse found about 10,000 young girls in Tokyo alone who were not in mission schools or other Christian schools. These girls needed shelter and some sense of community as they struggled to adapt to an urban setting. The Tokyo Federation conference recognized the need and the work was taken up by the Student YWCA. Canadian Y worker Caroline Macdonald (see chapter 6) used her furlough in Canada to raise funds for six hostels. New YWCA's were established in government schools and mission schools and a summer conference for women students was

54. Rowland, "Contribution," 118.

55. In Rowland's estimation, it was fortunate that Rouse had not been a radical feminist who would have insisted on women's equal participation in the Federation at the beginning of her appointment with the WSCF. With the opposition in some quarters to coeducational work, "there is no knowing what might have been the result of an absolutist position on the part of women." Ibid., 265.

56. Clements, Faith on the Frontier, 32.

organized.[57] At the Tokyo conference of 1907, the constitution agreed that the Movements should have one woman representative, as well as two men, on the General Committee. All the sessions were open to women and they took part in the evangelistic tours that followed the conferences.[58]

Rouse's visit in 1908 to Australia caused her to be "cast in the unusual role of a determined feminist," when she found the control of the movement entirely in the hands of the men. Although the Australian movement was organically one, the management and decision making was done by the men.[59] She participated in two women's conferences and left her mark on the organization. By the time she left, a woman travelling secretary had been appointed and five women members were on the committee. She also helped students find placements for student work in India and China through the YWCA Foreign Department.[60]

At the Oxford Conference in 1909, women from America, Britain, and Australia took their seats on the General Committee; followed by members from India and Sri Lanka (Ceylon) in 1911; South Africa and Japan in 1913. The Co-operating Committee was renamed the Women's Subcommittee. Ruth Rouse sent regular excerpts of reports of secretaries around the world to the members of this committee until it was disbanded in 1920 when the war required all to work together for a common cause.

Rouse argued that organizational innovations by women made a difference to the movement: "Certain SCM methods were developed first by women students; it was the women in most countries who originally extended the SCM into the normal schools and teachers' colleges and had the vision of influencing the rising generation through Christianizing the

57. Rouse, *WSCF*, 122.

58. Ibid., 104.

59. Saunders, "Women in the WSCF," *Evangel*, 179.

60. See Howe, "Australasian Student Christian Movement." Australian women volunteers found themselves caught between the cultural imperialism of the Americans and the colonial imperialism of the British-based missions. Rather than identify with either of these, volunteers pictured themselves as a new type of missionary that built up Indigenous resources in church and society. To this end they made substantial contributions to public health, social welfare and education (317). Volunteers increasingly preferred the MSUW and the YWCA and women students responded to opportunities in the Asian YWCA's, welcoming the independence from missionary boards and building on the cooperation between the YWCA and the Australian Student Christian Movement.

teaching profession." The "foyer method" that developed in Switzerland was another product of women's creative leadership.[61]

The presence of women in the WSCF coincided with the rise of women's education in the latter part of the nineteenth century. Rouse remarked on this connection: "It is significant, again, that the rise of the movement for higher education, and the opening of mission field after mission field for women's work synchronized in the period of 1850–1870, while in the next decades the Student Volunteer Movement awakened a world outlook and the vocation for the missionary life in women medical students, in women preparing for the teaching profession, in women students of the social sciences, just at the time when the missionary boards began to clamor for women doctors, educationists, and social workers."[62]

Education fuelled the demand for student organization and for a leader such as Ruth Rouse, who understood the needs of women students and who had the spiritual conviction that empowered her to speak in challenging circumstances. Although she had originally hoped to serve Indian students, her vocation was transformed into service to students around the world. She felt that the service motive of the WSCF was essential to the organization as a whole—to be redeemed was to become an agent of redemption in the nation and in the world.[63] Rouse believed the student movements had an evangelical purpose and that they carried a power that had "hitherto been unexplored for the Kingdom of God."[64]

Rouse found the women's work to be a "fascinating sphere of service." In many countries, women students were a new phenomenon. Because these women had fought for the right to study, they were often aggressively opposed to establishment values, which for many included Christianity. Rouse encountered a continuum of faith in higher education—the pioneers of women's education in the United States were largely Christian, whereas women students in Europe were generally "*religionslos*, and not seldom militantly anti-Christian." The British were in the middle of this continuum; women pioneers were absorbed in their causes and neutral in matters related to religion.[65]

61. Rouse, *WSCF*, 106.

62. Ibid., 106.

63. Ibid., 83.

64. Ibid., 24–25.

65. Ibid., 108. The aim of the movement, she believed, was to lead students to be

To prepare for her work as Secretary, Rouse decided to spend two months at Halle University studying German. While there, her work among students resulted in the formation of the Student Christian Movement among German Women (DCVSF)—the first women's student group in Germany. Rouse started a Bible study group and identified potential leaders. Although she was not registered as a student in the campuses she visited, she used creative strategies to publicize her lectures. In Vienna, for example, she hired men to parade with sandwich boards in front of the university inviting university women to her speech. In Brussels, a personal invitation was sent to every woman to attend a meeting in her hotel.[66]

WSCF CONFERENCES

Conferences sponsored by the WSCF were held in a variety of locations including Williamstown, 1897; Eisenach, 1898; Versailles, 1900; Soro, 1902; Zeist, 1905; Tokyo, 1907 (see the Appendix for a complete listing of WSCF conferences or General Committee meetings). Student evangelism was a popular topic at early WSCF conferences such as Eisenach (1898) and Versailles (1900) where delegates attended sessions on topics such as "A Spiritual Awakening in a University," or "What Can Our Movements do to Influence More Students to Accept Christ as Their Saviour?"[67]

Conferences were occasions to celebrate and welcome new student movement members. The movements of the SCM in Mission Lands developed into the Intercollegiate YMCA of India and Ceylon, the College YMCA of China, and the Student YMCA of Japan. At the Eisenach WSCF meetings in 1898, the SCM of France and the joint SCM of the Netherlands and Switzerland were admitted to the Federation. The Korean student movement entered as part of an affiliated movement and was reorganized at the WSCF conference in Soro in 1902 as a joint movement with the Chinese Student YMCA. The Italian Federation of Christian Students joined the WSCF at Oxford in 1909 in a movement with the French, leaving Holland and Switzerland together.[68]

---

disciples of Jesus Christ, to win the unconverted, to deepen the spiritual life of the students, and to prepare students to be strategic points in the world's conquest.

66. Ibid., 112.

67. Ibid., 83.

68. Ibid., 85.

Student movements followed each other's progress through conference proceedings and articles. Such communication sometimes turned to critique as at Eisenach (1898) where the Dutch movement declared that they were much more oriented to social questions than any other movement. This was echoed at the Versailles Conference (1900) when the Dutch made an impressive appeal for "emphasis on elements of high importance" which must not be left "latent" in Federation life.[69]

Conferences were held even when political events threatened to overtake the agenda or cancel the event. The Zeist conference in the Netherlands, with thirty nations and eighteen movements present, was held while the Russo-Japanese war was raging. At the conference Mott reviewed a decade of WSCF history and urged student movements to take up the study of social questions and social work. The Zeist event was groundbreaking in allowing women to attend the meetings of the Federation and in hiring a woman secretary to head a women's department.

The plan to organize a conference in Japan was postponed by the outbreak of the Russo-Japanese War (1904–1905). The Russian and Japanese empires fought over control of Korea and Manchuria. Even in the postwar phase, conference preparations were a challenge because "Japan was flushed with victory over Russia, a European Power. Nationalism was rampant; Japan was using what would now be called totalitarian methods in Korea; friction between Japan and an awakening China was rife."[70] As the first international gathering of any kind held in Japan or in Asia, the conference was a landmark event in the pioneering phase of the WSCF.[71]

The organization of the conference required immense tact and political persuasion; ultimately Japan was interested in opening dialogue with the West. World leaders, including President Theodore Roosevelt, King Edward VII, and King Haakon of Norway cabled greetings to the conference. Speakers had been chosen from leading universities on the basis of their ability to give sound apologetic lectures. Not everyone agreed on the outcome of those apologetics; a Count Okuma enthusiastically embraced the conference as evidence of a "universal amalgamated religion, which would be produced by the Japanese people."

69. Ibid., 136.

70. Ibid., 124.

71. Ibid., 316.

His claim caused Mott to quickly reassert the Christian intentions of their work and redirect the impulse toward syncretism held by some of the Japanese attendees.[72]

More than four hundred Japanese delegates and seventy-four Chinese delegates attended the event. Despite the conversions that took place as a result of the conference and the evangelistic campaigns held around the country afterward, not all Japanese were supportive of the notion of a federation. An anti-federation was formed in Japan, foreshadowing the formation of a similar protest in Peking in 1922.

Mott was convinced that the conference was important in uniting East and West and that it had started an advance which was unlimited. John D. Rockefeller Jr. gave half a million dollars to support this advance. In the next months, Mott collected a total of two million dollars from philanthropists willing to invest in this world movement.[73] Their concern for the world, however, was inextricably linked to their business connections in areas such as Latin America and Asia.[74]

Social questions increasingly became the focus of Federation work. Mott called students to greater social activism within the church. Already as a student at Cornell, Mott had participated in community service. He believed that in the face of immigration and industrialization, the nation would be saved by Christian character. College students, he believed, were to be involved in the service ideals and to live a life of character. The work of grace and the action of the Holy Spirit were less conducive to character than personal effort and willpower. Social service provided opportunities to develop character in individuals and communities, but did not address the structural problems that made it necessary. The development of moral character could take place in both domestic and foreign missions.[75]

Students were encouraged to read authors such as Jeremiah Jenks (1856–1929), Cornell professor of political economy, who believed that Jesus had not worked to change political structures, but to transform individual hearts.[76] Jenks' book, *The Social Significance of the Teachings of Jesus* (1906) was read widely through the college Y and the WSCF.

72. Ibid., 125.
73. Hopkins, *Mott,* 321.
74. See, for example, Colby, *Thy Will Be Done.*
75. Setran, *College Y,* 131–35.
76. Ibid., see chapter 6.

Other popular works included Raoul Allier's (1862–1914) *The Social Work of the American and British SCM* (1913); James Dennis' (1842–1914) *Christian Missions and Social Progress* (3 volumes, published 1898, 1899, 1906); Harry F. Ward's *Poverty and Wealth* (1915); Mott's, *The Future Leadership of the Church* (1908); and W. D. Weatherford's *Negro Life in the South* (1910). Canadians also read J. S. Woodsworth's *The Stranger Within Our Gates* (1909) and *My Neighbour* (1911) and wrestled with labor issues and immigration questions.

In the first decades of the twentieth century, although there was a general interest in social issues, national SCMs chose particular aspects or readings to support this interest. In 1908, for example, the Swiss movement featured talks on such topics as the "Relationship between Socialism and Christianity." Similarly, the French movement sponsored meetings between the students and socialist workmen in Lille and the industrial north. The Italian movement read Jenks' book, *The Social Significance of the Teachings of Jesus*. Scandinavian movements established settlements for working girls, and the German students worked in a settlement founded by Siegmund Schulze in Berlin.

The Oxford conference of 1909 focused on Bible study, apologetics, and social problems and examined the role of the Federation in Roman Catholic lands and the lands of the Eastern Churches, especially the Balkans and the Near East. They resolved to hold the next meeting in Constantinople even though there was little infrastructure available to help organize the conference. The resolution demonstrated a commitment to further opening the Federation to the world.

A key theme at Oxford echoed by a number of speakers—future ecumenical leaders such as Charles Grauss, Tissington Tatlow, Charles Gilkey, and William Temple—concerned social issues. The conference marked a turning point in the Federation as it expanded the notion of missions and evangelization as the "redeeming of persons and of the societies in which they live, towards justice and human dignity, in love."[77] A growing awareness at Oxford that the problem was external but was rooted in the very membership gathered there would again be raised in the postwar conferences and in Peking. The notion of repentance and the need for reconciliation would emerge in the West as the twentieth century unfolded.

---

77. Potter and Wieser, *Seeking and Serving the Truth*, 30.

Although not a WSCF conference, the Edinburgh World Missionary Conference (1910) involved student movement personnel in the organization and leadership of the conference. The organizing committee invited representatives of major Protestant denominations and missionary societies with the number of delegates based on the size of the budget of sponsoring organizations. Only Protestant denominations were invited; there were no Orthodox or Roman Catholic representatives. One hundred and sixty different churches and organizations were represented and one thousand guests attended in the gallery. The attendance figures demonstrate Anglo-Saxon dominance; out of 1,200 delegates, over 1,000 were British or North American and seventeen represented the non-Western world, not however by representing their national churches but rather as delegates of British and American mission societies.[78] No Asians were included on the planning committee of this conference.

To his position as chair of the conference Mott brought a variety of skills. He had gained a wide range of experience though leadership positions; at forty-five years old he was General Secretary and Chair of the WSCF, Chair of the Student Volunteer Movement for Foreign Missions (SVM), and President of the World Alliance of the YMCA. Also assisting with the conference was student leader Joseph H. Oldham.[79] Based on the conference, Mott wrote a book, *The Decisive Hour of Christian Missions* (1910), in which he argued for an urgent approach to non-Christian nations, lest the Christian world "lose its power on the home and on the foreign fields and . . . be seriously hindered in its mission to the coming generation."[80]

The conference was divided into eight study committees consisting of twenty members in each section who together researched a topic and provided a report prior to the meeting. Eight volumes were published based on these committees of inquiry and a ninth volume summarized the proceedings of the conference. Edinburgh challenged the churches and sending agencies to develop a new co-operative strategy. Despite this plea for unity, the conference did not celebrate a public liturgy in an

---

78. Hutchinson, *Errand to the World,* 135.

79. Oldham had attended the Keswick conference in 1894 and there gave himself to God after hearing Robert Speer speak. He was general secretary of the SVMU and the BCCU that became the SCM in 1898. He went to India in 1897 to do missionary work but returned for health reasons. See Potter *Seeking and Serving,* 31–32.

80. Mott, *Decisive Hour of Christian Missions.*

attempt to symbolize the goal of unity. Such celebration would require another decade of ecumenical thinking and growth. The conference marked the end of the classical period of Protestant missionary work for the nineteenth century and the beginning of the global evangelization movement in the twentieth.[81]

Mott served on a continuation committee after the conference that culminated in the formation of the International Missionary Council in 1921 and contributed to the later formation of the World Council of Churches in 1948. Looking back in 1944, Mott recognized that the event introduced the idea of looking at the world as a whole and of "confronting the world as a unit by the Christian church as a unit."[82] Cheng Ching-yi from China and A. Z. Azariah from India, representatives of "younger" churches, demanded recognition as equal colleagues on the world stage.[83] The speech by Azariah marked a new era as he noted the failure of the missionary enterprise to develop equal relations between foreign and indigenous workers. He challenged the missions represented there to reflect on the forms of domination of younger churches by foreign leaders.

A WSCF conference was indeed held in Constantinople in 1911 at the missionary-founded Robert College and Constantinople Women's College. The atmosphere was charged by political tensions between Turkey and the Balkan states that eventually resulted in war eighteen months later. An epidemic of cholera added to the complexity of organizing the event.[84]

To prepare for the conference, Mott and WSCF staff fanned out to call on the Eastern Church leaders in neighboring countries. Months before the conference Rouse visited Sofia, Bulgaria, and the Constantinople

---

81. See Sanecki, "Protestant Christian Missions," 10. See also Hedlund, *Root,* ix.

82. Rouse, *WSCF,* 97.

83. Potter, *Seeking and Serving,* 32–33.

84. Ibid., 36–37. In 1912 an alliance was formed between Serbia and Bulgaria that Greece joined three months later. When Turkey was defeated by Italy in North African and lost Libya and Tripoli, the Balkan league took advantage of Turkey's weakness to drive the Turks from Salonika, which the Greeks took immediately. In May 1912, the treaty of London brought an end to Turkey's role in the Balkans. But immediately after, the League broke up with in June 1913, Bulgaria fought with Serbia and Greece over Macedonia and Thrace. The Romanians took the opportunity to capture the border province from Bulgaria. During the Balkan wars two women workers served as nurses in the Bulgarian and Serbian armies.

Women's College, meeting with Greek, Armenian, Bulgarian, and Turkish students who represented Orthodox, Gregorian, and Muslim faiths. Armed with an official introduction from the Archbishop of Canterbury, Rouse met the Ecumenical Patriarch at Constantinople, the head of the Orthodox world, as well as the Armenian Patriarch, who gave her permission to visit the girl's schools. Through visits to Serbia and Romania in 1911, Rouse and French WSCF worker Suzanne Bidgrain made contact with students willing to come to Constantinople. Rouse also travelled with the Motts to Syria, Palestine, Jerusalem, Damascus, Beirut, Cairo, Alexandria, Smyrna, and Athens.[85]

As a result of this wide canvas, the conference achieved the most diverse representation of any previous conference, including delegates from the Eastern Churches, the Orthodox churches of Greece, Russia, Romania, Bulgaria, and Serbia; as well as the Gregorian, Syrian, Maronite, and Coptic Churches. The extensive preparations reflected the planners' awareness that they were holding the conference in the midst of "the greatest citadel of the Mohammedan world."[86]

The meetings were held in six different halls and conducted in French, Greek, Armenian, and Turkish. Dr. Mott addressed a packed audience at the Mohammedan University. Speakers included Cheng-ting Wang, who would later lead the Chinese delegation to Versailles (1919). Prominent educators from Europe and America, England, and Sweden gave lectures on apologetics.

At a General Committee meeting at Prinkipio a few days before the conference, members composed a more inclusive membership basis for the Federation that would allow participation of Roman Catholics, Orthodox, and Protestants. No student, they decided, should be excluded from full membership in any national movement within the Federation if they were prepared to accept the basis of the Federation. Thus, a student could be a member if he or she professed faith in Jesus Christ, studied the Scriptures, and prayed for the world.[87]

---

85. Rouse, *WSCF,* 153–54.

86. Ibid.

87. Hopkins, *John R. Mott,* 371. The Indian movement had already interpreted membership to included members of the ancient Syrian Church. The American movement had in place an alternative Personal Basis and the negotiations meant that they had to not exclude any members of the Roman Catholic or Eastern Churches.

Prior to the 1913 conference at Lake Mohonk, New York, the General Committee met at Princeton University. Reports from two pioneering areas, central and southeast Europe and South America, were presented. The committee also revised the "lines of activity" of the Federation and agreed to lead students to accept the Christian faith in God, Father, Son and Holy Spirit—according to the Scriptures—and to live as true disciples of Jesus Christ; to deepen the spiritual life of students and to promote earnest study of the Scriptures among them; and to influence students to devote themselves to the extension of the kingdom of God in their own nation and throughout the world.

By stressing the historic faith through the ages, the Federation facilitated outreach to Catholic and Orthodox students. The committee preserved the centrality of Bible study, but opened up the definition of missions to include both foreign and domestic missionary outreach.[88]

Delegates to the conference were housed in the New York City Y Training School and then taken to a reception at Grace Dodge's mansion at Riverdale. They travelled by steamer to Poughkeepsie and then on to Lake Mohonk. Unlike the Tokyo conference that concluded with a series of evangelistic campaigns, the Mohonk conference offered foreign students the opportunity to attend North American student summer conferences.

According to Rouse, the Lake Mohonk conference marked the end of the pioneering stage of the Federation. The conference itself was divided into four parts: four evening addresses on the themes the revelation of God and Christ as example; four-year reports by Mott on the federation; addresses on the influence of France and Germany, on the work in Russia, and on the African-American movement in the United States.

Rouse felt that this conference marked an interracial advance with progress in relating to visible minorities, particularly Blacks, as their representation had increased from just one African-American delegate at Williamstown, 1897; William Hunton at Tokyo, 1907; to a total of thirteen at Mohonk. Although the American student work continued to be segregated in the Y, the WSCF made it a condition of holding the conference in the United States that Black students be accepted on equal terms.[89] Delegate William Hunton in his speech to the gathering

---

88. Potter, *Seeking and Serving*, 40.

89. By 1913, there were 104 student Y's serving over six thousand students with

addressed the interracial theme where he observed the fiftieth anniversary of the emancipation of slaves. In addition to the African-American delegates, there were also other minorities including twenty Chinese, two Brazilians, three British Indians, four North American Indians, one Cuban, two Filipinos, nine Japanese, and one Korean—many of whom were students studying in the United States.

The fourth section of the conference was devoted to methods of setting up SCM's in various settings. At the end of the conference, Mott noted prophetically that "Our best days lie in front of us because we have greater dangers and greater problems than any preceding generation of students." Ruth Rouse observed that at Lake Mohonk, "the Federation found itself, as a world-embracing student Christian movement—international, inter-racial, ecumenical." A pervasive political unrest ruled many parts of the world, but most of the student movement was caught unprepared for the war that soon followed. When, a year later, they were faced with a world war Rouse wondered, "Would the movement stand the test?"[90]

Three major conferences were held in 1914 and all were chaired by Mott: the SVM conference in Kansas City with 5,031 participants; the North American student movement conference on social needs in New York in 1914; and a conference in Atlanta in May 1914 on the role of Blacks in American society. The creative interaction stimulated by this work ground to a halt by August 1914 when war was declared. Not only had the war been largely unanticipated but once it began, many thought that it would last only a few months.

Many continued to support the international ideals of the Federation even in the light of war. Dutch student leader Herman Rutgers, after a visit to Berlin in 1914, wrote that the federation's task lay ahead since the Federation "gives up great hope for the future, that the Christian spirit of love and brotherhood is maintained throughout the Federation."[91]

The Federation did its best to maintain contact with students across enemy lines. Leaders from neutral countries, including Dr. Fries, Fritz de Rougemont, Pierre de Benoit, Elizabeth Clark and Clarissa Spencer, and Herman Rutgers, travelled extensively to countries involved in the

---

black secretaries. The first student Christian Association had been founded at Howard University in 1869.

90. Rouse, *WSCF,* 175.

91. Rutgers, cited in Rouse, *WSCF,* 188.

war. Rouse and Mott travelled extensively to Russia, Western Europe, and Latin America. Experienced secretaries were sent out to countries in the East; Swedish secretary Ingeborg Wikander (1882–1942) travelled to China in 1915 and created a precedent for Swedish support of YWCA workers in the East.

In response to the war, Mott had declared that the Federation stood for the principles of Christ, not of war. That distinction grew more difficult to maintain once the United States entered the war in 1917; at that point some felt that the WSCF headquarters should no longer be housed in New York. In addition, Mott's mission to Russia on the request of President Woodrow Wilson created ill feelings among the Germans that would take years to heal.[92]

During the war, the WSCF continued to hold its day of prayer, to publish the *Student World,* and to send out surveys on the activities of national SCM's. Soldiers at the front received copies of student publications and were served in huts and canteens by volunteer workers. The Student Christian Movement Press in England was pressed to meet the demand for literature for these soldiers during the war years.[93] Foyers and self-help for exploding numbers of refugee students were organized. In London, the establishment of the Student Movement House gave many domestic and foreign students a place to meet.[94]

The end of the war in November 1918 witnessed a new wave of misery caused by famine, unemployment, homelessness, and diseases such as influenza, typhus, and malaria. Grief over the loss of student members and leaders like Charles Grauss affected the Federation deeply. Remarkably, no student movement withdrew from the Federation during this war. There were, however, animosities between countries as a result of the war that would take decades to heal. Plans for conferences that had been interrupted by World War I were rebooked. A much smaller conference gathered at Northfield in 1918. The theme of the Northfield Conference concerned the creation of world democracy. A four-point program was proposed which included Christian education (social gospel reading); personal commitment; recruitment of missionaries; and fundraising. The major change in the postwar missionary movement

---

92. Potter, *Seeking and Serving,* 57.

93. Rouse, *WSCF,* 202.

94. Potter, *Seeking and Serving,* 54–56.

was the breaking down of the walls between the Christian and non-Christian world.[95]

The war and the social change in the postwar period undermined the growth of the SVM.[96] The war, notes historian Nathan Showalter, stood as a challenge to the previously unchallenged missionary idea, and for the SVM, "the wartime propaganda could not completely dispel a sense that the military crusade was dealing a telling blow to the missionary crusade."[97] The previously assumed moral superiority of the West had been challenged by participation in war.

At the SV Conference in Des Moines in 1920, Mott challenged the almost 7,000 participants to become involved in building a new world. Students, however, did not want to hear about missionary work. Finding this Victorian rhetoric hollow, students demanded a greater share in planning conferences and in choosing an agenda. Not surprisingly, later that spring Mott resigned as chairman.[98] Although Mott still spoke with the optimism of the Victorian era, a generation of postwar students clamored for a message relevant to the times.[99]

In 1924, 6,150 delegates attended the Indianapolis Convention. Canadian Newton Rowell (1867–1941), representative to the First Assembly of the League of Nations, argued at that conference that Christian idealism should replace self-interest as the rule governing international conduct. Very little theology was discussed; rather, students focused on social issues, race, and war. The West, they felt, could no longer claim moral superiority; it was culpable for problems related to race, war, and industrialization.[100]

The Indianapolis conference marked not only a shift in emphasis from foreign missions to world missions, but marked a decline in numbers of missionaries sent abroad (in 1920 the U.S. sent out 1,731 and eight years later 550).[101] The SVM held its last independently sponsored convention in 1936, but Parker notes that the decline had started

95. Parker, *Kingdom*, 141.

96. Ibid., 137–42.

97. Showalter, *End of a Crusade*, 32. See chapter four for a discussion of how the war affected the missionary movement.

98. Hopkins, *Mott,* 567–69.

99. Parker, *Kingdom*, 150.

100. Ibid., 159.

101. Ibid.

already in 1921.[102] Student culture had changed during and after the war. In England, students were more intrigued by studies of internationalism and world religions than of missions or the Bible. They were critical of the church and of the church's mission abroad. In response, the SVMU committee was dissolved and its work transferred to the Student Christian Movement.

Troubles included budgetary concerns; a split in the movement that resulted in the formation of the Canadian Student Christian Movement in 1921; tensions over the failure of the SVM to address the demands of Black leaders; divisions between the demands of foreign missions and the desire for recognition of home missions. The needs of students of the postwar generation were beyond the grasp of Wilder, Mott, and Speer; they gradually faded from prominence in the SVM.[103]

The "Great War" not only decimated membership in the Federation but also turned thousands of students into refugees.[104] Postwar political treaties dismantled previous empires such as the Austro-Hungarian Empire and created Romania and Czechoslovakia. The Turkish Empire gave way to Iraq, Syria, Lebanon, and Jordan. Russia was changed, Poland reconstituted, and Estonia, Latvia, and Lithuania were created. Finland became independent. In the midst of such chaos and disunity, delegates to the 1920 WSCF Conference in St. Beatenberg, Switzerland, asked, "Do we still believe in the same Christ?"

It was a time to rethink the common basis that allowed the Federation to function. Although Mott's leadership had been questioned, he was nevertheless elected chair to replace Fries, a position he held until 1928. Suzanne Bidgrain observed that the conference upheld unity based on the "certainty that the fatherhood of God is denied and reviled by the divisions among men and that at the foot of the cross we *cannot* be anything but brothers."[105]

Responding to the charge of Anglo-Saxon dominance of the Federation required a restructuring that increased the representation on

102. Ibid., 187. In the U.S., the SVM was challenged by Inter-Varsity Christian Fellowship that had been established in 1939 as a conservative student organization.

103. Ibid., see chapter 9. Wilder resigned to serve as a missionary to West Asia and Africa.

104. Hopkins, *Mott*, 589.

105. Bidgrain, "Impression of St. Beatenberg," typescript, 2 pp. RG 46, 1–12, YDS Special Collections.

the General Committee from twelve to twenty. Because the number of Committee members rose from thirty to a minimum of fifty-eight, meetings could be held only every two years. To conduct business between meetings, an executive committee was empowered to meet yearly. Student movements that had previously been represented in combination with other countries were now allowed to be members in their own right. Of the two vice-chairs, one was required to be a woman—a requirement filled by the appointment of Japanese leader Michi Kawai. Rouse retired as travelling secretary and served as secretary to the Executive Committee until 1924. A more diverse executive committee and officers now included three Asians, four Europeans, three Americans, one Briton, one Australian, and one Canadian.

The office of the WSCF was moved from New York to Geneva where the European Student Relief, the WSCF, and the publication offices of the *Student World* were consolidated. Responsibility for raising the Federation budget, previously acquired through philanthropy, now rested with the members.

At St. Beatenberg the Peking resolutions were passed which affirmed the equality of the races and the need to oppose the causes of war. The restated purpose of the Federation read as follows: to bring students of all countries into mutual understanding and sympathy, to lead them to realize that the principles of Jesus Christ should rule in international relationships, and to endeavour by so doing to draw the nations together; and to further either directly or indirectly those efforts on behalf of the welfare of students in body, mind and spirit which are in harmony with the Christian purpose.

These resolutions marked the new "international" approach of the WSCF with a shift away from traditional evangelistic missions to a concern for social issues.[106] The speech that Mott delivered at the conference provided an overview of the twenty-five years of the Federation and was published by the WSCF in 1920 as *The World's Student Christian Federation: Origin, Achievements, Forecast.* In addition, the study commissions brought new information to the members related to methods of training secretaries and work with foreign students. Several student movements changed their basis of membership from a declaration of belief to a personal acceptance of the purpose of the Federation.[107]

---

106. Parker, *Kingdom*, 156–57.
107. Rouse, *WSCF*, 230–31.

New federation secretaries chosen at this meeting spent the following four years visiting as many student movements around the world as they could. Secretaries included Suzanne Bidgrain (France); Henri-Louis Henriod (Switzerland); Charles Hurrey (United States); Margaret Wrong (Canada); and T. S. Koo (China). They faced a complex postwar reality as student movements had been realigned by spiritual, political, and geographical realities. For example, as a result of the Versailles Treaty, many Hungarian Magyar students were located in the newly formed Czechoslovakia, at Poszony (Bratislava) and at Koloszvar (Cluj) in the Transylvanian territory transferred to Romania. The Hungarians in the latter group found themselves living under Romanian rule. All the transferred groups wanted to stay in touch with the Hungarian movement. To complicate the situation further, the Romanian movement was inexperienced and mostly composed of Orthodox. Because the Federation recognized only one national group, the Hungarian groups were not allowed to join the Federation as a separate entity.

In January 1920, Rouse went to Vienna to investigate student conditions that were reported to be dire. The Beatenberg Conference had voted to set up a specific unit to deal with relief, called European Student Relief (ESR). The relief effort was to be guided by the principles of self-help and intentional co-operation with other agencies.[108] Rouse reported on the urgent need among starving students and those in POW camps.[109] The ESR worked with a number of co-operating agencies including the Y, the Friends, the Red Cross, Save the Children, American Jewish Relief, American Methodists and Baptists, Imperial War Relief Fund, and others.

Key to the ESR relief effort was the principle that relief would be administered impartially without regard to race, nationality, creed, or any other criterion. Through its association with the ESR work, the WSCF articulated an ecumenical mission reaching out to respond to those in

---

108. The principles of relief in ESR included the following: 1.Every relief scheme will be as far as possible, on sound economic lines, no student being helped without most careful examination of his financial and other needs; self-help will in every possible way be encouraged. 2. We hope to co-operate with existing agencies. Our aim is by careful correlation of efforts to secure the maximum relief for the maximum number of students, in so far as we may do so, a) without endangering the principle of self-help, (b) without losing sight of the importance of developing human contacts. See Rouse, *WSCF*, 248.

109. Hopkins, *Mott*, 588.

need. Both the strategy and the apolitical vision allowed the WSCF to reinvent itself to meet the needs of the post and interwar period, and by doing so, ensured its survival in a new post-missions era. And the services were severely needed. Although founders of the ESR presumed that it would administer relief until July 1921, the agency in fact responded to a continuing series of world crises, setting a standard for relief work among university students for decades to come. The ESR responded to unfolding catastrophes in Poland, Russia, Greece, Japan, and Germany in the years 1921 to 1925. Through their work, new contacts were made with other student organizations such as the Catholic Pax Romana (established 1920). Students became acquainted with the Federation through the European Student Relief, which demonstrated to them the unity "between the gospel of service and the gospel of salvation.[110]

International student conferences and camps continued to develop the international aim agreed upon at Beatenberg. Students from hostile countries met in conferences of reconciliation and at leadership training events. In addition to national events and conferences, the Quadrennial Conferences of the SVM brought together international participants at Des Moines in 1920 and Indianapolis in 1924. Delegates pursued a similar international agenda from thirty-six countries at the Glasgow and Manchester Quadrennial International and Missionary Conferences in 1921 and 1925.

Evangelical students in Britain grew increasingly disenchanted with the SCM and by 1928 organized the Inter-Varsity Fellowship of Evangelical Students Unions effectively splintering the once united front of Christian students. In other countries, mission no longer held much appeal. In France, students were generally disinterested in mission. German students were hostile to the WSCF due to its perceived failure to improve conditions of the Versailles Treaty. The Australian Student Volunteer Movement was abandoned in 1921.[111]

Representatives of thirty-two countries gathered at Tsing Hua College in April 1922 for a conference organized completely by the Chinese student movement. Such capacity building had begun in

110. Rouse, *WSCF,* 261. The ESR was renamed International Student Service (ISS) in 1925. The first branch of ISS was formed at the University of Toronto in 1939. In response to WWII, ISS became World Student Relief. In 1950, the ISS changed its name to World University Service. Rouse detailed the story of ESR in her book *Rebuilding Europe*

111. Showalter, *End of a Crusade,* 120–21.

building native leadership at the beginning of the twentieth century in conferences such as the one held in Japan. Representatives from thirty-two nations and 500 Chinese delegates attended. The conference was divided into six forums—Christianity and International and Interracial Problems; Christianity and Social and Industrial Reconstruction; Presentation of Christian Message to Students of Today; Christianizing School life; Student's Responsibility in the Work of the Church; and How to Make the Federation a more Vital Force in World Reconstruction. Presentations by Dr. Michaelis, former Chancellor of Germany, clarified that nation's grievances against the Versailles Treaty and the war guilt clause.[112] The Peking conference helped prepare students to participate in the 1924 Indianapolis SVM conference which used the same forum technique and emphasized "war, race and industrial issues."[113]

Although several countries hoped that the conference would release a definitive statement in opposition to war, a consensus could not be reached. Instead, the conference released the Peking Resolutions that recognized the equality of all nations and the duty of all to fight the causes leading to war or war itself as a means of settling disputes.[114] According to Parker, the conference altered the purpose of the WSCF, affirmed both racial equality and the need to oppose causes leading to war. Robert Wilder wanted to reclaim a new missionary purpose, but instead, the WSCF moved away from evangelistic and social issues to a new international approach.[115]

The General Conference met in August 1924 at High Leigh, a conference site north of London, and welcomed ninety men and women from thirty-five nations. Delegates represented the ecumenical and growing interracial realities of the Federation. Responding to a previous recommendation to increase the numbers of student representatives, one-third of the representatives were college students. Several new movements were admitted, including the SCM of Hungary, Korea, and the Philippines, who were accepted as Constituent Movements and Bulgaria and Romania as Corresponding Movements.

Living out of an increased ecumenical concern, the Federation built relationships with other organizations such as the International

---

112. Rouse, *WSCF*, 276.

113. Parker, *Kingdom of Character*, 157.

114. Rouse, *WSCF*, 274.

115. Parker, *Kingdom of Character*, 157.

Missionary Council and the World Conference on Faith and Order. The new ecumenical hymnal *Cantate Domino* was used for the first time at the conference signaling a desire to embody ecumenical beliefs in worship practice.

In response to a deepening financial crisis, the number of secretaries was reduced from six to four. Rouse retired as secretary to the Executive Committee after nineteen years of Federation service. The federation grappled with the following topics: What conception of God does Jesus Christ reveal to us? How can our Christian Unions help to deepen the spiritual life of their members? What is the function of social service in the life and work of the Christian Unions? What is the function of international study and action in the life and work of the Christian Unions? No consensus emerged. However, in the end the group upheld the supremacy of Jesus Christ as the condition of unity.[116]

The Federation General Committee meeting at Nyborg Strand, Denmark took place in 1926, thirty years after the founding of the WSCF at Vadstena. At Nyborg the delegates attempted to clarify the relationship of the federation to different confessional groups. Acceptance of Russia as a movement in 1913 opened the question of the relationship of the Federation to Orthodox groups who defended exclusive participation in the Eucharist. The Federation clarified its position in a historic statement that welcomed members and non-members of Christian communions working for unity in Christ. Further, the Federation recognized the existence of confessional groups and was willing to enter into relationship with them as long as their aim of ecumenism was clear.[117]

The conference struggled with the meaning of the evangelization of the world in this generation and the context of postwar university life that was disinterested or intolerant of religion. The vocation of the Federation was to embody the reality of God at the heart of the university.[118] Respect for the diversity of its federated members challenged the unity of purpose that had guided the federation during its first decades.

Plans for a Pacific-Asia WSCF conference were brought to the Nyborg Strand meeting. The conference was intended to further explore questions of international, interracial, and economic realities. Political unrest in China, including in Shanghai where Chiang Kai-Shek

116. Rouse, *WSCF,* 302–5.

117. Potter, *Seeking,* 80–81.

118. Ibid., 82.

established power, left the area so unsettled that the conference had to be postponed. Eventually, in 1933 a conference was held in Java and in 1936 the themes that would have been addressed in 1926 were taken up at a conference in California.[119]

CONCLUSION

The WSCF was a federation of national student movements who affiliated with the movement and agreed with its purpose. Membership was restricted to one national movement in each country that could affiliate with the Federation. The organizational culture of the Federation resembled that of its component parts and retained a flexibility of structure among national movements. By contrast, the SVM was more rigid in constitution and in purpose—a feature that reduced its resilience in the postwar period as missions became associated with cultural imperialism and domination by the West. Students were now more interested in industrial relations, pacifism, and international understanding than in missionary campaigns.

Responding to the needs of the world proved to be a factor that allowed the federation to adapt and survive. The development of European Student Relief from the WSCF created a precedent for the distribution of relief without regard to race or belief, a precedent that has been continued in multiple relief organizations that serve students today on university campuses around the world. The desire to serve one's fellow student, to learn about her culture, to share knowledge and experience, was built on a notion of international friendship that was respectful and allowed for a mutuality that previous paradigms of colonialism and domination could never have appreciated.

The WSCF gradually developed an appreciation of the diversity of its federated member groups and became less focused on conversion to Western Christianity. This ecumenical stance gained the WSCF acceptance in countries where it would not have been tolerated if it had not ensured that students would be encouraged to maintain their allegiances to their own religious traditions whether Orthodox, Jewish, or Catholic.

Much of the WSCF's daily work and creative reimagining was accomplished through the women secretaries. Some found their location in the field an opportunity to experiment with programs and policies.

119. Ibid., 85.

Their instincts for fellowship and formation were based in many cases on experiences of hospitality in women's college and club life. Thus the home, the foyer, the sitting room became the place of engagement with questions that related to students' lives. Pioneering in universities hostile to Christianity meant that women secretaries had to create trust and common ground where all could be welcome. Overt and evangelistic Bible study and prayer meetings were still employed but were gradually replaced by studies of labor conditions and social problems.

Christian internationalism as a paradigm for a global movement proved inadequate for the modern and diverse world. Yet in the first decades of the WSCF, women secretaries expanded the mission of the federation in a variety of countries, working with student movements and national personnel, and developing new programs and initiatives. In their work, women secretaries functioned as diplomats and international personnel, promoting an agenda of friendship and women's empowerment around the world. Education provided both the rationale and the tools for this expansion.

Gradually the federation explored relationships to developing countries that attempted to rebalance the dominance of the West. The Edinburgh Conference signaled a desire by new churches to become independent and be equally in friendship with Christian neighbors around the world. Recognition of difference demanded more than mere toleration; the Federation tested new ways of developing a two-way dialogue with other beliefs and different cultures. The urgency that had fuelled aggressive evangelism gave way to a more measured assessment of the complexity of challenges that faced the world. In the next chapters, the experiences of secretaries in a variety of countries will be examined to better understand how the WSCF adapted to the challenges ahead.

FIGURE 1: Moscow students with Ruth Rouse in the middle and Kirsten Möller, Denmark on her left.

FIGURE 2: Vadstena Castle, Sweden

Figure 3: Michi Kawai at St. Beatenberg, Switzerland

FIGURE 4: WSCF Conference, Japan, 1907

FIGURE 5: WSCF trip to Japan, 1907

PART TWO

"But also to the world"

The Work of WSCF Secretaries

4

Russia

RUSSIA PROVIDED A VAST challenge for the fledgling student movement. On the one hand, there had been an expansion of higher education: university enrolment increased from 5,000 in 1859 to 69,000 by 1914; enrolment in specialized institutes from 3,750 to 58,000; and the number of women students had gone from 2,589 in 1900 to 44,017 by 1915. On the other hand, the country was experiencing great social and political instability. As a result of the unstable situation, Russian students migrated to universities in other European countries.

During the late imperial period (1855–1917) Russia's foreign policy and domestic priorities were closely tied together. Military defeats on the world stage led to a loss of international standing and Russian leaders sought to regain status as a world power through modernization. Yet improvements in these realms could not occur without advancement in political and social rights. Although the czars had some interest in the improvements that would secure Russia's pre-eminence and their autocracy, they were ambivalent about social or political changes that in any way threatened their control. From the latter decades of the nineteenth century until the early twentieth century, steps toward modernization or democratization were reversed at the first sign of political unrest.

The story of higher education illustrates a pattern of reform and retrenchment similar to that evident in politics, labor, and religious freedom. In the last half century of Romanov rule, the system of higher education that developed was characterized by diversity and, in the early twentieth century, by rapid growth. There were several types of educational institutions: closed schools (for training the government elite), military academies, specialized institutes (training engineers, surveyors, agronomists), polytechnic institutes, commercial institutes, private universities, and institutes such as Moscow's Shaniavskii University and state universities. In the elite "closed" schools, the cost of attending meant that enrolment was very low. Admission to the specialized institutes was by entrance examination only.

The Ministry of Education controlled the universities while control of the other institutes was spread over a number of ministries. In the latter decades of the nineteenth century, government control over education was based on distrust of the universities and student radicals. Events such as the St. Petersburg fires of 1862 and the Polish revolt of 1863 only served to increase the distrust of authorities toward students who were assumed to be involved in all radical dissent. Tighter government control in turn increased the demand for reform and student hostility to both the czarist regime and the Orthodox Church. Students rejected the religious and metaphysical roots of earlier generations in favour of science, materialism, and nihilism. The attempt by a student in 1866 to assassinate Czar Alexander II confirmed in the minds of many the revolutionary sentiments of students in general.

THE YMCA IN RUSSIA

The interest in modernization seems to have facilitated the beginning of the YMCA in Russia. The YMCA existed in Russia for twenty-three years from 1900 to 1923, employed 440 staffers in the country, and spent almost eight million dollars in operational costs during that period.[1]

YMCA work in Russia began in 1899 when Clarence J. Hicks, with the financial support of philanthropist and International YMCA Committee member James Stokes, a New York businessman, travelled to Russia to study the feasibility of introducing welfare activities for the railroad workers of that country. Although that project was not successful, Hicks won the approval of a highly placed Romanov to establish a young men's society in St. Petersburg and secured his personal protection for the organization. Called a *mayak* or lighthouse, it was essentially a YMCA. The new organization, directed by Franklin A. Gaylord, had its first home in a building donated by Stokes. Stokes also founded the James Stokes Society to support the work in Russia.

The early success of Y work can be attributed in part to the careful inclusion of both the government and the Orthodox Church. Stokes insisted that the society should preserve its Russian character. Orthodox

---

1. Davis and Trani, "American YMCA," 469–91.

priests directed religious activities in the Russian Y. The YMCA in St. Petersburg became an important educational centre offering courses in German, French, English, arithmetic, physical education, typewriting, music, and other subjects.[2] Eventually a library and a drama program were added. In 1908 an American director for physical education activities was secured and the best-equipped gymnasium in Russia was built in the courtyard of the *mayak*. An athletic field was constructed and basketball introduced. The success of the operation attracted the interest of Czar Nicholas II who, after about 1907, contributed five thousand rubles annually. Although such support must have seemed a guarantee of success to Y organizers, imperial support was soon to prove meaningless as revolution led to the overthrow of the Romanov dynasty.

Although plans included the expansion of the organization into Moscow, and despite a promise from John Wanamaker to finance another building, war and revolution prevented this. The First World War changed the nature of the work with the result that educational activity declined and the American YMCA found itself one of the main humanitarian organizations involved in prisoner-of-war work.

STUDENTS AND CHRISTIAN STUDENT
MOVEMENT LEADERS

YMCA work was only part of the American interest in Russia. John R. Mott was also concerned about student movement work and he planned a visit to Finland to discuss the possibilities of this work in Russia. Annie Reynolds had travelled to Russia in 1898 on an exploratory trip sponsored by the World's Executive of the YWCA. She recommended that student work be organized through either the Orthodox or the Lutheran Church with the added recommendation that only an Orthodox member should work with the Orthodox groups. If anyone tried to work with the Orthodox Church in its politicized state in Russia, she warned, that person "would be strengthening an organization which the evangelical Churches of the Christian world feel to be harmful." Both intense national pride and patriotism made any work undertaken by a stranger very difficult. Reynolds suggested that one or two Russians be nominated by the Czar to study the methods of the YM and YWCA in other

2. Ibid., 471.

countries, such as France, England, and America. After this exposure, they could return as workers to Russia.[3]

While visiting England prior to his trip to Russia in 1899, Mott had been introduced to an expert on Russian matters, the Bishop of London, Mandel Creighton. Creighton had attended the coronation of the Czar in 1894. Mott was given a list of introductions to officials including Over-Procurator Konstantin Pobedonostev. Mott wisely refrained from using the introductions when he realized that this approach would likely alienate students who had an active mistrust for church and government authorities. As secular head of the Orthodox Church from 1880 to 1895 and tutor to Alexander III and his son Nicholas, Pobedonostev opposed freedom of speech and democracy. Under his authority revolutionaries were hunted down and a severe plan of Russification was carried out.

When Mott and Karl Fries arrived in Finland in April 1899, recent steps toward Russification by the Czar's government provided him with an attentive audience among these Finnish students. Students were in fact so interested in discussions that Mott extended his tour at the University of Helsinki by several days. Mott and Fries were joined in Helsinki by Baron Paul Nicholay, who had been engaged in various forms of religiously motivated social work, some of it in Russia. Nicholay reported that the suppression of student freedoms during the national strike meant that public meetings would be unlikely, but he advised Mott to go to assess the situation for himself. Nicholay entertained Mott in his home in St. Petersburg and accompanied him on his visit to Russia.[4]

Baron Paul Nicholay (1860–1919) was an important contact and resource for the development of a Russian student movement.[5] The son of a Finnish baron, Nicholay was born in Berne, Switzerland. His mother was a devout Lutheran who had been formative in his spiritual development. After graduating from studies in law in St. Petersburg, he joined the Russian Bible Society in 1887 and began speaking to small groups.[6] He became acquainted with Alexandra Peucker, a wealthy woman who gave all her money to support gospel work. In 1888, Nicholay experi-

---

3. Annie Reynolds to James Stokes, 1897, RG 46, box 100–820, YDS.

4. Hopkins, *Mott*, 249–50.

5. Lagenskjold, *Baron Philip Nicholay*.

6. Lord Radstock visited Russia in 1874. Vasily Paschkov was in the audience and subsequently he founded a religious and literary society that was eventually banned in 1877.

enced a personal conversion and decided to dedicate his life to Christian service. He attended the British Keswick conference in 1890, after recovering from a serious illness. During this visit, he heard Charles Spurgeon (1834–1892) preach and became acquainted with Lord Radstock (Granville Waldegrave).[7]

Nicholay combined his love for sailing with his calling to do evangelistic work, sailing to remote communities in Finland and Sweden to distribute Bible tracts. He continued work with the YMCA and with German and Finnish temperance societies in St. Petersburg. With a German evangelist named Baedeker, he visited Russian prisons.

A spiritual movement had taken place in Russia that had lasting effects on religious expression in the nineteenth century. The preaching of Lord Radstock led to a revival in the 1870s. Despite persecution, this revival resulted in the establishment of the Evangelical Christian Movement that much later merged with the Baptists in 1944. Vasily Pashkov (1831–1902), a colonel of the Imperial Guard, was one who had been converted by Radstock's preaching.[8] Under Pashkov's direction, until his banishment in 1884, the new movement expanded outward from St. Petersburg, attractive partly due to its novel approach to crossing class lines. The Pashkovites preached from personal experience and emphasized changed lives through Christ rather than relying on theological arguments. Pashkov and his associates met with people individually to discuss salvation and belief. The society produced inexpensive reprints of the Bible and other biblical literature.[9]

The movement was characterized by large evangelistic gatherings, private meetings for prayer and teaching, and hospital and prison visitation. Social outreach included work in soup kitchens, homeless shelters, schools, and piecework to support poor women. The Evangelical Christian Movement ran a private publishing enterprise that produced more than 200 booklets and tracts.

Nicholay's brother-in-law had brought him into contact with the movement in the 1880s. His mother remained a member of the German church in St. Petersburg but was supportive of the activities of the move-

7. Charles H. Spurgeon (1834–1892) was a famous British Baptist preacher, whose Metropolitan Tabernacle could seat almost 5,000 people.

8. Online: http://www.wheaton.edu/learnres/ARCSC/collects/sc35/index.htm.

9. Lagenskjold, 1924. The author describes other minority religious groups as the Stundists, Baptists, Molokans and others.

ment. Several aristocrats in the movement were inspired to make sac-
rifices of property and money to serve the gospel. A Princess Sophie
Lieven (1830–1893) dedicated part of her mansion, specifically a hall
built of malachite, for the gospel work. Colonel Pashkov and his family
moved into a smaller apartment in one of their homes to allow the rental
of their mansion. Jenny de Mayer gave up her home, moved to the island
of Sakhalin, and later devoted her life to evangelism among Muslims in
central Asia.[10]

Although the Orthodox Church initially regarded the Pashkovites
as harmless, in the 1880s they began to persecute them. In 1884, Colonel
Pashkov and his associate Count Korff were banished from Russia and
their Society for the Encouragement of Spiritual and Moral Reading was
shut down.

Due to the ban on public meetings during his 1899 visit, Mott met
in private homes or under the auspices of a German Lutheran society. As
Mott spoke with students, professors, and other citizens he presented his
vision of the student federation. As he listened, Baron Nicholay realized
that he was in the best position to provide leadership to this new Russian
federation. Mott was convinced by his visit that Russia was a priority for
Federation and YMCA development. Tentative beginnings were forged
under Nicholay's leadership and through the YMCA *mayak*. After Mott's
departure, Nicholay gathered German students in St. Petersburg and
formed small groups of Russian students with the purpose of continuing discussion and building up the structure for a future Russian student
Christian movement. With the arrival of a German missionary named
Witt in 1899, the nucleus of the student Christian movement included
Witt, Nicholay, one Polish and four German students.[11] Nicholay's position and privilege allowed him to attend conferences in Abo, Finland
(1900) as well as the WSCF Conference in Versailles. He travelled to
Davos for a malaria cure where he became a friend of the China mission-
ary Hudson Taylor (1832–1905), who was there for a rest cure. While at
Davos, Nicholay translated Mott's book *Individual Work for Individuals*.

Accompanied by Leila, Nicholay, and William R. Stewart, and with
the assistance of Franklin Gaylord and Erich L. Moraller of the *mayak*,
Mott returned to Russia in 1909. This visit proved to be "one of the most
wonderful experiences that have ever come to me in all these twenty and

10. de Mayer, *Adventures with God*.

11. Witt, "Report of the Journey to Russia," 1900, RG 46, box 100–820, YDS.

more years work among students in different nations." Not only were the Russian students without religion but also they despised Orthodox Christianity because they regarded the Russian Church as "the instrument of oppression and cause of the crying social crimes with which they were familiar." Yet Mott found them possessed of "an essentially religious nature" and longing "for what only vital Christianity can give."[12]

In a decided shift from his policy in 1899, Mott sought out Orthodox leaders to assure them that he had no intention of proselytizing. Gaylord took him to meet the Minister of Public Education, the Over-Procurator of the Holy Synod, S. M. Lukianov, and the Former Over-Procurator Prince A. D. Obolensky. He also called upon Senator I. V. Meschaninov, president of the *mayak* board, Father John Slobotskoi, and Professor S. F. Plantonov. He spoke to some members of the Duma. He was advised to concentrate on the student centers of St. Petersburg and Moscow, with a shorter time at Dorpat (Tartu). Mott was astonished that he attracted 500 people a night to his public addresses. He felt that students were disappointed over the failure of the 1905 revolution and many were driven to religious introspection.

Although individual meetings with students were not feasible, Alexandra Dobroloubofff organized small group meetings in order that students could meet privately with Mott. In contrast to the laughter that greeted the name of Christ when Rouse spoke two years earlier, Mott found students uniformly quiet and listening intently. In their conversations, they raised the problems of evil and suffering, science and Christianity.[13]

He read a letter from Roosevelt at the annual meeting of the *mayak*. Although the halls were crowded, he felt that the time was not ripe for organizing a Student Christian Movement in Russia. He favored the organization of small Bible circles under Nicolay's leadership. Despite his successful visit, at the end, the Holy Synod decreed that Mott should never be allowed to return to Russia; however, he would return eight years later as part of the Root diplomatic mission and receive a welcome from Orthodox and other church leaders. [14]

12. Hopkins, *Mott,* 332–35.

13. Ibid., 334.

14. Ibid., 336.

WOMEN STUDENTS AND LEADERS

The situation of women students in higher education in Russia was a complicated one, again reflecting the pattern of modernization followed by retrenchment. In the aftermath of the Crimean War (1853–1856), there was a perceived need for more doctors in Russia. Consequently, women were allowed to study medicine and, in fact, Russian medical courses for women were far in advance of any European country. However, following the fires in St. Petersburg in 1862 and the Polish revolt in 1863, women were banned from universities due to suspected radical activities. Many fled to Zurich to continue their studies there. But in 1873 a special commission identified the need for female doctors and teachers and recommended establishing higher education for women; in 1876 Czar Alexander II permitted women's courses in Moscow, St. Petersburg, Kiev, and Kazan, as well as women's medical courses in St. Petersburg. By 1882, Russia had 227 woman doctors. Alexander II was assassinated in 1881. His son, Alexander III, succeeded him; under his rule, reforms were again reversed. When he died of kidney disease in 1894, his son, Nicholas II, succeeded him.

In this highly charged and unstable situation, a small but determined nucleus of women students invited Ruth Rouse to make a speaking tour in Russia.[15] Her first visit in 1903, two years before her official appointment as Women's Secretary of the WSCF, took place in an atmosphere of great suspicion and under police surveillance. When she arrived, the rented room was filled beyond expectation with approximately 300 curious students. She helped start a small Bible circle during that visit. On her return to Russia in 1905, she was surprised to see that the lecture hall was filled to capacity with nearly 1200 students eager to hear her lecture. Rouse described her experience:

> Everything had to be done in the form of a lecture without hymns or prayer. I shook a great deal beforehand, for a Russian student audience was an unknown quantity, and a fearful responsibility to address. The latter part of my address was distinctly evangelistic, the audience was clearly divided into two parts; some listened intently and eagerly; others talked to each other, laughed when I spoke of Christ and sin, and some went out. I nearly wrecked my career by innocently introducing an anecdote in which I spoke to

---

15. Rowland claimed that Russian Jewish students were restricted to only 2% of the total enrollment. See Rowland, "Contribution," 7.

a policeman, and was reviled for sympathy with the hated class. Some went out saying I was a paid agent of the government, or the "Recht" as it is the "Recht that speaks of Christ."[16]

Students were mystified by her presence and confused about her intentions. She was suspected of being an agent of "Protestant propaganda, or, again, of clerical Catholicism; of being employed by some political party—pan-Germanism in Austria, Czarism, or Social Democracy in Russia; of belonging to the Salvation Army; of desiring to spread Christian Science, theosophy, Tolstoi-ism, or free love; of leading an attack on the higher education of women, or on the Jews."[17]

At her third address, Rouse engaged in an open discussion in an audience hall that was crammed with men. As she spoke on the "Meaning of Life," the audience stayed quiet, but when she was finished, a male student jumped to his feet to attack and to point out the absurdity of being "poor in spirit and meek." In two minutes he was in the full swing of a revolutionary speech and a policeman intervened. Rouse reported the incident:

> If you wished to address a student meeting you had to notify the police ten days in advance when and where you wished to speak, and provide them with the text of your address. If they gave permission, uniformed police officers complete with swords, would be there in the front row to see that you or your audience did not stray from religion to revolution. A student by way of the Beatitudes started a flaming revolutionary speech: the policeman jumped up exclaiming, "Only Miss Rouse and Baron Nicholay [my interpreter] have the right to speak." After an uproar in which it looked as if students would attack the policeman, he allowed them to hand in their questions in writing. They kept me answering them till after midnight.[18]

The outlook for Russia in the early 1900s was very grim according to Nicholay. In 1905, he warned of an impending catastrophe similar to the French revolution. Russia's defeat in the Russo-Japanese War of 1904–1905 increased dissatisfaction with the czarist government resulting in the 1905 revolt. Labor unions, which had been allowed to exist under close watch, were now considered too dangerous by the govern-

---

16. Ibid., 158.
17. Rouse, *WSCF*, 113.
18. Ibid., 112–13.

ment. In response to this anti-labor stance, an Orthodox priest named Father Gapon led a march of the remnants of a union in St. Petersburg. Soldiers fired on the protesters and the resulting violence was memorialized as Bloody Sunday. More strikes and public marches followed.[19] In 1907 Alexander Maximovsky, head of the Russian prison system and a long-time friend of Nicholay, was assassinated, confirming Nicholay's sense of foreboding.

In addition to the volatile political situation, Nicholay believed that the Russian field offered challenges distinct from those encountered in places where no Christianity had existed. He claimed that Russians had fundamentally wrong notions of Christianity and no notion of salvation or inner reform. He wrote: "to most of them religion is feeling, no more."[20]

The movement among women students, though small, developed under the guidance of indigenous leaders. Alexandra Peucker organized initiatives among women students with an attendance of about twenty-five. When she left the women's' movement in 1907, she was succeeded by Marie Bréchet. Natalie Orgewsky was another of the influential Russian supporters of the movement. She was a devout and deeply spiritual member of the Orthodox Church in Russia and a Red Cross worker who became interested in the student movement during Mott's visit in 1909. She worked in the Paris student hostel where she tried to influence Russian women students to join the movement and helped the ambassador's wife, Mrs. Isnolsky, locate a house in the Latin Quarter to serve as a women's hostel for about fifteen students.[21] After her return to Russia after the revolution, she continued her work in poverty until her death.

A Miss Kulishov led five Bible circles; some of the members of the circles were women students from the medical school, as well as from other academic institutions. Rouse's visit to Russia in 1911 was complicated by student riots that restricted her travel. In critical condition due to a lack of supervision and conflict between leaders, the women's work in Russia needed to be reorganized and redirected. The newspapers were filled with attacks against the movement and against Christians. Christian students attempted to keep in touch with the movement by reading Russian translations of books by Robert Wilder and by J. H.

---

19. Service, *Russian Revolution*, 17.

20. Nicholay to Mott, 20 July 1908, WSCF, RG 46, box 99–805, YDS.

21. Orgewsky to Rouse, 17 November 1913, WSCF, box 100–809, YDS.

Oldham. Several of the Russian students were invited to help prepare for the WSCF Constantinople Conference of 1911. Because most of the women students, except the Bréchet sisters, were nominally members of the Orthodox Church, their input was important for Rouse and others who used the Constantinople Conference to further the WSCF position of openness to the Orthodox Church.[22]

Winnifred Sedgwick (1880–1922) made a visit to Russia in the spring of 1908. A graduate of Somerville College, Oxford, she served as a travelling secretary for the British Isles from 1903 to 1905 and as student secretary of the Swiss Student Movement in Geneva.[23]

She looked around Moscow for suitable lodgings and found a place in a hostel with a group of women students. Moscow had four or five hostels that were not officially connected with the "courses" women attended but were established with commercial or philanthropic aims by different societies. Sedgwick's hostel was supported by a philanthropic society and provided board and lodging for about fifty young women at a relatively cheap rate. The lack of oversight by a dean or matron had the disadvantage, she observed, of not developing collegial traditions such as one might find in England or America. Her communication with students was limited while she was learning Russian. She was able to lead a small Bible circle with women who spoke French.[24] Sedgwick observed in a letter to Rouse that the majority of women students lived in lodgings that were unhealthy. In her hostel, most students came from families of moderate or comfortable means and their outlook was not typical since they were less serious, more absorbed in entertainment, and not as keenly interested in politics as most of the women.[25] "I sometimes have a wicked desire to plant a Somerville or Girton don in this hostel & see what they would do!!!! I don't think the girls in the hostel are really typical, though, of the students. They don't work hard, & they seem to think chiefly of theatres & young men! There are some exceptions though— but on the whole, they have not got the student outlook."[26]

22. Rouse to Orgewsky, 4 Dec. 1911, WSCF, box 100–815, YDS.

23. Sedgewick served as traveling secretary for the SCM from 1909–1914 and as a warden of the British YWCA Training Center from 1915–1920.

24. Sedgwick, "Report on Moscow," 12 April 1908, WSCF, box 100–819, YDS.

25. Ibid.

26. Sedgwick to Rouse 25 March 1908, WSCF, box 100–816, YDS.

Alexandra Dobrolouboff [Dobroliubov], a student who had spent some time in Germany, made an impression on Sedgwick. Her German exposure led her to undertake the student work with an evangelical approach, quite unaffected by an Orthodox outlook. Sedgwick described the atmosphere in Russia in the following:

> Now to come back to the question of religious atmosphere here. I would like to know what you really feel about it—but I am coming to see it is not a question of external details like saints or images of confession or anything of that kind: but something in the whole attitude of faith. And the difference in actual life seems to me to be the difference between bondage and liberty. I never knew before coming here that I was a Protestant in this sense. To try to explain—the Orthodox lays the stress on his attitude towards Christ—Hence he is liable to forget what "grace" means—& to get tied up in an effort to assure, not his own salvation perhaps, but his own grasp of Christ. Hence, while theoretically believing in a complete work of Salvation—he yet puts in mediators between him and Christ; & exalts the saints who have reached heights of holiness "who have drawn near to Christ" (as Miss V. says so often)—So he can never be sure of his position before God—but only "hopes" & this seems to leave him with only half a Gospel to preach.

She felt that the Orthodox believer emphasized sins, while Protestants emphasized sin. The Orthodox would classify sins and exert an external form of discipline that would not reach the spirit. She felt that it was the sin and not the character that lay behind it that was the point of focus. This, she believed, was why there was a great emphasis on works. Her impressions, she realized, were based on conversations with students who might be misrepresenting the Orthodox position. She had not yet had the opportunity to study their catechism.[27]

After Rouse's visit a tiny circle of three Christian girls continued faithfully to meet for Bible study in order to become leaders of other circles. "The task before them is immense," wrote Sedgwick; "they are at the beginning of their experience; they need our prayers that they may grow in knowledge and wisdom, and have strength and grace for the work of leadership here." Gradually the work grew; four circles with about thirty members met regularly to study the Gospel of Mark. These circles made up the evangelistic work of the movement. In addition, about thirty

27. Ibid.

students occasionally attended the meetings. Sedgwick felt that Rouse's visit had cleared the way for further work. The increased interest was evident in the fact that students were willing to hear other speakers, some of whom drew audiences of about five hundred. Male students were also interested in following up what they had heard from Rouse and a circle for the study of the Gospel had been started for them.[28]

A few loyal leaders sustained the movement during difficult conditions. Marie Bréchet and her sister Lucie were members of a Swiss family living in St. Petersburg. They were for years the backbone of the work among women students. Marie also worked with the medical students in Russia. In 1912 they held a series of addresses in a large hall in St. Petersburg to draw new people into the movement. Out of this attempt, thirty women students entered Bible circles.[29] By 1914, many students had left school due to the war.

STUDENT WORK AFTER 1917

The rise of the Bolshevik regime with the overthrow of Nicholas II in the March Revolution of 1917 and the entry of the United States in the war in April changed the nature of YMCA activities. President Wilson sent a diplomatic mission to Russia, headed by former Secretary of State Elihu Root, to try to keep Russia in the war. When Mott accepted the president's request to accompany this mission to Russia on 25 April 1917, the Provisional Government had been in office in Petrograd (St. Petersburg) some six weeks and Lenin had been back in that city about ten days. The Russian Revolution was then generally regarded in the U.S. as the first step toward "a stable parliamentary system," and it was hoped that Russia would remain in the war as an ally. Wilson had recognized the new regime a few hours before Britain and France and in his war message had referred to the wonderful things that had been happening.[30]

The purpose of the mission was to assure the new Russian government of America's welcome into the circle of great democracies and to confer on how the U.S. could co-operate in the prosecution of the war and persuade Russia to stay in. This visit affected the rest of Mott's career with the YMCA and the WSCF. He met with political leaders and

28. Sedgwick, "Report on Moscow," 12 April 1908, WSCF, box 100–819, YDS.

29. Marie Bréchet to Rouse, 5 December 1912, WSCF, box 100–809, YDS.

30. Hopkins, *Mott*, 494.

religious heads of the Orthodox, Catholic, and Jewish faiths, as well as with the leaders of the Old Believers, the largest dissenting sect.[31]

During Mott's previous visits to Russia in 1899 and 1909, he had become aware of the needs of the Russian Army for the services that he believed the Y could provide, and he grasped the opportunity to obtain the Provisional Government's approval and support for a new program that was already in place for the British, French, and now the American forces in Europe. He had earlier established POW work in Russia.

The trip gave Mott the opportunity to converse with American men such as Hugh Moran and Robert Leonard who were doing prison work in Siberia, as well as with Donald Laurie who worked with prisoners and soldiers in Tomsk. Mott felt that this work offered the opportunity for scores of American workers to improve the morale and character of the troops. Meetings with various representatives of government, church, and American business interests provided different perspectives on the state of the Russian society and economy. The delegates were housed in the Winter Palace from which the czar had been removed, but his former servants provide a degree of comfort that belied the desperate situation of many ordinary Russians. Mott and the other Americans were oblivious to the enormity of changes underway in Russia, nor did they understand the principles of Marxism or Leninism. Mott met with the Prime Minister, Prince Lvov; Kerensky, the Minister of War; and A. Manuilov, the Minister of Education. He also met with a committee of the Holy Synod to discuss curriculum revision in theological seminaries. He outlined four new areas of study including missions, Christian social gospel, spiritual classics, and new apologetics. A serious misunderstanding arose when a speech that Mott gave to a group of Cossack officers was reported in a newspaper in China with some changes to his text. The changed speech denounced Germans as the enemies of civilization. Unfortunately the revised text was read by German missionaries in China who questioned Mott's fitness to lead the WSCF and the other neutral world movements with which he was involved. The issue emerged again in the postwar conferences with Germany and strained relations with the Swedish and the Archbishop of Sweden, Nathan Soderblum, as well.[32]

---

31. Ibid., 478.
32. Ibid., 501.

The experiences in Russia would motivate Mott to provide whatever help he could to the Russians or the émigré community scattered throughout Europe. Although the recommendations of the Root mission were largely ignored by the American government, Mott's relationship with President Wilson grew. On Mott's return, a large part of his energy would be directed to fundraising and organizing the YMCA's war work in Europe. He almost singlehandedly raised $3,000,000 in one month to support that work.[33] Supporters of the Y war work included the Rockefellers and United States Steel. Mott also raised $6,000,000 for expanding foreign work around the world.

From Baron Nicholay's point of view, the Revolution initially opened up possibilities for students to meet publicly. Nicholay arranged public meetings around topics such as "Why do we need a Savior?" and he would then invite students in attendance to join a Bible study group. He was troubled by the student isolation since student groups would form along ethnic and religious lines, such as Jewish students or Polish students

Ultimately, however, the aftermath of the Russian Revolution left the student movement severely damaged. Universities and institutes closed all over the country. Nicholay wrote that the state of anarchy made it difficult to assess what was happening: "I do not know if our headquarters in Petrograd . . . are existent or if they have been sacked by the Bolshevists. There have been so many general massacres in Kiev that I do not know if Prof. Slezkin, Mme. Orgeffskaia and Miss Kuleshova are alive or dead. Nor have I news from Miss Shesremeteva. Miss Bréchet is in Finland."[34]

Russian students suffered greatly during the wars and revolutions that affected their country and interrupted their studies. Russian students who had gone to other countries for their education were cut off from family and funds and left in desperate circumstances. The WSCF published a booklet in 1922 urging support to save Russian students from starvation, illness, and other adverse conditions.[35] Ruth Rouse must have felt a particular urgency to support Russian students who came from the movement that resulted from her visits. The optimism with which Mott and others had viewed Russia as a pioneering field waiting to be

33. Ibid., 524.
34. Nicholay to Mott, 29 September 1919, WSCF, box 99–808, YDS.
35. European Student Relief Series, No. 28, WSCF Geneva, May 1922.

developed was tempered by political events that virtually shut down student work and drove foreigners from the country. The SCM went underground and continued in exile.

The experiences of the Bréchet sisters provide some insight into conditions among student movement workers during this time. Marie wrote to Constance Grant from Finland in 1919:

> I have now been in Finland for 14 days and I can write more freely. The life of the past year has been a mingled one on the one side it has been sad and hard to bear, on the other hand my personal life has been full of joy in spite of all. Thanks to the Bolshevists I lost everything, all that I have, all my financial resources, but as I have been able to work in the Association for so many years without pay, I was persuaded that God would not desert me and I had all that was necessary by selling things that I could do without, doing needlework and making little paintings. The lot of the many bourgeois class has been dreadful. Some of our members have been employed sweeping the streets and cleaning out the barracks of the lazy soldiers. It was hard but for their faith in the living Christ. Their joy grew simply greater. Food is horribly dear and there is great scarcity . . . I had not felt ill. My inward joy increased my strength but at last my body began to swell. For some time I could not put my boots on. My family sold my little flat in the Autumn and my sister Elise and I lived at our little student hostel which was empty. Later on all the rooms were filled by students again. There were not many women students at the University . . . the atmosphere was intense and full of faith and the desire to receive still more from God. The year had taught us a great deal about friendship and love more than ever, for the hard and dangerous conditions of life bound us together very closely.[36]

Students were being rounded up in Petrograd. In 1919 there was famine and bloodshed. Marie Bréchet claimed that the war was unpopular among the students and especially among the Student Christian circle; many were jailed for their opposition. One student was put in an asylum because he was smiling and speaking of Christ. Some women students became nurses at the front or in hospitals.[37] Sometime after 1919, the Bréchet sisters went to Czechoslovakia to work among the

36. Marie Bréchet to Constance Grant, Sept. 1919, WSCF, box 100–809, YDS.

37. Marie Bréchet, "Women's Christian Student Circle of Petrograd and the Christian Student Association of Russia," typescript, 1919, WSCF, box 100–809, YDS.

Russian students there. Marie died there and her sister married Karl Bohaes, leader of the Czech SCM before World War I. Marie's work in St. Petersburg was, according to Ruth Rouse, most remarkable and far reaching. Lucie's escape was quite dramatic. She had been working outside Petrograd and she felt led by God to leave where she was. Had she stayed, she would have been assassinated. While in Kiev, she heard about the death that threatened her so she decided to go abroad. She waited several months for government permission to leave and then she headed for Switzerland.

Sophie Hintze Corcoran was another worker in the Russian student movement. Originally from Finland, she attended the High Leigh conference in 1924 and had worked during the 1920s in Russia. Called home in 1924 when her sister died, she brought back with her infant nephew who was less than a month old. When she returned, she found that many of the student workers had been arrested. The jailed student group began to read from the Bible together, specifically from the New Testament book of Acts. Three were released and the rest were charged with espionage, accused of supporting the Western bourgeoisie, and similar political crimes. Three were exiled for three years, "the first to the White Sea Solovetski monastery, the two latter, being women, to the Khrigiz steppe in southwestern Siberia."[38] Hintze and her husband were ordered to leave the country and they returned to Finland.[39]

WSCF RELIEF TO RUSSIA (1922–1924)

Rouse recounts the work of European Student Relief in her 1925 book *Rebuilding Europe*. In 1920, the doors into Russia were firmly closed. In 1921 when faced with famine due to the failure of the harvest, student relief was allowed in between 1922 and 1925. The American Relief Administration sent student leaders through the YMCA and YWCA. The Nansen Mission gathered all non-American relief organizations under its wing and worked with the international section of the ESR, administering all relief not raised in the United States. The two groups divided the field and worked in harmony; the Americans worked in the western cities of Petrograd, Moscow, Kiev, Odessa, and Ekaterinoslav;

38. The Solovetski monastery was turned into a prison camp during the Revolution.

39. Hintze to Rouse, Autumn 1924, WSCF, box 100–813, YDS.

the International section worked in the east in the smaller provincial universities.

Relief workers found 160,000 students in the area covered by the Soviet republics and eight universities in the actual famine area. Students were forced to eat roots, leaves, grass, and sometimes clay. Alleged cases of cannibalism were reported as well as the consumption of dogs and cats. The health of students was dire; almost half of the students had active tuberculosis; 47% had some contagious disease or illness and only 20% were in fair health. Supplies in the universities were non-existent, as were heat, light, and water.

An extensive relief effort was launched into this situation. Between March 1922 and July 1924, ESR invested more than half a million dollars which had been raised in various countries. Relief workers served meals and distributed clothing and medications. The ESR was determined to provide relief impartially but when they found they could no longer do so as a result of government interference, the relief effort ended and workers withdrew.

Rouse observed that "when the full story of the European Student Relief work in Russia can be told, the results in every realm, physical, intellectual, and spiritual, will be found far more commensurate with the effort put forth than the current record can convey. The seed of unselfish service rendered in the spirit of Christ cannot but bear fruit."[40]

CONCLUSION

The work in Russia focused on YMCA work and student work. Due to political circumstances, the Y work that had begun in the late nineteenth century was directed toward prisoners of war and soldiers and led by many American volunteers. The SCM was formally accepted into the federation at Lake Mohonk in 1913. The SCM work grew through small study circles led by dedicated volunteers and by Baron Nicholay until his death in 1919. His death spared him from witnessing the effects of the revolution and the hardships faced by the brave members of the student movement groups that he has fostered carefully for almost two decades.

The growth of higher education provided a fertile field for student work that grew out of these early YMCA initiatives in Russia. Students were however increasingly associated with political radicalism and

---

40. Rouse, *Rebuilding Europe*, 173.

viewed as enemies by both the state and the state church. In the face of such oppression, supporters of the student movement believed there was room for student organization that sympathized with the specific needs of students and that provided a sense of belonging to them. Such outreach demanded a difficult balance between supporting students' spiritual needs without appearing or attempting to proselytize them. Such strategy coincided with an increasing ecumenical sensitivity in the WSCF towards the place of Orthodox students in the federation. Both Rouse and Mott were deeply influenced by their travels and experiences in Russia—an influence that could be seen in the planning and events of the Constantinople Conference of 1908. The revised ecumenical basis of the Federation allowed Orthodox students to belong.

Although initial student work focused on men and the YMCA, visits by Annie Reynolds on behalf of the International YWCA and by Ruth Rouse soon turned attention on the growing numbers of women students in higher education. State repression of the freedom of women students forced many to immigrate to countries such as Switzerland to finish their studies. Such exclusion was undoubtedly an offense to the early graduates of higher education such as Rouse, who worked energetically to provide women students with a sympathetic community through participation in small groups and Bible student sponsored by the Federation.

The movement could not have taken hold without the participation of Russian leaders who risked their lives to maintain the student movement during the repression of the revolution. Although the methods of the movement were similar to those exercised in other countries, restrictions on student gatherings required students to meet in small groups and to develop a trust of each other that would be tested during later persecution. Russian leaders such as the Bréchet sisters and Alexandra Dobrolouboff provided invaluable assistance in translation, organization, and mediation with Russian bureaucracy. In addition, visits by Rouse, Mott, and Sedgewick brought hope and information from the student movement abroad for small group participants. In addition, Baron Nicholay, as a multi-lingual aristocrat provided important mediation between the class, political, religious and ethnic differences that complicated student movement work both within and outside of Russia.

Mott believed that Russia was an important pioneering field that would have an affect on the rest of the world. His hopes for the student movement were supported by an American political agenda that saw Russia as a vast treasure trove for American development.

Experiences in the Russian field were crucial in expanding the federation's ability to address the diversity of faith and ethnicity in Western Europe as World War I approached and refugees and displaced students would make their homes in cities like Paris, London, and Brussels. For this work, not only skilled secretaries, but the principles of neutral distribution of assistance and ecumenical outreach would be tested and would challenge the organization to meet acute needs of students which would only continue to increase in the decades ahead.

5

Switzerland

HOSPITALITY TO THE STRANGER

IN 1867, ZURICH UNIVERSITY awarded Nadaezhda Suslova the degree of Doctor of Medicine, Surgery, and Midwifery. The Russian Medical Council conferred upon her the right to practice medicine in Russia. Following her example, over one hundred women studied at Zurich University during the next five years. There were eighty-seven Russian women enrolled in Zurich's medical faculty in 1873. Eventually, alleged radical activities among the Russian students in there led the czarist regime to order all Russian women to abandon their studies in Switzerland.[1] Zurich, in fact, was reported as the centre of Russian revolutionary organizations abroad.[2] The commission charged with investigating these women students alleged that moral depravity had driven them to Zurich and that while there they had participated in anti-czarist organizations.

Several decades later, in 1890–1891, an American student named Elizabeth Clark began her studies of French and German at the more pastoral setting of Bryn Mawr, Pennsylvania. Bryn Mawr had opened in 1885 as a Quaker college for women; it was distinguished by its high academic standards. By 1893 the school was non-denominational and was offering advanced degrees. Clark did not complete her degree at Bryn Mawr; she transferred and graduated from the University of Zurich. After graduation, the intrepid Clark travelled to South Africa to teach at a Huguenot college.

1. Johanson, "Autocratic Politics," 426–43.

2. Meijer, *Knowledge and Revolution.* On migrants in general to Switzerland, see Madelyn Holmes, *Forgotten Migrants.*

On their tour to South Africa in 1906, John and Leila Mott accompanied by his secretary William Stewart as well as by Ruth Rouse,
held campaigns throughout the country. Mott spoke at schools and
universities to British, Afrikaner, and native audiences. Mrs. Mott and
Ruth Rouse addressed women audiences. The challenge in the African
movement was to develop a unified student movement out of the ethnic
plurality that characterized the country. In addition to the indigenous
peoples, the Afrikaners, and the British, there were Chinese and Asian
immigrants, as well as other groups.

After completing the tour of South Africa, the Motts travelled on to
South America, but not before approaching Clark to consider a position
with the WSCF. Since she was a young teacher with language skills and
professional experience, the Motts immediately recognized her potential
as a leader for work among women students in Geneva and convincingly
presented this option to her. A year previous to the Mott's South African
tour, the World Student Christian Federation, at the Zeist Conference,
had hired Ruth Rouse to head the women's department of the WSCF,
in acknowledgment of the growing population of women in higher
education.

The work with women in Switzerland had an added layer of complexity since it involved not only French and German language groups,
but also foreign students, like Nadaezhda Suslova, who had been migrat-
ing to Switzerland for their studies for several decades. In the period just
before World War I, Switzerland had 287 foreign students for every 1000
students enrolled. Open admissions policies at Zurich, Berne, Geneva,
Lausanne, and Neuchatel (though not at Basel and Freiburg) encouraged
the enrolment of foreign students. During the first decade of the twentieth century, the universities witnessed the highest rate of feminization,
with women representing 25 to 30 percent of the total enrolment; foreign
women accounted for more than 90 percent of the total female student
population. During the winter semester of 1906–1907, 1,832 women
were registered at Swiss universities of whom 1,696 were foreigners and
only 127 were native Swiss. Foreign women students came from Eastern
Europe as well as the Russian Empire (89 percent), most of whom were
Jewish, Catholic, and Lutheran. There were Slavs (Bulgarians, Serbs,
Romanians) as well as Germans, French, and Anglo-Americans.[3] This
work required a high degree of cross-cultural understanding, as well as

3. Tikonov, "Student Migrations."

an ability to work with students who were hostile to or unacquainted with Christianity.

Clark clearly had her own conditions under which she planned to do her job; she explained to Mott that she would be keenly interested in his plans for that country, while her own plans "would be naturally to some extent guided and modified by yours."[4] The independent-minded Clark was certainly not prepared to submit completely to Mott's authority in this new position—something that would become increasingly evident as she established herself as a foreign woman leader working with the Swiss student movement. As an outsider representing the Federation but placed in a somewhat unclear position in relation to the Swiss national movement, which was headed by men, Clark would find her authority questioned more than once.

One of Clark's priorities was the provision of room and board to a fledgling student movement. Funds were short for lodging and for staff; a Miss Veeder, presumably a student worker, had raised her own salary of $250 from outside sources with the remainder donated by Clark. Clark requested fundraising assistance for the Swiss work, particularly for Zurich where students needed a furnished room, a few cups and saucers, and extra chairs at a total cost of about twenty-five dollars a month for ten months. This room would function as a place for social and religions gatherings for women students—the majority of whom were Russian.

Some infrastructure was needed to establish credibility with the students, as Clark noted, for "in these continental universities where there is no natural basis of intercourse among the students, a little equip-ment is so much the more necessary, and so much the more effective." Her request included an allowance for print propaganda and funds for a series of student meetings. Such an organization, Clark realized, had to take into account the existing national student movement. Her letter concluded with a personal request to Mott to ask a Reverend McAfee to mention the student work at a prayer meeting at the home church of her mother and sister.[5]

Balancing the different requirements of students in Geneva, Lausanne, and Zurich was a great concern to Clark. Not only did these cities represent different language groups, but Switzerland also received large numbers of international students. Clark described the diversity of

4. Clark to Mott, August 1910, RG 46, box 164–1171, WSCF, YDS.
5. Ibid.

students: "We are coming more and more in touch with Slav students, Russians, and Bulgarians, who have little faith, but nothing strong or controversial enough to make it possible to hold their ground against modern Swiss theology as they meet it in our Foyers, especially at Lausanne."[6]

Student beliefs ranged on a continuum from liberal Christianity to atheism and agnosticism. One student in Lausanne complained that she would no longer attend the foyers since the sermons of the professors and the discussions of the theological students had resulted in her loss of faith. In conversation with religious leaders there, she learned that they accepted Christ as a perfect man, but not as the son of God.[7] In response to a lecture in Lausanne entitled, "Shall we regard Jesus Christ as mythological, historical, or divine?" most of the assembled group agreed that Christ was merely a historical figure.

Meeting the challenges of the student movement led Clark to work with an intensity that threatened her health. She admitted in 1912 that her work entailed greater mental and spiritual strain than she had ever experienced. Apparently she felt that the English helpers/student secretaries lacked training and relied on her too much. These inexperienced helpers felt the strain of working in another language and living in an unsympathetic atmosphere—a situation that required more careful supervision, leading Clark to note that she felt like a "peripatetic training institute." English student secretaries included Misses Veeder and Boyle in Zurich, Marion Grant in Neuchatel, Annette Tritton in Lausanne, and Constance Grant in Geneva.[8]

Theological differences among personnel led Clark to question whether the work with foreign students should operate independently from the YMCA work. The difficulty was compounded by the fact that out of six women workers, only Miss Veeder and Clark had academic status—a lack that apparently elicited objections from the Swiss.[9] Recognizing the abilities of Miss Veeder, Clark tried to reserve her for the Swiss German work and asked Ruth Rouse to consider offering her ten pounds a month.[10] The role of the student secretaries, and also Clark's

6. Ibid.

7. Clark to Mott, 7 Feb 1912, box 164–1171.

8. Clark to Mott, 13 March 1912, box 164–1171.

9. Clark to Mott, 9 March 1912, box 164–1171.

10. Ibid.

own position in the Swiss Federation, were ambiguous; she served as the Auxiliary Travelling Secretary for the Swiss Student Movement while simultaneously being an "Agent" for the Federation.[11] Such ambiguities were intensified by strains within the Swiss movement, as in 1913, when a serious conflict arose within the Swiss Federation. Although the French Swiss were largely loyal to the Federation, the German Swiss were inclined to withdraw and start an independent movement. The differences were located in organizational models and theology but undoubtedly also reflected rising tensions along ethnic lines.[12]

When the First World War broke out in August 1914, Switzerland proclaimed itself neutral. This followed a long tradition of political neutrality established at the Vienna Congress of 1815. Despite the official position, however, the war divided sympathies along language lines. The German Swiss sympathized with the Germans and the French-speaking with the French. Switzerland, already home to many foreign students, also was heavily engaged in refugee assistance through the Red Cross. One of its famous political refugees was Lenin, who played a leading role in the 1917 Russian Revolution. When Italy entered the war in 1915, Switzerland found itself surrounded by belligerent nations. The country was more dependent than ever on imports and exports, especially the import of food for a growing population of refugees and displaced persons as well as for its own citizens. The need to spend money on defence and secret intelligence further exacerbated economic strains.

In 1914, Clark was offered the position of General Secretary of the World YWCA. Since her training and experience had been primarily with students, her original plan had been to resume college teaching. Teaching seemed to offer the possibility of religious work and influence similar to the work she had done in Switzerland, but without the heavy demands of administration.[13] Her inability to leave Switzerland may have been influenced by the growing needs of students in light of political tensions connected to the war. Her letters express concern about other staff such as William Rose, the Federation secretary who was posted in Austria. Finances were difficult as well. Clark stretched the $500 sent by Rouse and a Mr. Seton to pay workers in 1914. In response to acute student needs for housing and food Clark arranged subsidy for housing

11. Clark to Mott, 20 March 1912, box 164–1171.
12. Clark to Rouse, 19 June 1913, box 164–1171.
13. Clark to Mott, 11 Feb 1914, box 164–1171.

fifteen girls and provided food for thirty to forty at such inconceivably low rates as thirty cents a day with the money being provided by a charitable committee composed of some university professors.

In Neuchatel, twenty-five women students, mostly Russians, were working as farm hands in the fields, for which they earned food and thirty cents per day. The situation was deteriorating, observed Rouse, and "with every new day, more and more of these women are homeless and penniless." Many women students were sleeping on straw, crowded together in conditions "that are not helpful for either health or morals."[14] That the work during the war was demanding is revealed in a letter from Clark to her father. She had enough food supplies to survive for a month, she reported, but was unable to cash any Federation checks or leave the country.[15] She noted that many students were living on one meal a day, with a cup of milk or coffee in the morning. She observed grimly, "I know of more suicides than I would like to count."[16]

To divert students from the dire circumstances, student leaders sponsored entertainments, such as expeditions to Mont Blanc and Lausanne as well as sporting events. Constance Grant wrote of one fundraising effort in Lausanne where she used her knowledge of the Maoris of New Zealand to develop a Maori hut complete with illustrations, straw, plants, and birds. The effort raised 350 francs for a university committee that collected funds for foreign students in distress and prisoners in Germany and Austria.[17]

The problems in the Swiss movement, exacerbated by the war, and lack of finances for basic support for foreign students took its toll on Clark. She confessed to Mott in the fall of 1914 that she was afraid of a breakdown.[18] Continuing to feel conflicted about her future plans and exhibiting signs of stress, she turned down Mott's offer to stay with the federation. She told Mott that her trip to Austria and Prague to observe student conditions there, had in fact been engineered by partisan political forces there to impress her with "the political righteousness of the Germano-Austro-Turkish cause and the utter perfidy of the English."[19]

14. Clark to Mott, 5 Sept 1914, box 164–1174.

15. Clark to William Clark, 5 Aug 1914, box 164–1171.

16. Clark to Mott, 5 Sept 1914, box 164–1174.

17. Grant, 4 December 1915, box 166–1187.

18. Clark to Mott, 31 Oct 1914, box 164–1171.

19. Clark to Mott, 28 Dec 1914, box 164–1171.

She suspected that Miss Spencer, who worked in Zurich, had been invited to Berlin to be swayed by political forces there. Clark's visit to Austria that summer had been both strenuous and enlightening and her subsequent report provides an interesting insight into the context in 1914. While visiting Innsbruck, she was stopped by police twice on suspicion of being an English spy. The enrolment of male students at Vienna had dropped due to the war but a number of men from the University of Cracow and from Lemberg fled to Vienna to continue studies there. Clark also noted the large number of women students, including hundreds from Poland. The foyer in Vienna, she felt, was unattractive, cheerless, and largely unsuitable.

In Budapest, Clark observed that the work was divided by gender. Margrit Pok, a Hungarian, was the secretary of women's work. The work included Bible circles for university women and high school girls, classes in first aid, hospital nursing, monthly social evenings, some education classes, and a library. Prague had six weekly Bible groups but had lost many members to the war. In Clark's opinion, the attempt in Austro-Hungary to fuse elements that by nature did not belong together would eventually fail. Her pessimism may have been informed by her experience of the growing split in the Swiss movement.

In Switzerland, the hardships were increasing, and to make matters worse, in a particularly cold winter, coal supplies from Belgium and supplies of petroleum were interrupted. The Swiss Federation assisted women representing twelve nationalities, the majority Slav. One such student, a Russian Polish girl in Lausanne, missed an appointment with Clark, too ashamed to leave her room because she had no soap for personal hygiene. This student had subsisted for months on bread and milk and had no wood alcohol for her lamp.[20]

Clark left Switzerland but was not at peace with her decision, so that by November 1916, she offered to return to continue student work. Her eagerness to do something for the war effort inspired her proposal for relief work in the camps for women and children from any "belligerent" country.[21] Yet organizational ambiguities continued to muddy the waters of the Swiss movement. That the Federation structure caused some misunderstandings is evident. Clark pointed out to the Federation Secretary for Women that her work had to be renewed annually through the Swiss

20. Clark to Mott, 19 Nov 1915, box 164–1171.
21. Clark to Mott, 7 Nov 1916, box 164–1172.

National Secretary in the hope that such steps would protect the Swiss movement from accusations of outside influence. Without clear status, Clark argued, she could not meet authoritatively with state officials. She criticized the Federation for being too short term in its planning. Her frustration with this situation was evident as she wrote, "Yet, you do not wish to call me to a definite position under the Federation, while I feel that so vague and temporary a relation as mine was, is no longer practicable; that the handicap is too great." Her lack of status in any organization had been a "source of confusion, hindrance, and actual loss."[22]

The student work was chronically underfunded, leading Clark to again request $3,000 to help women students in 1917.[23] She specified that the student work in Geneva should have two goals, namely, co-operative restaurants and self-support for the university students. She declared herself willing to travel on behalf of the Women's Educational and Industrial Union of Boston to raise the needed funds.[24]

Clark's salary in Switzerland was about $1,400 per year. She requested $1,500 with $35 per month for travelling expenses and postage, etc. Staples such as flour, sugar, rice, and butter were very scarce. The lack of coal in 1917 extended to all homes and led to further deterioration of health. Clark was forced to give up her small apartment and suffered two serious attacks of bronchitis. The treatment for this consisted of burns to her back in fifty-two places.[25]

Even in the face of such obstacles, Clark established a co-operative kitchen in Geneva that served two meals per day for twenty-two cents. Foreign students, slowly surrendering their lofty ideals that teaching was the only worthy occupation, were becoming more willing to do manual labor. Faced with a complete shortage of tea Clark wondered, "What was a Swiss foyer without a cup of tea?"[26] and donations of Ceylon tea were solicited from the WSCF Women's Committee. The purpose of the foyer—to extend hospitality—had been redefined in the war years to include the provision of basic needs, job retraining, and social support. The hospitality, which in British and North American women's colleges and dormitories had been, a natural extension of the common space in

22. Clark to Mott, 14 Dec 1916, box 164–1172.

23. Clark to Mott, 15 Dec 1916, box 164–1172.

24. Clark to Mott, 17 Dec 1916, box 164–1172.

25. Clark to friends, 17 Aug 1917, box 164–1172.

26. Clark, "Report to the Women's Sub-Committee," Nov 1918, box 164–1172.

residences and dormitories had to be generated in the common space created by foyers and soup kitchens. At a time when the Swiss movement splintered under its own differences, the WSCF sought a way to transcend the diversity of ethnicities, languages, and religions.

The Geneva student centre included both the *maison des étudiantes* and the foyer in the same apartment. The *maison* housed three Bulgarians in one room, one Serbian who shared a room with a Russian Jew, a suicidal Swiss woman, and another Russian Jew. The other occupant was a visually impaired Polish student. Marguerite Wohlers, as student secretary for the foyer, tried to institute daily prayers and attempted to make them "not too Protestant." Her multi-faith chaplaincy was accompanied by her work in the *bureau de travail* that assisted needy students to locate employment. She organized student work teams for farms to help with chopping wood, picking beans, and putting up preserves.[27] The hospitality at the foyer was thus based on very simple ingredients—heat, tea, and books. Despite their initial reluctance, the foreign students who arrived at the foyer found in the salon of the *Boulevard des Philosophes* "a warm welcome, a warm room, and a cup of hot tea."[28]

Student needs for employment, food, and shelter were endless. A typewriter was set up in a workroom for those who were willing to do transcription. The women students did needlework and the men worked in a carpenter's shop. Clark asked her American contacts for donations of clothing. In the appeal, she mentioned twenty to thirty women students who had just completed their doctor's degrees and whose wardrobes consisted of just one coat and shirt that were at least four years old.

Students also needed recreation and diversion. An American from Boston, Miss Jumblatt, and a Miss Ansch from England led the popular sports program in the Geneva foyer. A Greek student who had been educated at Robert College in Constantinople organized a basketball team. Another rented room served as a gymnasium. The expeditions to Mont Blanc continued despite the fact that some students had neither sports clothes nor footwear and had to walk in slippers.

Clark had overlapping commitments to the University Christian Federation of Students and the International Committee of Young Men's and Women's Associations. The work now included a home for women students, as well as women's and men's social foyers. Under the

---

27. Grant "Report to the Women's Sub-Committee," Dec 1917, box 164–1172.
28. Clark to Mott, 20 Dec 1917, box 164–1172.

strain of the work, Clark suffered from insomnia and, by 1918, offered her resignation, stating that the burden had become too great. An outbreak of Spanish flu that summer added to the stress by causing a great deal of illness among the students and rendering her usual clerical help unavailable.[29]

While on leave at her parents' house in Brooklyn, Clark wrote Mott confidentially that some of the workers and the national secretary had strong pro-German tendencies. In order to work around this situation, Clark was forced to act more and more independently without revealing why. This offended the Swiss and the women's secretary in Lausanne, Mlle Tschanz, had launched a complaint. Clark felt that if she let the Swiss know about the pro-German workers, there might be serious diplomatic consequences. Her own status remained ambiguous since she was no longer a WSCF representative, nor did the Swiss Student Movement officially recognize her. The Swiss did not need an accounting of the war relief offered to foreigners.[30]

The atmosphere of suspicion and uncertainty was reflected in Clark's reaction to a speech given by Felix de Rougemont, chair of the Swiss National Student Movement, on the subject of reconstruction after the war. Clark felt that this speech contradicted official WSCF policy to wait, say nothing, and do nothing. She was convinced that de Rougemont, one of the leaders suspected of pro-German sympathies, should not have delivered such a speech since undercover secret service agents in Berne, registered as students, would have been there taking notes.[31] De Rougemont argued that a national association should be completely autonomous. Citing competition between the YMCA and the WSCF in Switzerland,[32] he claimed that the foyer work attracted many foreign women and Swiss who had no interest in joining the national association since it was too Christian and too religious. He felt that the Swiss needed different approaches in discussion and study groups related to moral and philosophical issues, and that a group wherein Swiss and foreign women met would not succeed.[33] Whether this speech was intended to criticize

29. Clark to Mott, 26 Sept 1918, box 164–1173.

30. Clark to Mott, 17 Dec 1918, box 164–1173.

31. Clark to Barber, 2 Jan 1919, box 164–1174.

32. De Rougemont to Mott, 28 March 1919, box 166–1180.

33. De Rougemont to Mott, 2 Feb. 1915, box 165–1179.

Clark's methods and priorities for the Swiss student work is difficult to ascertain, but Clark certainly took his speech as criticism.

The critical attitude of the Swiss male leadership strengthened Clark's resolve to use her experience and credentials to find alternative employment. Seeing the need for a literary record of the work of the YWCA, she requested a six-month commission to write. Her ability to do this type of work was evident from her previous experience in South Africa where she had served as "Professor of English, with full British government recognition of that position, and with the accessory appointment as 'Assessor,' member of the examining committee for English, French and German, on the staff of the University of the Cape."[34] It was the first time, according to Clark, that an American had held such a position with reference to the teaching of English. Her proposed writing agenda included the phases of student life and what American students had done for the world in the past years. She felt that this information would counter the anti-American sentiment currently evident in Switzerland.[35] The work would thus allow her to set the record straight in the face of the distortions and allegations of the Swiss leaders.

Clark suggested that she travel to Washington in 1919 to clarify her position in Europe. Although the historical record leaves the details somewhat hazy, that there was a serious conflict is clear. A Mr. Harte had fallen under suspicion and Clark feared that the same could happen to her and that she would have no recourse.[36] In August 1919, Clark moved out of her apartment in Lausanne, while being deluged with complaints about the men's hostel. She tried to explain to locals that there were two committees, war work council and the International committee, but to the Swiss both were part of the YMCA. She was ordered not to have contact with Dr Harte.

The atmosphere of suspicion increased with accusations by Clark that Dr. Harte assisted women students who were not "worthy," a claim that Harte countered by accusing Clark of supporting "an unworthy loafer" named Perelman. At the end of 1919, after visiting England, Belgium, and Czechoslovakia, Clark returned and tried to discuss the conflict with Harte directly. Her attempts at reconciliation were futile since Harte was "not a man with whom a lady can discuss matters qui-

34. Clark to Mott, 18 Jan 1919, box 164–1174.
35. Clark to Mott, 12 Aug 1919, box 164–1174.
36. Clark to Mott, 28 Jan 1919, box 164–1174.

etly and impersonally. He storms, he brow-beats; but he will not listen, and he will not argue calmly—with a woman." Various tradesmen were collecting for unpaid bills and she was forced to pay 200 francs out of pocket to uphold the reputation of the Y in Lausanne.[37] By 1920, Clark was angry with Mott and declined an invitation to meet with him. She felt she had suffered intensely and without real support. In addition, she believed that someone named G. Kullmann had tried to obtain access to her private papers during her absence.[38]

Clark visited Bryn Mawr in the spring of 1921. During this visit, she asked Mott to listen to her account of events in Lausanne and her attempt to handle the situation in the best interests of the Y.[39] Although her motives may have been altruistic, her enmeshment in the complexities of the Swiss movement makes her perspective unreliable. When Clark refused to provide a reference for a Mr. Fiechter for YWCA work in Prague, she further aggravated tensions within the movement. Dr. Harte allegedly replied to this refusal to support his friend by threatening to crush her and have her turned out in disgrace.[40] Mott tried to clarify some confusion about Harte's original appointment, which had occurred without Clark's knowledge.[41] Matters deteriorated to the point that Mott did not invite Clark to the WSCF Beatenberg Conference, a decision that she could only have seen as a slight. Clark had her own secrets and plans; she had kept documents about Mr. Fiechter's intoxicated condition while working in the student foyer and his misappropriation of funds. Finding Mott inaccessible, she retained one document that she insisted she would show only to Mrs. Mott.

By late May in 1921, Clark wanted to return to Europe, particularly to rectify the situation for the American Y. The relationship between Mott and Clark showed no sign of being restored. She accused him of condemning her without a hearing and she blamed him for the loss of two employment opportunities– a lucrative teaching position and a post on a newspaper syndicate—because he misled her with the possibility of interesting work in Europe.[42] She invited herself to the Beatenberg

37. Clark to Mott, 25 June 1920, box 164–1174.

38. Clark to D. Davis, 14 Oct 1920, box 165–1176.

39. Clark to Mott, 22 April 1921, box 165–1176.

40. Clark statement, Sept 1919, box 165–1176.

41. Mott to Clark, 17 Sept 1919, box 165–1176.

42. Clark to Mott, 23 May 1921, box 165–1176.

conference but stayed only one day. By the end of May 1921, she wrote Mott a scathing letter comparing her situation to Naboth's vineyard, a reference to the biblical story in 1 Kings 2 where the king and his wife illegally obtain a vineyard they coveted by having the owner, Naboth, stoned to death.

Clark's feelings of having been betrayed arose out of tensions within the Swiss work over issues of American versus Swiss control of the student movement. The diversity of students in Switzerland provided a challenge for student movement organizers. In the foreign student population in Geneva and Lausanne in 1914, there were 138 Turkish, Greek, or Armenian students, forty-one Egyptians, and thirty-four Persians. The question arose whether there should be a separate association for Muslim students.[43] Clark tried to support students of diverse ethnic origin but her greatest block was her sense of exclusion from the Swiss national leadership who, according to her, tended to "treat every American as a caretaker with a big purse, unless the worker insists on something more."[44]

The case of Clark demonstrates some of the tensions of the WSCF secretary in relation to the executive of the WSCF and the national Swiss movement. From this distance, it is difficult to know for sure whether Clark's distress was due to overwork or if she was in fact treated poorly. Although Rouse and Mott had originally been strong supporters of Clark, this support gradually decreased with her erratic and demanding behavior. There is evidence that Rouse destroyed some of the correspondence when she established the archives. Rouse informed Mott of her intentions, remarking that most of the correspondence from the years 1920–1925 showed Clark's mental imbalance most clearly, and asked his permission to destroy the letters. Rouse wrote the following: "It is mostly about her grievances against AC Harte, who without question behaved badly to her and still more to the Swiss movement, but, as far as she was concerned, just happened to be the last straw which broke the back of her frail mind."[45] The stakes were high for WSCF work in Switzerland but ambiguities in authority with national committees and local control had to be worked out. To complicate the matter, Clark's status in working for

---

43. Warnery to Rouse, 7 Feb 1914, box 168–1196.

44. Harte, 27 Nov 1918, box 168–2000.

45. Rouse to John Mott, undated, RG 45, Series I, Box 77–1393, YDS.

various organizations that depended at times completely on American funding put a strain on the resources and individuals involved.

At the same time, however, Clark's work was truly formative. The methods that were developed during the war years for student self-support and hospitality in foyers were extended through the establishment of the European Student Relief (1920) which sponsored committees in forty countries dedicated to assisting students in the aftermath of World War One. The ESR was renamed the International Student Service in 1925 and extended similar relief to students living in parts of the world affected by natural and man-made disasters. The ISS changed its name to World University Service in 1951 and continues to support educational projects around the world and to fund the studies of refugee students.

Through training in co-operative self-help and international education, the ESR attempted to address the needs of students in an impartial way irrespective of race, ethnicity, and religion. Refugee students in Poland, for example, learned shoemaking, tailoring, laundry, carpentry, and soap making. Physical needs were met through the provision of dental work and tuberculosis treatment. Books were sent to libraries in Japan and to Russian students in interment camps in North Africa. ESR relief workers in Russia found that among students in the early 1920s, 12 percent in Kiev showed active TB, and of 1,833 students, 47 percent had a contagious disease. Conferences of the ESR brought together students of every nationality and such diverse faiths as Catholic, Protestant, Greek Orthodox, Greek Catholic, Muslim, and Jewish, as well as atheists and agnostics.[46]

The ideal of a worldwide fellowship established at Vadstena was severely tested in the conditions of the First World War and its aftermath. The notion of missionary outreach was eclipsed by the needs for survival, food, and shelter, and the ideal of universal understanding based on service and self-help emerged to respond to the very real demands of a diverse student world where students were made into refugees by political and economic situations and where higher education inspired migration of students. The work of Elizabeth Clark was both disruptive and creative and her work in Switzerland, despite the conflict and misunderstanding, led to innovations and shifts in student work that had lasting effects on the WSCF, ESR, and the YMCA and YWCA.

46. Rouse, *Rebuilding Europe*.

Switzerland became the central location for the WSCF and the offices of the ISS. It had a long tradition of hosting foreign students in large numbers and gradually also became home to a growing number of international organizations. Elizabeth Clark worked for the WSCF in Switzerland attempting to negotiate conflicts with the Swiss committee over power and money in a climate that was already full of suspicion generated by the divided loyalties of wartime Europe. The movement divided along language lines as well as along gender and religion. With scarce funds, Clarke attempted to manage a full-scale relief operation for refugee students stranded without resources. Mott may have been insufficiently focused on the situation in Switzerland, preoccupied as he was with the Root mission to Russia and the organization of war relief work through the YMCA, particularly as the United States entered the war. The real facts of the case will likely never be known in the face of the destruction of correspondence, but questions remain about the source of conflict. Clark's uncertain status as representative of the Y and the WSCF as well as her connection to American funding sources may have increased resentment against her; something that might have been heightened by her tendency to speak her mind. Despite the tensions, the Swiss movement during the war years pioneered methods, including foyers providing hospitality and inexpensive food, self help, training in handicraft and farm work for income generation, and study groups that became central to the WSCF and other student movements in the decades to come.

6

Poland

THE STUDENT MOVEMENT IN POLAND

THE ORGANIZATION OF A unified Polish student Christian movement faced daunting challenges. Prior to the First World War, Poland did not exist as an independent nation; its territory had been divided among Austria, Prussia, and Russia in a succession of partitions in the eighteenth century. Polish nationalists themselves fell into two camps; the right-wing National Democrats lead by Roman Dmowski and the Polish Socialists under Josef Pilsudski. Poverty and uncertainty exacerbated by the war and the fighting that went on after 1918 contributed to a fragmented and hostile climate as students struggled to continue their education in impossible conditions. A young Canadian couple on a vacation from their own academic studies became involved in the movement in ways they would never have anticipated during their undergraduate years in Manitoba in the early 1900s.

William Rose was born in Minnedosa, Manitoba in 1885. He attended Wesley College between 1900 and 1905 where he studied classics, winning a Rhodes scholarship to Oxford. He returned to Manitoba to teach Greek and Latin. With his wife, Emily Cuthbert Rose, William travelled to Leipzig to pursue a doctorate in classics while Emily studied music. Rose had been a member of the YMCA as an undergraduate in Canada. In response to an urgent request for his help, he agreed to cut short his studies to go to Prague as a student secretary for the SCM. He realized that his lack of Czech language skills or any background in the history and politics of the region inhibited his effectiveness in the proposed student work, so he decided to study the Czech language. In attempting to organize a student conference, Rose was challenged by the need to unite students who represented a number of ethnic and religious groups. Baron Nicholay, leader in the Russian SCM, who was a "tower of strength" as he addressed groups in French, German, and Russian, assisted him.[1] The first Southeast European Conference in approximately 1914 was a landmark, bringing together Slavs, Germans, and Magyars but also Protestants, Catholics, Jews, and "free-thinkers" in one place.

While the Roses were visiting friends in the summer of 1914 in the Polish district of Silesia, war broke out. The couple was allowed to live in the village of Ligotka rather than suffer internment to which, as British subjects and enemy aliens in the Austro-Hungarian Empire, they could have been subject. Rose organized a summer school in 1914 in the parish of Ligotka, part of the duchy of Teschen, with other leaders such as Elizabeth Clark, the American leader of the WSCF work in Switzerland. Rose studied Polish and read through the library of his host, Lutheran pastor Karol Kulisz. Kulisz had studied in Vienna and Erlangen and shared a social gospel perspective with Rose, who had been influenced by the Prairie social gospel of J. S. Woodsworth.[2] Kulisz believed that every church needed an inner core of spiritually active members who would help establish the kingdom of God on earth. His desire to find ways to serve his village had inspired travels in 1907 to the Keswick conference and to orphanages in Bristol. These orphanages had been established by George Müller (1805–1898), a Prussian-born English evangelist and philanthropist.

Rose and his wife became deeply engaged in the life of the village, establishing a youth choir and teaching classes in Christian education. Rose read history and literature and studied the Polish language. He decided to edit and translate sociologist August Cieszkowski's (1814–1894) four-volume work on the Lord's Prayer. Cieszkowski made the case that human effort and human prayer were the two things that would bring about the kingdom of God on earth. In 1919, Rose showed the resulting manuscript to Tissington Tatlow, general secretary of the SCM of England, and the SCM agreed to publish it.[3] Such acceptance indicated an openness to service as well as gospel as part of the postwar religious climate among SCM leaders. The Canadian couple also engaged in energetic letter and journalistic writing; Emily wrote letters to the students

1. Stone, *Polish Memoirs*, 17.

2. Allen, *A Social Passion*.

3. Stone, *Polish Memoirs*, 57.

who had left their Bible School work to go into the military and she also learned to knit so that she could create cuffs, knee caps, and other warm items of clothing.[4] Rose wrote a newsletter on such topics as "Decision" and "Suffering" for distribution among the troops.[5]

In a letter to John Mott, Rose described their confinement in Ligotka: "For a month we have not had a line from the outside world. The last letters from home (Winnipeg) were written early in June. We are here still. No trains to take us back to Prague and I'm not sure I shouldn't be arrested on the way if I tried to get there. Things are in such a nervous state we can only hope by keeping quiet to avoid all danger." Wounded people were arriving and the villa in which they were staying was to be given over to the Red Cross Society.[6] On the subject of the Russian Revolution, Rose wrote that, in his view, the only way to break Bolshevism was by means of a religious awakening. He believed that Warsaw was waiting for the work of the Federation and the Red Triangle (YMCA).[7]

Emily Rose began a Bible study class for girls but she realized with dismay that it would be a long time before she would be fully able to lecture in Polish. At the same time, her perspective as an outsider allowed her to see the needs of the people that others had ignored. For example, she commented that even in the Protestant part of Poland, a stupor paralyzed the pastors and made them unwilling to help the peasants. But the worst news, in her estimation, derived from Vienna where food was scarce and students were longing for spiritual light and hoping for help from the Federation.[8] When Rouse visited Vienna, she found ample evidence of the accuracy of Emily's report.

Others did not share the social gospel perspective of the pastor and his guest in Ligotka with connections to student work. Eberhaard Phildius, a Swiss student leader resident in Vienna, wrote critically about the Federation and particularly the North Americans. He observed that "The American idea of friendship is a work of the devil—putting fleshly experience in place of the Love of God." Whether his attack was intended

4. Emily Rose, 19 Jan, 1915, WSCF Archives, RG 46, box 188–1361, YDS.

5. W. Rose, "Report to the Women's Subcommittee of the WSCF," 16 Nov, 1915, box 188–1361.

6. W. Rose to J. R. Mott, 21 Aug, 1914, box 188–1361.

7. Extract of letter by W. Rose, to WSCF, 22 March, 1919, box 188–1361.

8. E. Rose to the WSCF, 25 Nov, 1919, box 188–1361.

for the Canadians working in Poland or not, Mrs. Rose attempted to address his comments by agreeing with him that nothing could take the place of the Bible, yet "one cannot stand over the students with a hammer in one hand and the Bible in the other and say: 'Believe or be damned.'" Her sense was that the hard exterior of students that had been created by much pain and sin had to be broken off by practical kindness, at the same time as one pointed to Christ. She noted that "every student who came to Christ at the Bible school in 1914 has told me that it was not the lectures or even the Bible classes so much as the friendly, innocent atmosphere which changed their attitude toward Christianity."[9]

In 1917, Russia withdrew from the war, signing the Treaty of Brest-Litovsk with the Central Powers in March, 1918. This withdrawal, along with America's entry into the war, brought an end to British and French reluctance to support Polish self-determination. In 1918, the collapse of the Austro-Hungarian monarchy ended the Roses' confinement. The Polish National Committee, led by Roman Dmowski and headquartered in Paris where it acted as a quasi-government, asked Rose to report to the Allies on the desire of the Silesian Poles to join a Polish state.[10] Rose made an epic journey to Paris and then to London where he reported to the foreign office and the war office. The Polish question was complex because there were two rivals—Dmowski, the head of the Polish National Committee, and Josef Pilsudski, who had seized power from the Germans in Warsaw. Eventually Pilsudski became head of state and Dmowski the head of the Polish delegation in Paris.[11] The lengthy negotiations about Poland's redrawn borders meant that fighting continued on several fronts after the armistice of 1918.

Between 1918 and 1920 Pilsudski fought six different wars. The task he faced was overwhelming; over 10 percent of Poland's wealth had been destroyed in the war; the Germans had ransacked the territory. He had to rationalize nine different legislative systems and he had to reduce five currencies to one. In Paris, Dmowksi and his committee promoted a greatly enlarged Poland to act as a check on Germany and Bolshevism. Their Poland would have minorities of Germans, Ukrainians, Belarusians, Lithuanians—40 percent of the total population—all ruled by the Poles.

9. E. Rose to Ruth Rouse, 4 Dec, 1919, box 188–1361.

10. Stone, *William Rose,* 53–105.

11. The negotiations are well documented in MacMillan's fascinating book, *Paris 1919.*

Pilsudski was prepared to accept less. He was willing to complete a federation with the Lithuanians or with the Ukrainians in which they would
work as equals.[12]

The area of Upper Silesia, with a majority of Polish-speaking inhab-
itants, was greatly contested due to its mines and iron and steel mills. In
the end, a four-country panel awarded 70 percent of the area to Germany
but gave most of the mines and industrial centers to Poland, a loss the
Germans deeply resented. Poland was also in conflict over the Austrian
province of Galicia. The duchy of Teschen, where Rose had spent the war
years, was subject to a tug of war between Poland and Czechoslovakia.
Poland from 1919 to 1920 also engaged and repelled Russian Bolsheviks.
Eventually the Treaty of Riga in 1921 gave Poland its eastern boundary
and added four million Ukrainians, two million Jews, and one million
Belarusians to its population.[13]

Rose observed that the existence of the YMCA (the Red Triangle)
as a war mission created a great deal of confusion since people thought
that the Red Triangle and the Federation were the same organization.
The association with the Y was also problematic in the women's work as a
letter from Ruth Rouse indicates: "I feared . . . that an American Y.W.C.A.
worker will not find herself free to take an active part in building up
a Polish Student Christian Movement such as Mr. Rose and others are
helping to bring into existence. It has seemed to me that the policy of the
American Y.W.C.A. has developed in such a way that either they must
do an exclusively secular work or on the other hand a work which is
entirely dominated by authorities of the Roman Catholic Church."[14] A. S.
Taylor, who represented the YMCA in Warsaw, believed that the Student
Movement should become a "definite department of the Association
movement" in Poland in order for there to be one central organization.
He felt that students worked with the Y so that they could be of service
to others, as opposed to the tendency in the student movement to "dwell
entirely in the realm of ideals and metaphysics."[15]

The overlap of the work of the YMCA and the Federation continued to be the focus of debate among organization leaders in New York,
England, and Poland. The YMCA, under the European leadership of

12. MacMillan, *Paris 1919*, 210.

13. Ibid., 228.

14. Rouse to A. S. Taylor, 17 June, 1921, box 188–1362.

15. A. S. Taylor to Rouse, 24 June, 1921, box 188–1362.

Darius A. Davis, wanted the Federation to do student work in connection with the YMCA. Davis wrote: "I understand that one of the greatest difficulties will be to harmonize the fact that the YMCA work in the army has up to the present time been a social work with Christian inspiration, whereas the Student Christian Federation has been essentially a religious work with a social outreach."[16]

There were other problems and political difficulties within the Federation in Poland. Some felt that Rose was too identified with political interests in Poland to be eligible for the post of senior secretary there. Apparently the Czecho-Slovak authorities threatened to court martial Mrs. Rose. The Czechs felt that the couple was working against their interests in Silesia.[17] Mott continued to counsel Rose to stay out of any political agitation and activity and concentrate on the spiritual ministry. For Mott, that distinction was perhaps more easily drawn than for Rose whose years in the country and whose inclinations were to combine politics and religion to work for the kingdom of God in the place where he found himself.

Student summer conferences were held in 1921 and 1922, the latter at Sandomierz on the Vistula with eighty students. The study circles discussed methods of work and argued about the basis of belief of the Federation. A Catholic priest and professor named Father Wladyslaw Kornillowicz who supported a Catholic direction to membership in the Federation had influenced students from Warsaw. The term "Christian" did not satisfy him and the presence of non-Catholics was an "offence."[18] Other students felt that conscience provided the sole authority and preferred to keep revealed religion out of the organization. The majority of students resolved to hold to a middle course based on the full teaching of Christ and the divinity of Christ as the final appeal. This would admit every believing Christian as well as those who were still seeking.[19]

There were a handful of local student Christian unions by 1921 in such cities as Warsaw, Crakow, and Poznan. The local study circles focused on the Gospel of Mark or other New Testament work as a basis for studying life problems. Since nine-tenths of the members were Catholic the leaders found that "we cannot do evangelizing work just

---

16. D. A. Davis to Rouse, 12 Feb, 1920, box 188–1363.

17. Mott to Rouse, 21 Oct, 1919, box 188–1361.

18. Stone, *Polish Memoirs,* 126–28.

19. William Rose to Mott, 6 July, 1922, box 188–1361.

as it is done in the West. For the same reason we cannot use corporate audible prayer."[20] Context was shaping and at times limiting the methods that could be used in ways that had not been predicted by Mott and other leaders.

YMCA Work in Poland

The work of the YMCA remained essential in postwar Poland. YMCA leader Davis described the suffering in the Brest-Litovsk area as acute. In one area, where the Y was the sole organization providing relief, they found men suffering from spotted typhus, dysentery, and wounds of all kinds. Secretaries from the Y were distributing cigarettes and cocoa to the men. Despite the threat to their own safety, Y workers were determined to remain with the Polish army as long as there was one. They continued to offer athletic classes and opened railway canteens in practically all the cities where there was a Y. In Siedlice, which in 1920 was the front line of army headquarters, they served about 30,000 men in their canteens that were open day and night. Portable YMCA huts were also set up in a number of other strategic points and secretaries were attached to the rear of the fighting divisions. The work was intended to support morale and to prevent starvation. In case of a dire emergency, an evacuation plan was intact for Poland whereby the secretaries in the south would evacuate through Crakow and those in the north around Warsaw, and a few from headquarters would continue front line service to the end. As Arthur Taylor noted, "As long as there is a Polish army, the YMCA will be with them."[21] Although they tried to keep the women secretaries away from the front lines, a hut was established for the Polish women's fighting battalion called the Legion of Death. They had originally organized themselves in Lemberg while it was occupied by the Bolsheviks and were instrumental in driving them out of the city.[22]

What values were being taught through YMCA activities? Athletics taught team play, honesty, and clean living as far as that was possible in wartime conditions. Further, there was an emphasis on the democratizing influence of the Association. Literacy classes were offered in French, Polish, and English and courses on other subjects as well. According

20. William Rose, "Reply to Questions, Aug, 1912", typescript 2 pp., box 188–1362.

21. Arthur Taylor to D. A. Davis, 3 Aug, 1920, box 188–1363.

22. D. A. Davis, "Report on YMCA work in Poland," typescript, 13 pp., box 188–1363.

to Taylor, the YMCA's conception of the task was not to make people Protestants, but to "leave the superficialities of the different confessions to those who delight in them and emphasize that which is central to both," which then would bring unity to Poland.[23] Thus, Taylor concentrated on the creation of good citizens rather than the conversion and evangelization the early WSCF had supported.

The aims of the student movement continued to be contested by various sides. William Rose questioned whether they were "a movement which aims at moral uplift by national processes?"[24] He proposed rebuilding one of the most battered villages not too far from Warsaw to create a model community, a model farm, and a place that would provide a centre for Fresh Air Work. Rose was delighted that his friend, a Mr. Chambers, who had worked in the city mission work in Winnipeg, was willing to come and work with the Army YMCA workers in Warsaw. Poland, Rose believed, was caught between Lutheran Prussia and Orthodox Russia. It would thus be foolish for anyone to think that they could turn the Polish into Protestants, but one could "hope to make true and useful Catholics of them, a thing which they are not at present." Although he hoped to help reform the Protestant church of Poland, he felt that it was necessary to apply the teaching of Jesus in the epistle of James and "hope to set these Polish Catholics an example of Evangelical Christianity which will not offend them as Lutheranism has always done and may even win them out of their exclusiveness for some kind of cooperation."[25]

REFUGEE WORK

Rose had the opportunity in the postwar period to engage in the work of relief and rebuilding. The task was enormous since the war had left the country stripped of infrastructure. One of the many agencies engaged in rebuilding was the Hoover relief agency also known as the American Relief Administration (ARA).

Refugees presented an urgent problem as prisoners of war and uprooted people tried to return to their homes. The European Student Relief depended on Rose's skills and experience particularly in the immediate postwar period from 1920 to 1921.[26] The headquarters of ESR

---

23. Taylor quoted in Davis, "Report on TMCA work in Poland," 7, box 188–1363.
24. William Rose, "Report Krakow," Feb, 1922, box 188–1364.
25. William Rose to Major J. H. Wallace, 20 Nov, 1918, box 188–1365.
26. Wrong, *Ideas and Realities in Europe.*

was located in Warsaw under the leadership of J. C. Manry (Harvard) and secretary Jean Chisholm of Scotland (later Mrs. J. O. Wilson of Quebec). Rose headed the Cracow office and liaison work since he was one of the few foreigners who could speak Polish. He also cared for the faculty there who were in dire need of food and basics. The ARA provided regular delivery of sacks of food. A diverse group of agencies worked in the territory including the Red Cross, the ARA, Friends' Service Mission, the Joint Distribution Committee (Jewish-American), and the European Student Relief. Another group called the Grey Samaritans comprised Polish-American women who focused on care in the villages. They had been trained by the YWCA and were sponsored in Poland by the White Cross.[27]

The student population numbered approximately 20,000, some of whom were still mobilized. Those who hoped to return to their studies were inhibited by the lack of the most basic necessities of housing, food, and clothing. Students wore pieces of various soldier's uniforms and slept under bridges and in the railway stations. Some had been prisoners-of-war in Italy and Russia. Cafeterias were established to feed the students, and relief workers attempted to find clothing, school supplies, and books. Students shared one textbook among a large group or made notes of a text to distribute. The cumulative sufferings of the war years and the effects of tuberculosis rendered some incapable of resuming their studies. The universities of Central Europe had traditionally maintained their own sanatoria but the war had destroyed the facilities. Rest homes in the mountains were established and the ESR supported them through food aid.[28]

WSCF women's secretary Ruth Rouse's visit in 1920 provides some insights into the situation in postwar Poland. There were a total of six universities in Poland with the addition of two from the former Austrian empire, namely, Cracow and Lemberg. The Polish University of Warsaw had become Russian under the Russian regime and had been attended by Russians and Jews. Under the German occupation, this pattern was abolished in favour of a Polish university. Three new universities were established in Vilna in the extreme north, Posen in Poznania, and in Lublin. The latter was a Roman Catholic university, open to all Christians and closed to Jews. Because the men were still enlisted, the

27. Stone, *Polish Memoirs*, 116.

28. Ibid., 120.

majority of students at that time were women. Although Rouse sensed a unity among the Polish people, she observed political strife everywhere, as she noted: "Students are violently political and are formed into political societies of every kind"[29]

Such divisions among students encompassed the full political spectrum from right to left and included a club of aristocrats who were reactionaries; a national club of students who were primarily patriotic and secondarily religious; the regeneration club which was a social centre trying to free itself from politics; the club of National students who were strongly socialist and claimed to be free from any denominational affiliation; and the communists who were primarily Jewish.

Rouse felt that the restlessness among Polish students was a result of the fact that they were searching for new goals. During decades of Polish partition, students had maintained secret societies that existed through all of German, Russian, and Austrian Poland and aimed at a free and united Poland. Once they had achieved their aim, the leaders were aware that a new moral or spiritual purpose was required. Some turned to the American YMCA in Poland to ask for some form of affiliation and for help in reorganization.

Women students belonged to various movements. In Warsaw, women students helped with the Girl Guide movement. Both Guides and Scouts were Roman Catholic organizations. In Cracow, some of the 1000 to 2000 women who attended university were interested in the social work done by the YWCA. Their societies included *Jednost* (unity) that originally had included Jews but in 1913 moved toward exclusion. Their aim was economic help for students and they hoped to set up a hostel and then a co-operative for supplies. Another society was called *Zjednosnie* that consisted of a student union that included both men and women. The Forge (*Kuznicz*) was originally a radical society that was pro-Pilsudski until he came into power. The Torah (*Zagiew*) was a Jewish organization that included both men and women and at the time Rouse investigated was also pro-German.

Jewish women made up about one-third of women students and were mostly concentrated in medicine and law. Rouse was unable to get much information, nor could she totally trust the information given her about this society, since her sources had an obvious anti-Semitic bias.

29. Ruth Rouse, "Report on Visit to Poland, March 14–20," typescript, 7 pp., box 188–1365.

Another women's society was the Children of Mary, a Roman Catholic student society with one hundred members. The group did social work and hospital visitation, organized factory girls' clubs, and sponsored other religious work and discussion meetings. The meetings centered on a variety of topics such as "What should be our attitude toward the Jews?" In order to become a member, one had to go through a Novitiate for six months followed by lifelong vows.

Rouse identified the challenges to student work as the relationship with Polish Roman Catholicism and the presence of anti-Semitism. Rouse noted that anti-Semitism was rampant in Poland and the proportion of Jewish students in the university was large. Rouse asked: "What is to be the line of any Student Christian Movement toward the Jews?" In all other countries the movement accepted Jews along with anyone who wished to become a member of the foyer and share the advantages of the institutional work. She felt that if the Federation started a foyer in Poland, Jews would crowd into it and exclude the Polish students whom they hoped to conscript into the movement as the backbone of the nation. The foyer would then become a Jewish institution. The problem was complex since "If we on the other hand do anything to exclude the Jews we are acting in an unchristian manner and shall be justly reproached by the Jews for doing so."[30]

When Rose had originally decided to stay in Europe in 1913 to follow a call to serve the Student Christian Movement, he had not anticipated that the call would extend into the next decade. However, in 1921, that same purpose called him again. The student spirit was entirely different: "Now, when a call came, minds and spirits were responsive as never before; both men and women were eager to fit themselves for the highest service."[31] Some alumnae/i remembered the visits of Robert Wilder and Ruth Rouse before 1914, but the postwar generation consisted of a different group of students with different values and ideas.

Dr Mott visited in 1920 in his role as official head of the YMCA war work. He gathered student representatives to a conference in Warsaw and delegates were chosen to attend a French SCM conference and the WSCF conference in Beatenberg, Switzerland. The war with Russia, however, prevented their attendance at this conference. Poland by 1920 still had unsettled boundaries. Russian Poland had an illiteracy rate of 70

30. Rouse, "Report 1920," box 188–1365.
31. Stone, *Polish Memoirs*, 122.

percent. As the struggle against the Bolsheviks ended, Rose estimated that the student body of 20,000 would greatly increase. Rose took Mott on a tour of universities. He also received information from Harriet Taylor of Bristol University who was sent out by the Friends' Relief Mission. One of the problems for university students was that, for example, at Wilno, only 5 percent had enough funds to finish the school year. At least 10 percent lived in "cubbyholes . . . in which there was neither heat nor light in the winter, and the sanitary conditions were indescribable." Many students had no clothes other than those they were wearing. Women students in Warsaw had very little food. Books were extremely scarce. Scientific literature in Poland could not be published so there were no medical texts. Books from outside the country were expensive.[32]

Rose occasionally lectured at the university and built contacts in the postwar academic community. Groups were set up at the various universities to discuss social and spiritual issues and to plan summer conferences in Golészow in the Carpathians. Thirty student leaders participated in a leadership conference and fifty others attended the general meeting. The leaders' conference worked out a basis for membership for the newly constituted Christian Union of Polish Students.

As a result of Mott's visit, a Provisional Committee was formed in 1920 for organizing a Student Christian Federation in Poland.[33] By the fall of 1921, Rose felt that a milestone had been passed in the development of a student organization in Poland on a Christian basis with the successful organization of the Golészow Conference. The student conference began each day with morning devotional times of which four were given to the discussion of prayer, including a discussion of the New Testament teachings on prayers—the vine and the branches, Mary and Martha's dispute with Jesus, and Jesus' withdrawal to the mountain to pray. They discussed the value of communion with God as a spiritual service. Concerning the atmosphere at the meeting, Rose observed that, "Although audible prayer was not used at the conference, the spirit of prayer pervaded it throughout."

The Polish Student Association elected a Mr. Krzywoszewski of Warsaw as General Secretary and complete unanimity was reached about the aims and basis of the structure. The Polish movement agreed to have contact with the World Federation once they were established. On the

---

32. William Rose to Miss Lowenfeld, 15 June, 1920, box 188–1365.
33. Arthur Taylor to Ruth Rouse, 22 June, 1920, box 188–1365.

question of whether to be considered a moral or a religious movement, the students decided that any questions of dogma would be matters of private conscience rather than public decision.[34]

The second Southeast European Conference of Students was held a few weeks later at Sonntagsberg, near Vienna (1921). An Easter leaders' conference was held in Cracow. Rose described how Father Wladyslaw Kornillowicz, a guest at the conference, was unhappy with the basis of union since he wanted the movement to be Roman Catholic. Two factions characterized the movement at that time; one wanted it to be theologically Catholic and the other desired complete independence from creeds. Some members in the middle supported the ideal set out in the Golészow basis. In the end, the vote showed that the majority was in favour of the Golészow basis. A splinter group that disagreed with this basis formed a new organization.[35]

Rose observed fear on the part of the Catholics with respect to foreign Christians in the country. The newcomers "were charged with propagating indifferentism," meaning that one way to heaven was as good as any other. There was also a fear that these Christians would proselytize Catholics away from their churches. A third summer conference of the SCM was held in 1923 in the People's University at Dalki, near Poznan.

In a report written in 1924, Rose observed that equality of opportunity was established in the universities. In Warsaw, the Protestants had a flourishing Theological Faculty—the first in Polish history. The Orthodox Church also had a theological faculty. He felt that rumors about how Jewish students were disadvantaged were not true, explaining that students wanted to limit their presence in clinics and dissecting rooms where they were highly concentrated; some wished to restrict Jews to one-seventh of the university, but officially the universities did not recognize this limitation. Overall, living conditions were still poor but were improving. Engineering students at Lemberg had built their own residence in 1922 and in Warsaw a women's residence was being constructed.

Student organizations were of three types: economic self-help; scientific and general study; and political, moral, or religious self-development. Rose questioned whether the Student Christian Alliance was

---

34. William Rose, "Report of Student Work in Poland," Autumn, 1921, typescript, 4 pp., box 188–1365.

35. Ibid.

perceived to be as necessary as it had been in 1921. He found students to be interested in or consumed by party politics, earning a living, study, and sports and games. Inner needs received little attention. There were a few exceptions to this rule, though, and they included the ex-Scouts who managed to transcend political differences to do service work. The Pan-Polish groups who were quite narrow in their views attempted to restrict membership and to be anti-Bolshevik as well as anti-Semitic. The third movement was the Renaissance movement that was strictly Catholic. Even in these groups, he observed that politics set in and students became dogmatic. He observed a note of social gospel and an element of service in religion—a promising trend, in his view.

The Student Christian Alliance had not fully developed due to a lack of personal outreach by members, dropouts in the groups, too little real devotion to the idea, insufficient attention to raising up leaders from the first year students, and a lack of financial backing. Further obstacles from the outside included: the growth of nationalistic sentiment, the efforts of Roman Catholic leaders to hinder a joint organization among Christians, problems arising out of poor housing conditions which led to the failure to establish a foyer, and the poverty of the best students who simply did not have time to work for the SCA. The students did decide that the SCA was still a necessity.[36]

Part of the task for Rose was to train workers in summer programs. With support from New York and workers from Cracow, Rose rehabilitated a barracks. Training included an early morning period of meditation and discussion, a second period on methods and principles of social work, and a third dealing with education and Polish history. The summer school attracted many visitors, including Richard Morse, leader of the American YMCA who in 1924 was eighty-three years old. The school trained community workers, social workers, and workers for the Y and the Polish Federation. By 1925, the school named Osada was given over to the Polish board of education for a peasants' high school based on the Danish model.

The Polish YMCA was organized in 1923 with the motto "Serving Poland through character, education, and health." The service of American Y volunteers during the Russo-Polish war in 1919–1920 had brought comfort to the troops. When the volunteers left, the Poles

36. William Rose, "The Students of Poland," March, 1924, typescript, 3 pp, box 188–1367.

created their own YMCA primarily as a youth organization. The organization consciously established a Catholic ethos while pledging to not exclude members of other faiths. The Y supported theatres, pools, clubs, and hostels and carried out an outreach program with the poor and illiterate. The newly formed Y supported the principle of lay responsibility for leadership in youth guidance. Rose was still employed part-time by the SCM but the YMCA in Cracow had sufficient local leadership.

In conclusion, unforeseen circumstances left Canadians William and Emily Rose stranded in Silesia as hostilities related to the war broke out. A combination of Prairie social gospel and deep interest in language and culture shaped how the Roses approached this unplanned interruption in their lives. They studied languages, read broadly, engaged with local churches, planned programs, and worked to improve the conditions of the people.

Centuries of partition left Poland vulnerable to a variety of countries that sought control over resources and land both before and after the war. Rose's linguistic abilities and his understanding of the local situation presumably led to his conscription as a delegate to Paris and London to meet with the foreign office and the war office.

Poland's student movement faced a variety of difficulties, not the least of which included overlap between the work of the YMCA and the WSCF. Under wartime conditions, with scant resources and little communication, it is not surprising that the mandates of the organizations were sometimes confused. Although Mott counseled Rose to remain politically neutral, such neutrality may have been impossible in the politically charged climate during and immediately after the war.

Relations with the dominant Catholic culture required a different kind of diplomacy because some priests were offended by the work of the WSCF and sought to keep control over students within their own Catholic-sponsored activities. Far more urgent to many student movement workers were the practical needs of health and shelter and sanitation. Rose chose to work with the student movement in ways that supported the peasants and farmers; a social gospel approach to the needs he saw in the war-ravaged countryside. Rose continued to be useful as the work of the European Student Relief focused specifically on the needs of refugee students. A variety of groups were active in the area requiring the coordination of an experienced student worker such as Rose. Student work methods were adapted from the Swiss movement as cafeterias and foyers were set up to house and feed displaced students. A student movement fractured by gender, ethnicity, and religion would require continued care to build and create loyalties based on Federation and Association values. Such organization building would demand patience as the priorities in Poland rested with basic needs. By 1920 a Student Christian Federation had been organized in Poland.

Realizing that their stay had extended far longer than they would have dreamed, William and Emily Rose packed up and left in order that William could pursue graduate work and eventually build an academic career. With some time available, Rose decided to return to graduate work with Professor Stansilaw Kot in the history of education, graduating in 1926. In 1927 he became an assistant professor of Sociology at Dartmouth College, Hanover, New Hampshire. He was appointed to the School of Slavonic Studies in London in 1935. After his retirement, he taught at the University of British Columbia as a visiting professor. In 1956 he moved to the United Church of Canada's retreat centre, Naramata Christian Leadership Training School, in the Okanagan Valley where he worked until his death in 1968.

Lasting peace was not an attainable goal for Poland at this time. The price of war included the deaths of 450,000 soldiers; yet, the terrain remained contested. Despite this lack of overall political resolution, the student movement provided invaluable help with reconstruction, self-help, and student-sponsored relief. William Rose would witness the continued contest for Poland's resources, peoples, and land; however, he would do so from his new post in England and later in Canada. His life's work was formed forever by the chance encounter with a country and its people; an encounter of Prairie socialism with Polish nationalism that left many lives changed in the development of the WSCF, the student relief, and the YMCA war work.

7

France

MARIE SABINE KAUFER, A Polish student at the Sorbonne in 1910, met a student movement secretary during a critical time in her life. Her Polish roommate had committed suicide the night before. After having spent the night in despair, the student wrote, "The next morning, about 9 o'clock, half stiff with cold, and exhausted with grief, I saw a young and beautiful girl come into my room carrying a sheaf of roses. She understood. Quickly she shut the window, threw a coat around me, and drawing me quickly to her heart, she said, pointing to my friend: 'She has gone to heaven; I love you like a sister.'" [1] The student secretary, Rose Cullen, helped the Polish student to make arrangements for the funeral. When Marie decided to return to Poland, Cullen helped her pack. In such ways the secretaries of the WSCF worked with foreign students who needed emotional support, practical help, and fellowship in the desperate and acute situations they often faced away from home.

Rose Cullen (1880–1924) had graduated from Victoria College, University of Toronto, in 1903, then travelled to Paris to work with the student foyer.[2] Paris was attractive to foreign students and the numbers of women students there led to the organization of a foyer designed to build community. In the years just before World War One, France had the third largest population of foreign students, and the second largest

---

1. Marie Sabine Kaufer, "Impressions of a Polish student re: the work of Rose Cullen, then secretary of the Foyer Internationale, Paris." Paris, Feb 1925, WSCF papers, RG 46, Box 298–2740, YDS. All subsequent references will be to this record group unless otherwise indicated.

2. Cullen married Edward Wilson Wallace and the couple traveled to West China to serve as missionaries. Cullen died in 1924 of pneumonia, leaving her an eight year old son and husband to continue to serve the mission. Her husband was appointed Chancellor of Victoria University in 1930 and was a supporter of the SCM. See Austin, "Wallace of West China," 111–33.

number of foreign women students. Women were legally admitted to French universities in approximately 1880. The bulk of foreign women students were from Russia and most of them studied in Paris.

THE PARIS WORK 1905–1915

Paris was the site of British-American YWCA work. This included the management of a student hostel at 93 Boulevard Saint-Michel in the Latin Quarter, established through the generosity of an American woman. The building, formerly a convent, could accommodate twenty-five students. Unlike many university dormitories for women that tended to impose control over the lives of residents through curfews and regulations, this hostel required only that women who were staying out late inform the head of the house of their whereabouts.[3] In addition to providing shelter, the hostel served as many as 100 to150 non-resident students per day and offered baths, medical help, and advice from a trained nurse. A small hospital contained two beds for sick students—and the beds were rarely empty. The great majority of students served at that time were British or American, but many students from a variety of countries also used the hostel's services.

The leaders of this hostel work were a Dr Richardson; a Mrs Jackson, head of the hostel; and Rose Cullen, student liaison. They directed the religious work of the hostel with the help of English student leader Annette Tritton. Religious practices consisted of morning and evening prayers (apparently rather poorly attended), a Bible class conducted by Miss Cullen once a week with an average attendance of sixteen, a few Bible Circles with a "somewhat precarious existence," a mission study class once a week, and a service every Sunday afternoon with an atten-dance of between twenty-five and one hundred.[4]

Margaret Bretherton, British student secretary, wrote a report in 1906 that encapsulated the tensions within the student movement about goals and methods. She noted that anyone with experience of the British Student Christian Unions would feel that the French student movement gave too much to the students and asked too little from them in the form of service to others. She wrote: "Still, I think something might be done

3. Margaret Bretherton, "Report of French Visit," March, 1906, typescript, 8 pp., box 151–1114.

4. Bretheron, "Report," 1906.

if the secretaries more deliberately attempted to throw responsibility on the students and gave them committee work in connection with the religious writings, etc."[5] Prioritizing the physical needs of students risked losing focus on the spiritual work. The work among the 150 foreign students needed a different approach from the work among English-speaking hostel guests.[6]

Bretherton observed that the French women students who used the hostel were not bluestockings, nor did they feel any need to live or dress in a way that showed they had been "delivered" from traditional expectations. They considered belief in Christianity to be anti-intellectual and they were anxious to avoid anything associated with religion; social and moral questions were more compelling to them. Bretherton felt that French women students, many of whom belonged to French Protestant families, were similar to the French male students whom she had observed at a student conference in Bordeaux. Their reserve on religious subjects meant that methods such as prayer meetings or Bible circles would not likely succeed. French students, however, did not share the narrow Pietism of the German students and thus were willing to work for a good cause. The tolerance exhibited by students allowed them to forge bonds with many types, including free-thinkers, but because of that same tolerance they could easily lose their focus on religious experience. In addition, their tolerance included any belief as long as one lived according to Christian principles—something that others interpreted as a shift toward Unitarianism. They wanted to express their faith by doing something practical, but were not concerned with details of creeds. French male students and professors, Bretherton noted, welcomed the presence of women in university life, in contrast to men in Germany; in fact, French men hoped that women would help them transform the moral tone of the university.

5. Bretherton, "Report," 1906.

6. A Dr. and Mrs. Shurtleff, an American clergyman and his wife, devoted themselves to Christian work among English speaking male and female students. They opened their house in friendship to the students and organized a Sunday evening worship service that drew about 100–200 otherwise "unchurched" students. The service consisted of hymn singing, Bible reading, good music, and an address by Dr. Shurtleff. The work was based on the idea of extending the home life to students and providing them with both faith and friendship.

Jeanne Pannier was one of the principal leaders of the early years of the Paris student work.[7] Her husband was the secretary of the Cercle Protestant d'étudiants in Paris. She regularly gathered twenty or thirty women students in her home. By 1906, this group formed the basis of the women's student work of the French women students of Paris, known as the Fédération française des étudiants chrétiens. Pannier had a gracious and charming personality and she provided mature leadership to the circle. She persuaded the group to keep the designation "Christian" rather than replace it with "moral." Her eye for prospective leaders was useful and her ability to network kept women students in touch with the men's groups. She encouraged the first women delegates to attend the Federation conference. Gradually, after a year or two, the number of women delegates at these conferences grew to thirty.

Pannier and Natalie Orgewsky, who had migrated to Paris from the Russian Student Movement, formed an effective team. They also worked with the British-American student hostel (the Foyer Internationale) at 93 Boulevard Saint-Michel and later with the American YWCA secretaries who came to France during and after the war. When Professor Pannier retired as secretary of the Protestant club, he became the director of the Maison des Missions (the Training School) of the Paris Mission and Jeanne added groups of future young missionaries to her circle of student friends. Her health inhibited her from accepting many invitations to conferences in other countries for the WSCF and YWCA but despite this limitation, she served for many years on the executive of the World's YWCA.[8]

By 1913 YWCA secretary Lizzie Meyer had eight new groups with a total of 300 members. These groups gathered for Bible study, missions or met as reading clubs largely under the auspices of the YWCA. The residents of the foyer requested help with their moral life and they also attended association meetings. The Paris Y's members were studying a book by Malcolm Spencer, *The Hope and Redemption of Society*, in addition to attending Bible discussions given by pastors.[9] A new spirit

7. Some of the other workers in the French student movement included Alice Bianquis; Lizzie Meyer (Madame Pierre Maury), 1911–1914; Professor Raoul Allier, 1915–1918; Mlle. DeLord (Grenoble), 1915; Miss Mabel Morgan, 1916, Foyer Internationale.

8. Notes by Ruth Rouse on Jeanne Pannier, box 151–1110.

9. Jeanne Pannier to Rouse, 20 Jan, 1914, box 151–1110.

of friendliness and enthusiasm in the association was noted. Madame Orgewsky's work for the Russian girls and women was developing well.

The growth of the movement was not always matched by an equal increase in resources or trained personnel, something requiring negotiation and careful allocation of the few existing funds. Madame Pannier requested Lilli Kellerman's services for one term in the Paris foyer to be followed by a second term visiting universities and establishing Christian Association work. Anticipating complications with the funders, Rouse did not agree with Pannier's plan to divide the work in this way. The original proposal had suggested that the position would be funded by the Société d'évangelisation laique, a Protestant society that aimed to gather people into the Protestant church. This was, however, not considered a good ideological match for the WSCF, since the aim of the latter was "to Christianize the Student World and the individual students"—not to endeavour to win students from one form of religion to another. To support her argument, Rouse referred to resolutions passed at the WSCF Constantinople conference in 1911. Even the statutes of the French women's association claimed that all were welcome, irrespective of the denomination to which they belonged. By contrast, the men's association retained the word "Protestant" in its title and upheld a more conservative approach to other denominations and religions.

Rouse believed that, if the women's travelling secretary worked simultaneously for a protestantising agency and for the Federation, then the ecumenical stance of the Federation would be substantially weakened. The public would not distinguish the two agencies with the result that the Y would be accused unjustly of trying to turn Catholics into Protestants.[10] The WSCF could not afford to have such a claim made against it.

Rouse was careful to reassure Pannier that the Federation was not attempting to dictate policy to the French student movement. She felt obliged to protect the interdenominational policy established in Constantinople in relation to interdenominational work. To solve the problem, Rouse suggested that the money the Federation had planned to give to support the women's secretary should go to Miss Kellerman's work in the Paris Y and Miss Meyer's work could be supported by other sources. That compromise was accepted.

10. Rouse to Pannier, 27 June, 1911, box 151–1110.

The competition for students was reflected in Meyer's observation in 1918 that it was essential that the associations do more recruiting. She noted that the Catholics were uniting around similar goals for student work and, following the instructions of the Archbishop of Paris, were carefully observing Protestant methods, which he thought were effective. Anticipating that there would be some struggle and difficulty during the winter, she wrote: "We need strength, and we shall only be strong when we have more members."[11]

Secretary Lilli Kellerman held a planning retreat in 1915 attended by twenty women. Proposals included a study circle on the apostle Paul; social issues including temperance and immorality; popular evangelization; and a mission study circle on Madagascar.[12] The religious meetings would include either Bible studies or prayer. In addition to retreats, general meetings were to be held two Sundays per month with a similar focus on moral, social, pedagogical, or religious subjects. Invited speakers were M. Grauss on the French Federation, Mlle. Hugenin of the Swiss Christian Movement, Dr. Claupaudel of Geneva on personal purity, and a Madame Vermeil on women's suffrage.[13]

For the Paris secretary Lilli Kellerman, an average day began with breakfast at the student foyer, followed by an open house between 12:30 p.m. and 3 p.m. She sent letters, organized reunions, gave advice, and visited students, especially the sick and isolated. As a student herself, she knew "the material difficulties and the intellectual and moral struggle of the French students, profoundly Christian and desiring above all to serve God and to know Jesus Christ, she won the confidence of the students and became friend and confidants among them."[14]

The war had a devastating effect on the universities and the student movement. France was unified in identifying German aggression as the cause and in opposing Germany. In the first four months of war, France suffered 850,000 casualties. Civil unrest increased and strikes, inspired by the example of the Bolshevik Revolution in Russia, became widespread in the fall of 1917.

The need to train student secretaries remained an issue—particularly with the loss of leadership that resulted from the war. Professor Allier

11. Meyer to Rouse, 12 Oct, 1918, box 151–1112.

12. Kellerman to Rouse, 30 Nov, 1915, box 151–1112.

13. Rapport de L'Association Chrétienne D'Etudiantes de Paris, box 151–1115.

14. S. Bidgrain to Rouse, box 151–1114.

observed in 1915 that the war had increased the need for more trained women: "With us, women will have a very important role to play now that the terrible slaughter has deprived us of so many of our young men. The question of the Christian education of women ought to stand in the first rank. You see how much I ought to lay stress on a vigorous continuation of the work among women students and school girls."[15] As part of this effort to train secretaries, Rouse urged Meyer to attend a student conference in America and suggested that she stay in America to attend the six-week summer secretarial school in New York City. The program included Bible Study, history of the Student Christian Associations in different parts of the world, and careful study of the different methods of work. Although not all the methods taught in this school would be suitable for work in France, Rouse believed that comparing methods with those doing student secretarial work in America would yield methods suitable for France and would provide inspiration.[16]

The war strained existing resources. Jeanne Pannier was committed to women's work in her own district; for example, she hosted in her home a branch of the Red Cross that employed sixty women. Secretaries Suzanne de Dietrich and a Miss Dorio were doing outreach work with students who were stranded without money and supplies. At the beginning of the war needy students were very much in evidence, but within a few months, many had left Paris with the exception of some Russian women students. The Federation had sent money, which Madame Pannier put in a reserve fund, to help the Russians.

The foyer, under Suzanne de Dietrich, was open daily for students who had nowhere else to go. The student hostel had been transformed into a hospital and most of the English and American students had left.[17] Secretary Mabelle Morgan described life in the Paris foyer in the following:

> The tea house, library, and office continue to be open and we are very busy indeed. Since the first of the year we have enrolled about 200 girls representing eleven nationalities. I enclose our bulletin and entrance card which will show you conditions. We need not only to look after the girls in giving them a quiet, safe

15. Allier to Rouse, 12 Aug, 1915, box 151–1112.

16. Rouse to Meyer, no date, box 151–1109

17. Jeanne Pannier to Rouse, 26 Aug, 1914, extracted for Women's Committee of the WSCF, box 151–1110.

place to rest and study, but to aid in clothing, finding employment, etc. We have given two girls, a Russian and a Roumanian, work in cataloguing our library. We are helping a student who is ill to have a long vacation by the sea. These are just mentioned to show you something of the way we are meeting the needs of the hour. In the month of June we served about 850 teas. The girls pay no fees nor do they pay for their tea or the use of the library. It is through the beautiful generosity of Mrs. Hoff that we are able to continue the work for students at this sad time. Mrs. Hoff is still at her Chateau, but she keeps in close touch with our work.

The work has grown so much that at our last board meeting Miss Loos, whom you know as in charge of our dispensary before the war, and who has been nursing soldiers for the last two years, was called to take the position of assistant secretary. She is most capable and helpful. We are now able to add three consultation hours a week to our schedule. Miss Loos, at these times, advises free of charge any girl who is ailing and directs her to the proper medical advisor etc.

Our office for information etc. is open for all women from 2–4 pm. The other privileges are offered only to student girls from 15–35 years of age. Please do not think of us as lonely or unhappy. It is a glorious opportunity of service, and though these two years have not been easy, and though they must from the very circumstances be filled with sad experiences, yet we rejoice and count ourselves happy to have a part in doing service in this great world crisis.[18]

The French federation also organized summer camps, such as those held during 1917 and 1918 at Malons. Some students came seeking and encountered Christ, according to secretary Mademoiselle Herman, but others were looking for strength for their lives, however long they might last.[19]

SUZANNE BIDGRAIN (1879–1961)

The work in Bordeaux developed under the leadership of Suzanne Bidgrain (1879–1961). She had been born into an agnostic family in Normandy, but discovered the Bible when she was twenty-five years old. She served as a founding member of the Union chrétienne des jeunes filles (UCJF) of Normandy and was its leader from 1911 to 1912. She

---

18. Morgan to Rouse, extract, 1916, box 151–1112.
19. Herman to Rouse, 6 Aug, 1918, box 150–1106.

studied theology at Marburg where she founded a women's branch of the German Student Association in 1912. Bidgrain graduated with a Master of Arts from Glasgow University in 1916.[20]

Prior to her work in Bordeaux, Bidgrain had gained valuable experience in Germany. In 1914 she spent three months in Heidelberg working with the German Christian Student Movement for Women (DCSVF). She joined one Bible study group and then became the leader of a second. A Catholic student, Thea Tillisen, became a close friend, a friendship that would be of great help when Bidgrain had to "win Catholics" working in France. She noted that they frequently discussed the difficulties of Catholic-Protestant understanding and the work of the federation to "unite the members of all churches."[21]

The work of the student federation in Germany, Bidgrain believed, could be more effective if the leadership were not so intimidated about being seen to adopt a liberal theological position as part of their method. They tended to attract members who had been brought up in pious families and who would make social connections, but they were not the kind of members with whom one could form a missionary society. She objected to the underlying narrowness of vision that limited the way the work was done.

Bidgrain attended a conference in Freudenstadt at which she observed the marginal status of women's concerns. A woman delegate who had been asked to speak on women's concerns was rescheduled at the last minute for the last and much less favourable time slot. When she protested, the organizers gave her two minutes to summarize her work. Despite this rearrangement, the women students saw the opening as a hopeful precedent for women's place in future conferences.

Student leaders who worked in more than one region of France had ample chance to compare the student movement at different universities. As a Federation worker employed to work with students in Bordeaux, Bidgrain observed in 1916 that that university had a particular identity. Women students were very preoccupied with their academic work and constituted almost the entire membership of the General Association of students—an association that was neither anti-religious nor religious, but provided a venue for students to meet. The Catholic Association had

---

20. Bidgrain studied French Language and Literature, German language and literature, and Logic.

21. Bidgrain to Rouse, 23 July, 1914, box 150–1102.

been in existence for ten years and it was quite vibrant with thirty-eight members. A priest led Bible studies, conferences examined Catholic dogma, and social activities were organized in town. At Bordeaux, the *libre-penseur agressif*, presumably more prevalent in other locations, was virtually unknown. Bidgrain concluded that the enemy to student Christian work in the south of France was not liberal thought but rather inertia and indifference.[22]

Tensions between Catholic and Protestant students complicated Bidgrain's attempt to bring Orthodox students into the movement. Two Serbs were elected to the Foyer committee, one of whom had already been a member of the Geneva Foyer. The second, Emilia Yeksitch, had not previously been involved in the Federation. They both belonged to the Orthodox Church and had a great deal of influence with other students. At a meeting of students in Montpelier, a woman had invited the students, including the Serbians, to her house. Bidgrain wrote:

> It was a fateful meeting for me at any rate. E. Yeksitch spoke of the World Federation and of the unity of Christ's Church. She spoke of the beautiful thought that all the Churches have the same root and bear the same fruits and only differ in their exterior appearance. I prayed in French, and E. Yeksitch in Serbian. After that we had a good tea and the Serbians sang popular songs and their national anthem, etc. I am very happy about some of these Serbian girls; I was able to buy some books on medicine that they were unable to buy. My sister who is still with me gives lessons to those who know enough French to follow their lectures. One girl arrived from Salonike, ill and tired out, having lost all her family. We are not going to call it a "foyer" here, because there is already a Y.W.C.A foyer, it will be the "Chez Nous" as in Paris.

Whether the emphasis of student work was outreach or conversion varied with individual leaders. One key leader of the French movement, Raoul Allier (1862–1939), served as Dean of the Protestant Faculty of Theology in Paris. He gave priority to conversion and described the conversion experience of one of his students:

> A year ago, this young girl, Mlle. Goldschild, was a radical free-thinker and belonged to the most violent faction of the revolutionary party. During the first days of October, 1914, she came, by

22. Bidgrain to Rouse, extracted 20 Feb, 1917 by RR to the Women's Sub-Committee, box 150–1102.

chance, to hear one of my lectures. From that time, she attended all my meetings very regularly. At first, it was only an intellectual interest which led her to this. She simply wished to know what Christians thought about certain questions. Little by little the nature of the interest which she felt changed. At the beginning of December, she began to be troubled in conscience. The day on which she heard my lecture "Christmas and mourning" she felt that God was calling her to be converted. As yet, I did not know her. In January, after much hesitation, she came to see me. She had heard that I improvised the form of my lectures entirely and that I had no notes at all to serve for their publication. In taking these she has rendered me a very great service. It is thanks to her stenographic notes that the publication of my talks has been possible. Once having entered into relations with me, little by little she gave me her confidence. She has told me that she belonged to a Jewish family, but one hostile to all religious ideas. She revealed her troubles to me, and during several months I helped her in a tremendous crisis. Terrible was the internal struggle in this soul absolutely sincere, wedded to the Truth, conscious of a terrible pride against which she must fight. The struggle only ended by one of the most beautiful conversions I have ever seen, a conversion total, radical, absolute. This young girl was baptized on Sunday, July 4. As she lives in an atmosphere where religious ideas are constantly ridiculed, I wished her to pass some time in a Christian family and I have brought her here with us for a fortnight. With the help of Divine Grace I am witnessing the unfolding of this soul. I must say that during this crisis I was strongly seconded by my daughters Mlle. Kellerman and Mlle. Viguer, who surrounded this soul with unceasing prayer.[23]

The French movement relied on the Americans for funding, for example, hoping to cover a deficit of 6000 francs in 1916 by appealing to American supporters.[24] The financial support, however, obliged them to listen to the advice and leading of Americans such as WSCF leader John Mott. He criticized an article that had appeared in the Federation journal, *Le Semeur*, regarding the interconfessional position of the WSCF. Mott felt that the article would not help their efforts to expand the movement in the Roman Catholic Church. Mott observed: "You will recall the policy and the principles of our World's Student Christian Federation as agreed upon at the time of Constantinople Conference and therefore

23. Allier to Mott, 3 Aug, 1915, box 148–1091.
24. Allier to Mott, 3 Aug, 1915, box 148–1091.

how important it is that we let those guide us, not only in our World's federation but in each of these Movements which belong to the World's Federation."[25] Allier was quick to respond that since 1914, the Roman Catholic Church interpreted the war as one of Protestantism represented by Germany versus Catholicism presented by France.[26]

Allier was further annoyed in 1915 when Suzanne de Dietrich asked for money for the Paris student work. He asked Mott for clarification of her work there since he felt that she was neither a founder of the movement, nor a secretary of the work, and that all she actually did was meet the Slav students who frequented the movement. He wrote:

> I am very much struck by the spiritual value of this young woman; hers is a chosen spirit; she does good to all those who come to her; you see, I have a most complimentary opinion of her; unfortunately, I must add that the practical powers of Mlle. de Dietrich are not equal to her spiritual faculties; she has not the gifts necessary for organizing and vitalizing a work. She can speak to souls; she does them good, she instructs them; she encourages them, she comforts them; but she must not struggle with practical questions. As soon as she attempts this kind of question she loses herself in Utopia, or else she changes her plan every day; she does not follow out consistently affairs of this kind. In this respect, I have undergone a real disillusionment; she is a force in the spiritual work of our Federation; she would be a source of weakness for an Association taking her for a secretary.[27]

In another case, Allier requested money from Mott to support the work among Slav students that was led by Lilli Kellerman. The Slavic students, he noted, were very poor and their resources had been cut off by the war. He described the nature of the work and then followed it with a statement of need: "The 'Students' Foyer' which my wife founded and which is the center of the work among the young girls of the Latin Quarter, attempts to aid materially these poor Slav students. To some we give free meals. We help others to buy their books or to pay the rent for their rooms. I have hunted for and raised the money for this special work among the poor Slav students but I have not as yet all the resources which I need. I lack about 500 francs."[28]

25. Mott to Allier, 16 Nov, 1917, box 148–1092.

26. Allier to Mott, 7 Dec, 1917, box 148–1092.

27. Allier to Mott, 7 May, 1915, box 148–1091.

28. Allier to Mott, 7 May, 1915, box 148–1091.

Complications and tempers which had simmered just below the surface were exacerbated by the tensions and propaganda generated by the war. A declaration formulated at a conference in Montpelier in 1915 claimed that although the Federation work had been born in Protestant countries, it counted among its members adherents of different Christian churches, whether Orthodox, Catholic, or Protestant. In fact, the report from the Montpelier conference stressed that "It [the Federation] never seeks to detach its members from their own church, whatever that may be. It recommends to each of its members, on the contrary, the most complete loyalty to his particular church. The Federation seeks in no way to become a new church in competition with the others."[29]

Rouse continued to look for opportunities to extend the student work through the presence of individuals such as Father Nicholas (Professor Velmirovitch) who was interested in placing a Serbian travelling secretary in France. He was deeply concerned with the spiritual needs of the Serbian students there and was willing to use all his influence to persuade the Serbian government to back the proposal. Rouse also met with a Professor Popovitch, a professor at Belgrade University in charge of the Serbian students in England, where there was an organization that functioned in the same way as the *Bureau scholaire serbe* in France.[30] She also maintained contact with a Professor Jovicic, formerly teaching at Belgrade University, who had been converted by one of John Mott's visits to the area.

The French women students eventually took over La Maison serbe. The program included a club and restaurant.[31] Developing such programs required staff with the necessary skills but also involved subtle debates about gender expectations. So Rouse wrote to Allier,

> As regards my suggestion about Mlle Bidgrain I do not think you have quite understood it. I do not mean to suggest that Mlle Bidgrain should work to any extent amongst the Serbian lycéens and étudiants. As you say, as a woman she would have less influence with them than a man. What I proposed was that she should go to the same towns as M. Jovititch and work amongst the Serbian women students whilst he was working amongst the

29. R. Allier, S. Bidgrain, Marc Boegner, Henri Bois, Daniel Couve, Suzanne de Dietrich, Lilli Kellerman, Report adopted 6 May, 1915, after Montpelier Conference, typescript, 2pp, box 148–1092.

30. Rouse to Allier, 8 June, 1917, box 150–1101.

31. Rouse to M. Holmes, 15 Jan, 1918, box 249–2040.

men, thus enabling him to have the benefit of her advice and experience from the French point of view. Mlle Bidgrain has of course a unique advantage in having been to Serbia, as well as having made a special study of the Serbian mentality and the circumstance of the Serbian too will be a great benefit. I fear that it is almost impossible that you should find a man traveling secretary who has had such experience as she has had in dealing with this special problem. Indeed, apart from yourself, does such a man exist in France? But I am hopeful, of course, that you will succeed in finding someone of sufficient weight and experience to travel with M. Jovititch.[32]

To fulfill her own desire to contribute to the war effort, in 1917 Rouse worked for a few months under the auspices of the YMCA with soldiers in Le Havre. Unfortunately, she was wounded, forcing her to limit her Federation work while she recovered from shell shock. She worried that she could not afford to scale back her responsibilities since the Federation in Europe faced such a crisis. With Dr Mott at a distance and with her own physical limitations, she feared much ground would be lost unless she could overcome these difficulties. A reshuffling of staff released Louis Henriod from the British Student Federation work to act for all foreign matters in London and transferred Suzanne Bidgrain to Paris.

Another crisis faced the student organization at the end of the war. The men who returned from the front were apparently furious to find that the university was full of both women students and Serbians. The sense of a takeover by women was also reflected in the workplace as women had entered the workforce in large numbers during the war. The men felt that the women were too liberal and too progressive to take up leadership in the movement. Bidgrain found that they were had strong opinions on both the methods and the membership, as she noted:

> The letters from the Front which I sent you prove further that our ideas of breadth in the matter of interconfessional relations have reached them in one way or another. Some of our leaders fear that it will be difficult for all to work together harmoniously. One wrote to me three weeks ago to put me on my guard. He says that they are asking, "What has this woman outsider to do with us? She does not know the French Federation before the War, *our* Federation and it is *our* Federation which we must have

32. Rouse to Allier, 30 June, 1917, box 150–1101.

back. Why is this Woman's Federation to meddle with us?" It is only an annex, a side show. It is the men's Federation which is the Federation.[33]

SUZANNE DE DIETRICH (1891–1981)

An Alsatian by birth, Suzanne de Dietrich was the youngest of seven girls. Her mother suffered from a congenital condition that also affected four of her daughters, including Suzanne, whose limbs were malformed. She walked with two canes and experienced chronic pain but rarely complained. Her mother was a German baroness and her father owned iron works in Alsace. The family held daily worship services in their chapel and attended German-language Lutheran Sunday services. Her religious education had been undertaken by a French-speaking pastor, Rev. Breitenstein, in the evangelical chapel in Strasbourg. Breitenstein had heard Mott speak at the first Swiss Student conference in Sainte-Croix.[34]

When both her parents died, her uncles helped guide de Dietrich's choice of engineering at a technical high school in Lausanne where she studied from 1907–1909 followed by engineering at the University of Lausanne. In her class at Lausanne, the only other woman student was a Russian named Lydia Menzinger, who returned to Russia in 1912 and corresponded with de Dietrich for the next several years. She became a member of the Russian SCM and served as a nurse during the war.[35] During her studies, Suzanne met another student named Renée Warnery, a Swiss medical student who served with the Swiss student movement.

De Dietrich attended her first student movement study conference at Sainte-Croix in 1909. When the women's foyer in Lausanne opened up that same year under the leadership of Annette Tritton, de Dietrich served on the leadership team. In order to follow Rev. Breitenstein's courses, she convinced her guardian to allow her to study in Geneva for a year. During this time she joined the Geneva SCM and led Bible study groups. A speech by General Secretary of the French SCM, Charles Grauss (who died in the war in 1918) convinced her to join the French

33. Bidgrain to Rouse, Extract, 26 Dec, 1918, by RR to the Women's Subcommittee, box 150–1102.

34. Breitenstein was ordained as a Reformed pastor in 1897 and became chaplain of the Evangelical Free Church in Strasbourg until he left to serve a church near Geneva in 1907.

35. Weber, *Courage to Live.*

SCM. The French SCM had grown out of the YMCA (est. 1852) and the YWCA (est. 1894). The French federation of SCMs had been accepted as a member of the WSCF in 1898. In 1914 there were about 400 men students, 300 women, and 450 high school members.[36]

In 1915 de Dietrich tried to gain the confidence of the Polish and Russian students by organizing literary evenings in her room.[37] She described this work as meeting with some success:

> I have had much to rejoice ever since last I wrote to you! I have asked a Polish woman to help me gather the women students together at my house on Saturday evenings and to organize little literary discussions. The first evening she spoke to us about Krassinski; there were thirteen of us, eight strangers, Poles and Russian Jews. It was in my room, a real student gathering with six cups and one tea spoon among twelve people, but we parted friends,—and much more, in the course of conversation one of them asked me to study the Bible with her! Others have asked if they may join us, also we have decided to have a Bible Circle on Thursday evenings. The first was not all that I could have wished but they will come again; some of them came to the circle held on Sunday led by M. Marc and they were delighted.[38]

De Dietrich tried to build trust among the various non-French women students. She brought Poles, Lithuanians, and Russians into the discussion group representing Orthodox, Catholic, and Jewish faiths. They used Federation money from Mott to provide an inexpensive breakfast at the foyer which fifteen students attended daily. The Russian foyer offered dinners to about ten students who were mostly Orthodox and Catholic. The Slavic students, de Dietrich observed, were less reliable as they would seem enthusiastic one day and then would disappear without a word the next. She felt that, for them, religion was a matter of feelings more than conscience.[39] Two Jewish students studied the gospel with her and had come to stay for a week in a room associated with the YWCA. They sometimes joined in evening prayer; the others were greatly moved to hear them "praying to Christ for the Jewish people."

36. Ibid., 38.

37. Letter by de Dietrich to Rouse, 5 Jan, 1915, extracted, box 150–1104

38. De Dietrich to Rouse, 7 Aug, 1915, box 150–1104.

39. De Dietrich to Rose, 5 May, 1915, box 150–1104.

Jewish students, she concluded, needed to be reached by other students of their own faith.[40]

Another group of volunteers, Volontaires du Christ, arose out of the ranks of the French federation movement; this group sought to work for the evangelization of the world. In 1916 de Dietrich became a member, with a particular vision of sending a health team to Muslim countries. She held a meeting in her room with two volunteers and three young women to pray for France and for Germany.

De Dietrich continued to struggle with the notion of war and the culpability of the nations, believing that in the question of the war, no one was completely blameless.[41]

She noted the self-righteousness of the Germans and their "pharisaic pride" but she reflected that she was no longer sure that the French were any better.[42] She believed that there should be a revival of French Protestantism wherein all fighting Christians returned to the foot of the cross, "so humiliated by their fault for accusing each other—to dream again and to judge and condemn each other mutually. This day seems very, very far away, it is with the eyes of faith that one can imagine and wait for it, but I believe in the future of the Federation Universal."[43]

Part of her work included federation development in Strasbourg—a development that she was convinced would need a great deal of tact and a thorough knowledge of the Alsatian character. The French and the Germans were quite separate and the existing Association was identified with the latter. The situation was complicated by the long history of the region, as she noted in the following: "The people have fraternized with our troops with a rush. Enthusiasm was unanimous and passed all that I had ever dreamed of. It came from the heart, but it is not without result that they have lived without enthusiasm for 47 years. The intelligence of many has been corrupted through being

40. De Dietrich to Rouse, 7 Aug, 1915, box 150–1104.

41. De Dietrich to Rouse 7 July, 1916, box 150–1104.

42. De Dietrich to Rouse, 28 Oct, 1914, box 150–1104.

43. De Dietrich to Rouse, 7 July, 1916, box 150–1104. In his biography of De Dietrich, Weber notes that in the 1930s she had not read the whole of Karl Barth's *Dogmatics*. She felt that she did not like the intellectualist and dogmatic stance of his followers. She appreciated his theocentric way of thinking and his theological interpretation of the Bible. She felt that what she herself had learned through study and suffering was confirmed and deepened by Barth's writing and preaching. See Weber, *Courage to Live*, 65.

obliged to play a double game. Their whole mental makeup must be renewed. I am frightened at the task."[44]

Her preliminary investigations in the region revealed that there were very few women students registered at the university and there was no sign of a women's student Christian association. The pro-French Alsatians avoided the men's association, mostly composed of Germans. Any attempt to organize a student movement would be interpreted as either pro-German or pro-French. Students, de Dietrich found, exhibited one of two positions: either a very strong religious indifference or a narrow and dogmatic Lutheranism.

After receiving a warm reception to the proposal of the establishment of a foyer for women students, she prepared a survey for the Alsatian students to see if a foyer would meet their needs. She admired the absence of hatred among the Christians in Alsace: all were open to reconciliation with the pro-German Alsatians. She found the German tendency to platitude "sickening" and in sharp contrast to their previous arrogance. The Alsatians suffered various indignities in the war; pastors were forced to preach political sermons or face imprisonment. She concluded that having an official religion was a calamity since Alsace seemed to her as irreligious and unbelieving as France—all was tradition.[45]

A month later, de Dietrich had made contact with twenty women students at the University of Strasbourg including a few Catholics, several Jews, and a number of Protestant pastors' daughters. The social side of the Federation interested them much more than the religious side. De Dietrich would have preferred opposition to the polite indifference with which she was met. "This is a country where one is *born* Protestant, Catholic, or Jew. At the University I believe, the fashion is to be materialist."[46]

Yet, her dedication to reaching diverse student groups made some of the male leaders uncomfortable. As noted earlier, Raoul Allier wanted Mott to clarify de Dietrich's work in Paris since she was not an official secretary and she had not founded the Paris movement, yet to his annoyance, she was asking for financial support for the work

Bible study had been a central activity in the WSCF since the early summer conference at Mount Hermon. Lectures by learned

44. De Dietrich to Rouse, 21 Dec, 1918, box 150–1104.

45. De Dietrich to Rouse, 7 Jan, 1919, box 150–1104.

46. De Dietrich to Rouse, 10 Feb, 1919, box 150–1104.

biblical authorities were the traditional way to communicate knowledge. Students were encouraged to practice daily Bible study in the form of a devotion called the Morning Watch. In pioneering movements, students were pulled into the movement in a variety of ways related to hospitality in the foyer movement (see chapter 6) and then they would be invited to join small groups to study the Bible under a leader. The next step was to train leaders so that these groups could multiply.

De Dietrich developed new methods for Bible study that replaced the traditional lecture style approach that had been in use until 1914. She led Bible studies in camps and study circles of the women's branch of the Federation and the French YWCA. A small-group format with between twelve to fifteen members allowed for fellowship within the group and transmitted a method.

The method of letting the biblical passages speak with only minimal interpretive comments by the leader proved to be a good approach for newcomers, because it allowed the words of Jesus, Paul, or the prophets to make their own impact. For texts which needed background information, one or several group members might be asked to prepare and to introduce the study, leading to a general discussion. A study outline could be given out beforehand with questions to help members in their personal preparation; the group could then share and discuss the insights while the leader was careful to see that it was the biblical text that was discussed and not the study outline. This method relied on good leaders, persons who would not monopolize the discussion and would bring it back to the text when it went astray, who were prepared to comment on questions raised when no one in the group dared to speak. Finally, Suzanne pointed to the need for study material and biblical commentaries written in French and for lay people.[47]

De Dietrich's biographer, Hans-Ruedi Weber writes: "Today these comments about Bible study may sound commonplace, so much have they become part of our practice. But such participatory studies were revolutionary in 1920. Later Suzanne spoke and wrote much more about the 'why' and 'how' of Bible study, but the main lines of her life-long commitment to it are already present in that early report."[48]

47. Weber, *Courage to Live*, 59.

48. Ibid. In 1925 de Dietrich attended a seminar given by Henry B. Sharman, an engineer from California who bought a wilderness camp in Minnesing in Algonquin

Because of de Dietrich's work in the Latin Quarter with Orthodox and Roman Catholic students, she was well prepared to pioneer an interconfessional Bible study—a form that became more relevant after the adoption of an ecumenical policy by the WSCF. Yet her understanding of the importance of ecumenism was not shared by some of the male leaders of the WSCF; they referred to her "ecumenical impatience." [49] She read Walter Rauschenbusch's *The Social Principles of Jesus*, published in 1917, which influenced her own thinking about the importance of the gospel.

De Dietrich argued that Bible study should have several aims. First, Bible study in groups was important for the growth of fellowship; members could enter into honest conversation in which they could share their own doubts and personal experiences. Second, the best way to share the Christian message with newcomers was to share the texts with them, listening to their objections and entering into their problems. Third, Bible study developed and strengthened faith. For many students it became a main part of their faith and practice throughout the rest of their lives. Bible study also provided a good school for acquiring an understanding of the biblical message, of how to approach the Bible, and of how to let it guide one's life. She found this approach completely lacking among French students. She argued for a "historical-critical approach which freed the text from our presuppositions." [50]

De Dietrich suggested several ways to conduct Bible studies. While not wanting to prescribe fixed rules, she recommended that study groups should have no more than twelve to fifteen persons. In a newcomers group the participants could read the passages to hear them first hand without too much commentary or interpretation. For texts that needed background information, one or several group leaders might be asked to prepare and introduce the study, leading to a general discussion.

The war, however, caused a shift in mood and interest in this type of Bible study. The New Testament, which had served as the preferred

---

Park, Ontario, for annual Bible study camps. His emphasis on students encountering the historical Jesus influenced Suzanne greatly, as well as generations of students. She felt that the contact with Sharman cured her of her inclinations towards Catholicism. She translated some of his studies. Sharman used a Socratic method and challenged participants to read for themselves the meaning of Biblical passage and arrive at their own sense of truth about the meaning. See Weber, *Courage to Live*, 64–65.

49. Ibid., 62.

50. Ibid., 58–59.

text for Bible study in the pre-war period, was replaced during the war, by Suzanne and others, by the Old Testament. The prophets were found to be fruitful sources for biblical reflection in that political context. A tremendous wartime demand fuelled the publication of articles and Bible study guides that attempted to answer questions concerning the meaning of suffering. Rouse noted that the British SCM press was so successful during this time that the publication of this type of literature became a source of income. Some of the bestsellers on the topic of Bible study included H. Wheeler Robinson's *The Cross of Job* and W. B. Selbie's, *The Nature and Message of the Bible*. In addition, during this time (1915) there was an increased interest in evangelism—a looking outward that gradually became inspired by increased social consciousness.[51]

The WSCF sponsored a consultation in 1922 in Hardenbroek, the Netherlands, to gather Bible study leaders. De Dietrich was an active participant in these meetings. The purpose was to develop an intellectually honest and open kind of Bible study. As a result of the growing acceptance of an interfaith stance at the Constantinople meeting in 1911, the notion of opening up the membership to Roman Catholic and Orthodox believers drove the demand for interconfessional Bible study. This ecumenical movement had been the point of tension in the French leadership with de Dietrich leading a move toward an aggressive ecumenism and others holding on to the historic privileging of the Protestant roots of faith.

The Beatenberg conference allowed member movements from other continents to participate in decision-making but did not include non-Protestant member movements. A rising demand for inclusive practices was equalled by a downward trend in evangelization in North American contexts in the 1920s. This tension was acknowledged by some in the rising ecumenical context of three ecumenical world conferences in the 1920s—Stockholm in 1925, Lausanne in 1927, and the IMC assembly in Jerusalem in 1928.[52] For de Dietrich, the type of study engaged in by the WSCF during the 1920s led her to re-evaluate the role of the church

51. Ibid., 62.

52. Ibid., 74–75. The WSCF at this time chose to follow a process of mutual listening and witnessing in the context of the changed world situation. Part of this extended study method included reflecting on the question of unity with the church of all ages and thereby finding unity not in one particular manifestation of the church but in the unity represented by God's call. De Dietrich was a central participant in this process called "message study." See ibid., 76.

as the body of Christ. The WSCF shifted to an interconfessional policy and then in 1928 to a policy where they recognized the "existence and approved the formation of confessional groups and sought to enter into relationship with them, in order to foster ecumenism."[53]

RUTH ROUSE AND THE FRENCH FEDERATION

Ruth Rouse's role as advisor to the French movement is evident in her correspondence with women secretaries. She encouraged Jeanne Pannier, for example, to continue the camp work at Malons and to extend it to the rest of the country. She also played a mediating role between the national movements and the Americans as, for example, in correspondence where she noted that M. Allier might be of help to the American secretaries by bringing them in touch with people who understood foreign affairs in Paris. She told Pannier that she did not see how she could "write to M. Allier myself about it until the American secretaries act themselves but as you have close relations with Miss Taylor you could easily bring the matter to pass as far as the women at least are concerned."[54]

Rouse understood the different cultures involved in the Federation and, in a letter to Pannier, gently urged cross-cultural understanding: "It is very important too that you should get into *spiritual* touch with the American friends who are helping you. Sometimes I think that because their form of religious expression is different from yours we do not credit them with the spiritual fervour that is really there. I think it will be well to take all possible occasion to join in their religious meetings when asked to do so and to ask them to join in yours. If these new hostels can be begun in a real spirit of prayer on the part of all the workers I think many difficulties which you fear will disappear."[55] She also gave advice on the placement of staff and the internal politics of the Federation. Concerning the impending move of Suzanne Bidgrain to Paris in 1916

---

53. In 1932 an historical event in the form of an ecumenical retreat was organized in the village of Moutherhouse in the Vosges that combined Orthodox, Roman Catholic, Anglican, Lutheran members for almost a week. Most participants were from Europe but two Asians and one American were also present. From this small gathering, de Dietrich continued to contribute to ecumenism on a world scale writing reports and attending meetings for both the WSCF and the World YWCA. Her work contributed to a biblical and liturgical renewal that led to publications of an inter-confessional WSCF hymnal in 1924 and a prayer book in 1937. See Weber, *Courage to Live*, 82.

54. Rouse to J. Pannier, 13 Dec, 1918, box 151–1110.

55. Ibid.

she advised Pannier to write the movement in the provinces to express her appreciation for the willingness to share Suzanne, not with Paris, but with the world.

Another matter where Rouse gave counsel was on relations between student secretaries. In response to a reported difficulty between M. Allier and Suzanne Bidgrain, Rouse suggested that it was helpful that "Susanne's 'oecumenical' operations are concerned with other countries and not with France only. It will make them more natural and less pointed. I hope you gather my idea. The difficulty of M. Allier's attitude to Susanne can perhaps be mitigated by very great care on the part of the Federation to consult him in all matters in which he is really concerned, so that he will not feel that Susanne has taken Federation responsibilities away from him, but we must guard these points carefully."[56]

By 1917, Rouse felt that the women's work in France had improved greatly on a number of fronts. Women students were better prepared for their studies and they were younger and healthy. Some fine leaders were emerging. The religious side of the work had greatly deepened and there was also a growing interest in social questions and in providing assistance to foreign students. The movement was growing in ecclesiastical breadth from its early years of very narrow Protestant focus. Rouse credited Suzanne Bidgrain for this increasing openness since she firmly maintained that the movement was open to all students who accepted its aims, regardless of their particular denominational membership. Increasing numbers of Catholics were joining the movement.

Such progress in inter-faith work was unexpectedly rapid and would require the Federation to clarify its direction in the postwar period. Rouse wrote: "It must either drop its ecclesiastically Protestant character and become really inter-ecclesiastical, or it will stamp out the lighted torch of unity. What is necessary is the avoidance of things which will make Catholics feel like outsiders in this Association." The French Movement would need to hold its meetings in neutral places, have fewer pastors and more lay speakers, and drop such references as "we Protestants" and "the days of the Persecution" in order to be more welcoming to the Catholic members. These questions were not relevant during the war since conferences were not being planned, but they would become more of an issue postwar. Besides, she perceived that progress was being made inter-ecclesiastically among the women "where it is always easier."

56. Ibid..

Rouse felt that in the future, the women's work should be allowed to develop its own lines so that after the war they could provide an object lesson to the men.[57]

In 1920, some leaders of the women's movement (de Dietrich and Tritton) organized a conference at Chateau D'Argeronne, France. Attendees were mainly students from Paris representing Europe, North America, England, and Madagascar and various faiths including Roman Catholic, Protestant, free thinkers or those with no church affiliation; most had never heard of the Federation. The program consisted of Bible study, addresses, and discussions on philosophy and religion, the relation of the Federation to the church, the Christian attitude to international affairs, reports from the different countries represented, and an explanation of the WSCF.

The leaders assumed that not everyone would want to take part in an optional evening service, but to their surprise everyone came and many considered the service the highlight of the day. Margaret Wrong (1887–1948) WSCF secretary, noted that what most impressed her were the "spirit of good fellowship which prevailed and the attendance at the evening service. The general life together was perhaps the best exposition of Christian internationalism and a revelation to many of the students present."[58]

Such a spirit of internationalism raised hopes for the postwar student work in France. Tensions were evident, however, as men returned from war and found an altered terrain. The postwar context offered new challenges to the movement which had struggled in so many ways to continue its work with scarce funds, few workers, and many demands. A conference was held in Montpelier in 1920 to unite the French student movement. The General Secretary called out all the names of the delegates and then continued by calling out all the names of those who had died in the war. This solemn moment also underlined the difference between the former leaders of the movement who were remembered by the returning soldiers, but not by the high school students and most of the women university students. The returning men felt a little disturbed:

57. Rouse, "Impressions of Women's Work, April 1917," box 152–1116.

58. Margaret Wrong, "Report on the International Conference at Chateau D'Argerrone, France, 23 July—5 August, 1921, box 151–1114, YDS. Margaret Wrong was the daughter of University of Toronto history professor George Wrong. See Brower, *Modern Women, Modernizing Men.*

"They came back to the old home . . . and the garden had been re-shaped, the trees had grown, the house had been painted anew and new carpets were on the floor!"[59]

The returning students had been used to the close connection between the French movement and the Protestant church. During the war, the connections that the women's movement made to Catholic students created a new attitude and a need to meet in neutral locations and to avoid holding communion services which would exclude Catholic members. The men were very shocked by these changes and they felt that it was not fair to the Protestant body in France which had started the movement and which had provided the movement with its best leaders. The conference theme promoted the need for thorough study, rather than practical action without the necessary intellectual equipment. Sessions focused on Bible and mission study.

Gender relations were not the only challenge for the postwar student movement. Relations between French and German students demanded a great deal of reconciliation before students could work together for Federation purposes. During the war there had been debates among the French wherein some felt that the Germans should take absolute responsibility for the war. De Dietrich had started a World Day of Prayer event as early as 1915 which included prayers for German students in the army.

One of many postwar student conferences brought together French students and German students in Switzerland to discuss their respective student movements. They observed the following about their differences and commonalities:

> We came to the conclusion that in particular we were in agreement in our conception of the Kingdom of God (this subject was chosen as an introduction to the discussion) and we did not fail to avail ourselves of the connection which there is between this religious idea and the national divisions which separate us. But we quickly got to the root of the question and put forward at length our respective points of view as regards the relation of our two countries as well as the deep sentiments which we feel the one for the other. This explanation was made with absolute frankness, we did not extenuate, hide or pass over anything. The Germans described to us the distress in their country, moral more than material, explaining what they believe to be the causes. We on

59. Fritz de Rougement to Mott, 8 March, 1920, Box 151–1115.

our side told them of the distrust which was inspired by their militarism, their unwillingness to make reparation. Also we laid emphasis on the question of the responsibility for the war, the violation of Belgium, etc. These interviews were often painful but always courteous, each listening to the other with respect.

We then examined the practical means by which we could seek for the truth which should dominate all our activities (the starting of circles, exchange of documents, correspondence, etc.). In our personal opinion this meeting at Bale could become the first of similar meetings, which we hope will one day lead to a complete agreement. Altogether we have the feeling that the result was very real and could be made an excellent starting point.[60]

In conclusion, the French student movement would face renewed challenges as it struggled to find common ground among different world religions, students in exile, and students in countries that were political opponents. In the postwar climate, the WSCF would enter a period of self-evaluation in an attempt to determine the nature of its mission. As the myth of Christian nations, or of the Christian West, crumbled, how could the WSCF respond to the new world situation? The WSCF provided the common ground for such opposing points of view in conferences such as Beatenberg, 1920. Yet alliances would crumble in later decades in the rising tensions that erupted in World War Two.

60. Anonymous, "The French Students' Christian Movement," 1919, typescript, 3 pp., box 152–1116.

8

Japan

NIIJIMA JO WITNESSED THE arrival of Commodore Perry and his American mission to Japan, and then secretly left that country for the United States in 1854, just before Japan opened its doors to foreign trade and diplomatic relations. While a student at Amherst College, the young man, now renamed Joseph Hardy Neesima by his sponsor, served as a translator for the Iwakura Mission that brought the first Japanese students to the United States for American education. Neesima graduated from Amherst College and Andover Theological Seminary in 1874. After a fundraising campaign in the United States, he began a school in Kyoto in 1875 that later included a school of theology (1882). Although Neesima died in 1890, his school continued to grow and evolve into Doshisha Women's College in 1901 and Doshisha University in 1920.

In the late 1860s, the increasing leniency of the Meiji government led to the repeal in 1873 of the edict against Christianity that had been in place since the early seventeenth century. With the loosening of restrictions and increased missionary presence, the rapid growth of the Roman Catholic, Protestant, and Orthodox churches led some to believe that the nation would be converted. Several bands of young Samurai who were converted in the 1870s became leaders in both the country and the indigenous church, presenting a powerful model of indigenous leadership. At the same time, missionaries were busy developing schools and competing vigorously for adherents.[1]

During the Meiji Restoration (1868–1912) the Japanese actively sought the assistance of Western educational experts who could help with the task of modernization. Compulsory elementary schooling for boys and girls had been instituted in 1872. At the young age of six, Umeko Tsuda went to the United States to study as part of the Iwakura

1. Beasley, *Modern History of Japan*.

Mission (for which Neesima had been a translator). In 1871 that organization dispatched a group of leaders and fifty-nine students to the United States. The five females in the group were charged with bringing domestic science to Japan, whereas the men were to obtain technological knowledge. This educational tour signaled the increased value placed on women's training for a state-defined ideal of motherhood. As Patessio notes, women like Tsuda were public figures working in government schools opened for aristocratic and upper-ranking samurai girls in Tokyo in order to "further women's advancement in fields that were allowed, if not considered necessary, by Japanese society."[2] Although women missionaries who arrived in the 1870s considered themselves superior to Asian women and stressed the importance of family life and Victorian models of womanhood, by opening girls' schools, they also offered "alternative understandings of women's position in society."[3]

For Tsuda, and later for Michi Kawai, the goal of training girls and women for the ideal domestic life opened up a realm of opportunity for their own work in establishing schools and in organizing the work of the YWCA, as long as those initiatives were associated with prevailing gender expectations. Eventually, a growing resentment of American influence brought to a halt the progressive mode which had motivated this educational exchange and resulted in a return to repressive and hierarchical Confucian-based policy in all of life.[4]

The YMCA had been established in Japan in 1880 by Hiromachi Kozaki, a twenty-four year old who later became Niijima's successor as leader of Doshisha University. Yale graduate Jonathan T. Swift arrived in 1888 as the first foreign secretary to the YMCA. While officially employed as a teacher of English, Swift worked with the Y and hosted Luther Wishard's nine-month stay in 1888–1889. His work in the ten years between his arrival and Mott's first visit yielded concrete results; the YMCA grew to eight associations.

Swift held evangelistic meetings at Doshisha University in Kyoto which resulted in over a hundred baptisms and the formation of twelve local YMCAs. He organized a student conference attended by 500 stu-

2. Patessio, "Creation of Public Spaces," 155–82.

3. Ibid., 167.

4. McCue, "Meiji Maiden," 29, 140. For information on the influence of women missionaries on gender roles and racial ideologies in the United States, see Seat, "*Providence Has Freed Our Hands.*"

dents of whom one hundred were women. His groundbreaking work ultimately led to the establishment of forty-two YMCA's in Turkey, Persia, India, Burma, Ceylon (Sri Lanka), China, and Japan. The WSCF had ambitious hopes for Asia and for Japan in particular, as Ruth Rouse noted: "If Japan can be made a Christian nation, it will have a vast influence throughout the entire East and Pacific Island world."[5] The YMCA was able to reach places where a church or missions organization would not have been tolerated. A convention at the Tokyo Y in January 1898 resulted in the formation of a national Student YMCA movement. The majority of the delegates were Japanese. The organization stated their purpose as "To bring students to become disciples of Jesus Christ as only Saviour—*true God and true man.*"

When Mott arrived for his first tour of Japan in 1898–1899, thirty years of Meiji rule had consolidated the Emperor's power and the policies of modernization for the country as a whole. In 1895, Japan had emerged victorious from the Sino-Japanese war which rendered Korea a protectorate and forced China to cede Taiwan. A few years later, in 1904, Japan would declare war on Russia and, after defeating that country, sign the Russo-Japanese peace treaty. Russia ceded railway lines in southern Manchuria and turned over the Liaodong Peninsula and the southern part of the island of Sakhalin to Japan. Although Japan had embraced aspects of Western culture, the country remained ambivalent about the compatibility of Christianity with Japanese conservatism and nationalism. Japanese political leadership emphasized loyalty to the political and social structures of the land, whereas the Christian elements, among whom were 40,000 Protestants, stressed the transcendent perspectives of the Christian faith and the Christian command to obey God, not "man." During this tour Mott addressed evangelistic meetings, spoke at forty-two educational institutions and converted over two hundred students.[6]

Mott's second visit in 1901–1902 was supported by his friends Mrs. McCormick and John D. Rockefeller Jr. Mott met with students and business leaders and held evangelistic rallies that resulted in hundreds of conversions. In 1903 the Tokyo Y Association achieved financial independence and in 1903 the National YMCA comprised fifty-nine student Y's and nine city associations. Future bishop Yoitsu Honda served as chair from 1903 to 1909 and was succeeded by K. Ibuka from 1909

5. Rouse, *WSCF,* 72.

6. Hopkins, *Mott,* 201.

to 1930. While the YMCA was developing into a national association in Japan, Michi Kawai (1878–1953), future leader in the Japanese YWCA movement and the WSCF, was pursuing studies in the United States. Her elementary education had been completed in a school run by a Presbyterian missionary from New England named Sarah Clara Smith. When Smith opened a new school in Sapporo, she took Michi along as an apprentice teacher.

Michi was awarded a scholarship to enter a preparatory school prior to admission to Bryn Mawr.[7] College life allowed for participation in many rituals and customs which had been carefully inculcated by her American missionary teachers. Concerning her college experience she observed that, "The things I learned in the class-room may slip from memory; but the things the girls said and did under this circumstance or that can never be erased from my mind. Even now my decisions are affected by such things; and I pity our Japanese people who go abroad to study and get nothing outside of intellectual education."[8]

Her attendance at a YWCA summer camp at Silver Bay in Lake George in 1902 would prove formative for Michi's later YWCA work. The experience at Silver Bay sharpened her sense of vocation: "Thus my narrow ideas were being broadened; I began to realize that I belonged not only to Japan, but also to the world, God's world. With this new light I came to appreciate the missionaries in my own country."[9]

In the summer of 1903, Michi travelled to Europe chaperoned by a Bryn Mawr professor who was going there to work on her doctorate. Although she would make this trip many times in subsequent decades, she observed that her first trip made the greatest impression. She wrote: "it was my first trip that stretched my mind so that I could begin to think internationally, and set me to pondering on how my own country could have a part in the mutual development of the human race."[10] With a vision of international friendship that was rooted in the Christian voluntary organizations of the West, Michi returned to Japan in 1904 after

7. Ume Tsuda at the age of seven, traveled with seven women to America for education in 1871. After graduation from Bryn Mawr, she became head teacher in the Peeress' School and Professor in the Tokyo Normal School for Women. She eventually started her own school with the help of American women such as Anna Hartshorne and Alice Bacon.

8. Michi Kawai, *My Lantern*, 83. Hereafter referred to as *ML*.

9. Kawai, *ML*, 91.

10. Kawai, *ML*, 98.

an absence of six years, not imagining that her optimistic vision would be severely tested by a world at war.

CAROLINE MACDONALD AS YWCA AMBASSADOR

Work with women in Japan was focused on the needs of young women who moved to the cities to find jobs. A request to the World's YWCA brought a North American worker named Teresa Morrison to Japan followed by Caroline Macdonald of Canada. Caroline Macdonald (1874–1931) had attended secondary school in Ontario before graduating from the University of Toronto. While a student in Toronto, she was a member of the YWCA. After graduation in 1901, she worked for the London, Ontario YWCA with women factory workers. She met Sara Libby Carson, a Wellesley College graduate, who helped develop the Evangelia Settlement House in Toronto.[11] Carson recommended Macdonald for national Y work that later led her to work in Japan. Macdonald became interested in penal reform in Japan and established a settlement house in Tokyo to support the families of prison inmates.

The first decade of the twentieth century was "epoch-making" in the field of women's education in Japan.[12] Several schools had been established, such as Ume Tsuda's school, Nihon Women's University, and a growing number of high schools for girls. Tsuda's school had been supported by a Miss Anna Hartshorne who raised half a million dollars for Tsuda College's new buildings. Michi began her teaching career at the Tsuda school, but she quietly nurtured her own ambitions about establishing a girls' school. She taught a combination of history, translation, and English.

After she had been at the school for six months, the Canadian YWCA representative Caroline Macdonald arrived. Macdonald had been sent out under the auspices of the World YWCA to organize a national Y in Japan. With an eye for talent and a dedication to building up national leaders, Macdonald persuaded Michi to help as a volunteer—a valuable training opportunity for the latter which would eventually lead to her role as leader of the National Japanese YWCA. When Caroline rented a house, Michi invited girls from Miss Tsuda's school for Bible

---

11. Prang, *Caroline Macdonald*. This marvelous book details Macdonald's work in the prisons, as well as her personal views on the Y and the WSCF. On Carson, see James, "Practical Diversions," 48–66.

12. *ML*, 115.

classes, while Caroline taught literature and advanced English Bible. According to Macdonald, Michi and Miss Tsuda did not work together as well as they might and she saw that as a "case of two really big women who do not understand each other."[13]

The influx of women from the provinces to study in Tokyo fuelled an increased demand for housing. The National YWCA and the local Tokyo YWCA responded by jointly raising money for their first student dormitory. With this success in hand, they then organized a summer conference, based on the Silver Bay model, at the Aoyama Jogakuin (Methodist Girls' School) in the summer of 1906. It was a fitting celebration for the friendship between Macdonald and Michi that had commenced with their meeting at Silver Bay. One hundred and sixty-five students attended and heard speakers such as the first Japanese bishop of the Episcopal Church in Japan. The program encouraged the women to interact and to study and included an overview of social issues in Japanese society. With no prior experience in this type of organizing, Michi quickly learned all the basics—from printing programs to fundraising.

In addition to her Y work, Michi was also involved in the WSCF, particularly when the WSCF Conference took place in Tokyo in 1907. She translated and met many foreign leaders at this conference, who in turn invited her to England and Germany to observe the student movement there.

With two secretaries, the YWCA work began in earnest. A magazine was published under the title *Meiji Girls*. A National Board of the YWCA was established by 1905 with Umeko Tsuda appointed president. Priorities included the establishment of an international week of prayer in concert with the rest of the World's YWCA membership and the opening of the first dormitory for women.

TOKYO WSCF CONFERENCE 1907

Five years after his first visit, Mott travelled to Japan to attend the first International Conference in Asia. The Y was enjoying popularity particularly due to its service to Japanese soldiers during the recent war. In 1907 there were fifty-eight student groups with 2,000 members and nine city Associations with as many members. The Tokyo Conference of the WSCF was the first international gathering of any kind in Japan or in

13. Caroline Macdonald to Rouse, 30 Sept, 1910, box 228–1791.

Asia; the conference became a national event that gained the attention of the world.

Mott described how the Federation united university students in forty nations. Over 627 delegates, (including representatives from Burma, Ceylon, Korea, Philippines, and Thailand) heard talks given by a variety of academics. Several high-ranking officials such as the Minister of Foreign Affairs, Viscount Hayashi, gave receptions for the WSCF delegates—the first time those of high rank had received Christian representatives in such a regal way. The Tokyo conference generated a great deal of interest in voluntary organizations and Bible classes. Unlike the Peking WSCF Conference in 1922, which focused almost exclusively on political issues, the Japan conference centered on the religious life.

After the conference, deputation teams went out to various student centers including Yokohama, Hirosaki, Okayama, Kyoto, Shidzuoka, Osaka, Moji and Kumamoto, Kanagawa, and Fukishima to hold evangelistic meetings. Bishop Yoitsu Honda, the first bishop of a United Methodist Church of Japan, wrote in the first issue of the WSCF magazine, the *Student World*, and covered the events of the conference. Mott was convinced that the possibility for Federation work in the East was limitless and he proposed that priority be given to building up national movements with indigenous leadership. In the next months, after a conference at the White House, Mott raised two million dollars for buildings around the world that would provide a place for movement work.[14]

Michi Kawai helped plan and facilitate the WSCF conference in 1907, not only bringing attention to the needs of the YWCA but also breaking new ground in her role as a woman leader in this international effort. This public event increased interest in the Y; lectures and Bible studies were held in mission schools around the country and as a result a number of school YWCA's were founded. Students who attended the conference were also interested in organizing branches of the YWCA in their schools. Many young women attended Bible classes and several requested baptism.[15] The evangelistic campaigns that followed the conference encouraged student leaders to make a commitment to study the Bible. Macdonald, for example, taught Bible classes in some schools under the guise of English literature, including the Bible as one text in this literary study.

14. Hopkins, *Mott*, 317–21.
15. Macdonald to Rouse, 1907, box 228–1785.

The students came from a range of schools—sewing schools and high schools, as well as the other academic schools. Upper-class women such as a Madame Niwanda, who had a large and prosperous school for upper-class Japanese women, and who was a devout Buddhist, became interested in the work of the YWCA.

The interest of many women in the YWCA had also been encouraged by the acceptance of YMCA work in the Japanese army and navy. In addition, the Red Cross Hospital in Tokyo hosted a meeting of 150 nurses and doctors who were addressed by Sir Alexander Simpson of Edinburgh and Annie West, a Presbyterian board missionary in Tokyo and member of the National Committee.[16] The conference thus stimulated interest in and sponsorship of student voluntary work among Tokyo society.

Japanese women ran local YWCAs. Hanako Ibuka was elected National President and Michi Kawai became the General Secretary. Most women in Japan had no previous leadership experience in such an organization so foreign helpers and Japanese women who had studied abroad were in demand to provide necessary skills.

The YWCA was not the only Christian organization seeking to reach Japanese women. The WCTU was organized in 1874 by American Protestant church women and expanded rapidly and formed an international body, the World WCTU in 1883. As missionary for the World WCTU, Mary Leavitt, a divorced school teacher arrived in Tokyo in 1898 to campaign against alcohol, tobacco, and other drugs as a missionary for the World's WCTU. Leavitt was one of at least twelve women with World WCTU titles who travelled or worked in Japan between 1886 and 1913.[17] Through contacts made by Presbyterian missionaries working in girls' schools, Leavitt was introduced to Japanese women's reform groups. The notion of reforming society through collective action required women to associate in public spaces and to hold meetings, an important step in allowing new discourses to take place and enabling Japanese women to construct new subjectivities that incorporated such public action. Not all had access to such freedom; reform platforms were upheld by upper-

16. Report on Japan, n.d., no author, box 228–1791.

17. For more information on the WCTU in Japan, see Yasutake, "Men, Women, and Temperance in Meiji Japan," 91–111. Leavitt's tour led to the formation of the Tokyo WCTU in 1886 and this group worked for the elimination of geishas, concubines, and prostitutes. Temperance was never adopted with the same fervor as it had been in the United States. Temperance societies were also founded among men.

middle-class women and expressed in terms of their own nationalism. The rhetoric of new freedom and rights was couched in the rhetoric of the importance of women's role in upholding the state and the family. Women's education was the platform that allowed women to argue for increased rights in home and society, and in the process invalidated the separation between moral (private) and political (public) spheres.[18]

Canadian YWCA worker Caroline Macdonald noted that there was competition among voluntary organizations and constituencies who were attempting to gain the allegiance of Japanese women. Competition had intensified between the Y and the WCTU, as she wrote:

> The W.C.T.U. has been very energetic recently in worrying us, but we discovered that the Japanese W.C.T.U. knew nothing of it, & that it apparently emanates from a few foreigners who are rabid W.C.T.U.ers. However it will all settle down—we appointed a committee to explain our position. Extremely kind of us, wasn't it? The whole problem resolves itself into this that the W.C.T.U. knows it oughtn't to be in the schools & that in the end, we shall get in whether we try to or not. We can afford to wait, I believe, until we can go in without let or hindrance, which won't be so very long & we only ask to stay in. It is the remarkable attitude they take. They insist they go in any place we are asked to. But you need not be bothered about details of our work like this. We had such a glorious National Committee meeting on the 13th of February.[19]

Caroline Macdonald supported social movements rooted in the gospel that provided the "right" type of motivation, a type that she distinguished from the agitation promoted by the suffrage movement in the West. Modern movements were not the way she envisioned change:

> I think we cannot be too careful about contributing the *essential* Christian factor in all these movements of the day—namely "the power of God unto salvation to everyone who believeth." Because in the long run this is the only basis for reform. I do most surely think that we have not given half enough attention to the study of social problems. I know I am ashamed of my ignorance & shall try not to perpetuate it, but most distinctly,

18. Patessio, "Creation," 170–71.

19. Macdonald to Rouse, 8 Feb, 1909, box 228–1786, RG 46, WSCF Papers, YDS. All subsequent references are to this collection and record group unless otherwise indicated.

I do not believe that "women's suffrage" for example—is a very deep solution for women's wrongs. I do not think many outsiders view that movement in England with anything more than considerable contempt so for at least the militant method people are concerned. People who break the law in this effort to make it, do not strike the people in the outskirts of the Empire as a very sure foundation for Empire building. What are they to learn of true womanliness from such a movement? I believe most emphatically in the freedom of women but one's heart aches sometimes to see in the Eastern papers stories of the English women who are fighting for their rights. Of course, I do realize that it is difficult to understand the enormity of the social problems here—as English people think of it, but I confess I do not see the ultimate solution in these decidedly modern movements.[20]

Another Canadian—Emma Kaufman from Kitchener, Ontario—further supported the YWCA work. Kaufman, a graduate of the Ontario Ladies' College in Whitby, continued her studies at Victoria University and the United Church Training School, and then at Columbia Teachers' College. After a trip to Japan in 1909 and a short-term teaching assignment to Tsuda College, she returned in Japan in 1913 and was appointed to the Tokyo YWCA staff as a volunteer secretary.[21]

The gospel of true womanliness was to be rooted in education and the gospel. In a report to the World Missionary Conference in 1910, Macdonald attempted to clarify the aims of the work in relation to girls' higher education. She believed that educational missionary work provided a training ground for future professional and lay leaders and that this work would build the foundation for Christian community. The Christianization of a non-Christian society required more than just the conversion of a person from one set of beliefs to another, no matter how "superior" the beliefs might be. A new background, outlook, and deeper conception of the reality of the present life had to be substituted. No better method could be adopted to promote Christianity than through education founded on Christian principles together with the direct influence which Christian teachers brought to bear on a Christian life. Macdonald believed that evangelization without educational foundations would produce superficial Christian character. Missionary organi-

20. Macdonald to Rouse, 30 Sept, 1910, box 228–1786.

21. Kaufman Personal Papers, Microfilm, 1881–1979, Victoria University Archives, Toronto.

zations that stressed education were the strongest groups in Japan. She concluded that, "in a non-Christian country, the idea that religion is a sphere by itself apart from the material facts of life and morality must not be propagated or tolerated."[22]

Voluntary organizations imported from the West contained implicit organizational values rooted in Western ways that included gender, race, and class assumptions in addition to the religious message that was being transmitted. In her study of the YWCA in the United States, historian Judith Weisenfeld notes that the white majority controlled the involvement of African American women in that context.[23] Japanese women who wanted to participate in the YWCA in Japan were exposed to a model of leadership and participation that provided training in Western assumptions, but they continued to inhabit a culture that limited public opportunities for women. Opportunities to engage in philanthropic and educational activities were directed to privileged women, whereas efforts at benevolence were concentrated on working-class women in factories. For many non-Western countries, the WSCF and the YWCA offered the only public leadership training for women at that time, and the close association of these groups with evangelical Christianity presented women's education, moral development, and social reform in one discrete package. Macdonald and Kawai hoped that pioneering work in the YWCA would develop indigenous leadership to assume leadership of national movements.[24]

The development of women's education travelled an uneven course. In 1911, Caroline Macdonald observed that the situation in the girl's schools was somewhat grim. "The Woman's University is a little down on its luck at its present. They have closed up their Japanese Literature Department altogether, and very few are in the English Department. It has practically become a school of Domestic Science. There have been many ups and downs in girls' education during my absence. The Minister of Education was awful conservative and suggested that Shinto shrines be put in schools and that girls only need to be educated along

22. Macdonald, "Report to the World Missionary Conference, 1910, Commission III Education in Relation to the Christianization of National Life," box 228–1786.

23. Weisenfeld, *African American Women*.

24. See Kwok Pui-lan, *Postcolonial Imagination* for a discussion of why the notion of conversion to Christianity appealed to women in China.

domestic lines, etc." [25] Macdonald's vision for women's education did not support the more radical groups in the women's movement, either in England or in Japan. She explained that there were two societies in Japan called the Blue Stocking and the Real Woman, the "latter being a protest against the eccentricities of the first, but having in turn quite as many eccentricities of its own." Both organizations, she felt, protested against the status of women in Japan and their watchword was "self-realization" for women as well as for men. She offered to put Rouse in touch with some of the leaders but cautioned her against meeting them in a public way, presumably lest the cause of the WSCF become linked with theirs. Graduates of the Women's University had been exposed to ideas that left them vulnerable to such organizations. However, no institution could be held completely accountable for such movements because women's protest was in the air.[26]

What was the status of women's education in Japan at the beginning of the twentieth century? Education for women took place in elementary schools, ninety-five higher girls' schools, and one High Normal School with about 2,000 students in Tokyo. Schools emphasized domestic arts and sciences and physical culture, the latter involving the girls tying back their kimono sleeves and participating in the Swedish system of exercises. According to a report by American Y secretary Bertha Condé, by 1909 there were approximately 10,000 women studying in Tokyo who had arrived from all parts of the country. The Peeress' school had been established by the nobility to educate their daughters. Ume Tsuda had returned from her education to open a school that attempted to maintain high standards in English and literature. The Women's University enrolled 1800 students and offered all levels from kindergarten to college, a level that in reality matched high school more than college. There

25. Macdonald to Rouse, 3 Nov, 1911, box 288–1787.

26. Macdonald to Rouse, 1 Sept, 1913, box 228–1786. She wrote further that, "Early in January is the annual meeting of the Federated Missions. I think there will be no difficulty in your being given ample time there to say what you please about the significance of the women's movement and its relation to the whole advancement of civilization. The men's missionaries in Japan as a rule are inclined to calmly ignore the women's side of it all and there are practically no women on the committee appointed by the Federated Missions. There are one or two exceptions to this. If you could go to Sendai when the University is in progress it would be worthwhile to go, to meet the three women who have been admitted as regular students to the Imperial University whose Science Department is situated in Sendai. This is the beginning of real University education for women."

were fifty-two Protestant girl's schools in Japan with an enrollment of more than 3,000 students including Joshi Gakushin (one of the most elite girls' schools of the period), Aoyama Gakuin, and Kobe College that provided close to a college level education for women.[27]

Increased numbers of women students created new problems and the demand for housing in the cities. Graduates found it difficult to find jobs or to return home educated when their mothers were not. Some students lived in boarding houses. Dormitories for women students became a major campaign among supporters of women's education. Funds to support women's education were raised within Japan and in England, Scotland, Canada, and other colleges, such as Vassar.

The YWCA continued to grow. There were ten student associations in Japan including those at Miss Tsuda's school; Joshi Gakuin in Toyko (Presbyterian); Miss Barernfeind's Bible School, Tokyo (German Evangelical); St. Margaret's School, Tokyo (American Episcopal); Ferris Seminary, Yokohama (Dutch Reformed); Miyagi Girls' School, Sendai (German Reformed); Bishop Poole's School, Osaka (Central Missionary Society); Wilmina School, Osaka (Presbyterian); Doshisha School, Kyoto (Congregational); and Hiroshima School, Hiroshima (Southern Methodist). In addition to these, there were ten city associations in Tokyo, Yokohama, Tokushima, Kagoshima, and Hakodata. The hostels for women offered the possibility of modeling and mentoring through Christian women's leadership and provided opportunities for Bible teaching outside of the school context. St. Hilda's Mission, run by a Miss Phillips, was one such hostel for women offering Bible study. The Society for the Propagation of the Gospel ran a hostel under the leadership of a Miss Weston, who also led a Bible study class.

Fundraising efforts led to the building of an eight-room centre for the Tokyo YWCA. The National Committee and the Tokyo city board were made up of equal numbers of Japanese women and foreigners who were clear about their intention to eventually be replaced by Japanese women.

Bible classes continued to be a focus of the work. Ten classes were organized with representatives from the major girls' schools. Michi Kawai taught in Miss Tsuda's school, Girls' Higher Normal, and in the Friend's School. Caroline Macdonald sent personal notes to students

---

27. Report on Japan, no author (possibly Bertha Conde), date approximately 1907–8, typescript 7 pp., box 228–1791.

who had signed cards at an evangelistic meeting that followed the WSCF conference. She invited them to her house on a Sunday afternoon. The young women arrived long before the appointed time from various parts of the city. The atmosphere was chilly at first and the students seemed perplexed. Macdonald guided the conversation using an interpreter and gradually led to a practical talk that concluded with a "deeply spiritual message." After this talk, three students expressed a desire to become Christians and all promised to return.[28] Another American Y secretary, a Miss Matthews, taught Bible classes at Miss Tsuda's school. She tried to help the girls in the various difficulties in which they found themselves, including financial, housing, jobs, and relationships.[29]

Patessio notes that the early Meiji women's movement was limited by class; aristocratic women were too limited in movement to be able to participate and lower class women were expected to work to help their families survive; thus, only a very few seemed to be interested in the fate of women of the poorer classes. The women who were concerned about social conditions turned their attention to helping factory girls.[30] Women were working in the government arsenals, cotton spinning factories, wool factories. Many women workers were isolated in dormitories where they were virtually prisoners with only two holidays per month. The authorities gradually allowed Christians to give talks to these employees. In one factory outside Tokyo, the YWCA organized an event with a speaker who was a gifted storyteller and who held the attention of the audience by telling Old Testament stories. They also learned to sing a simple hymn, something that was a new experience for the 1300 women assembled. The organizers hoped that they could build a central building to hold night classes that would be educational, recreational, and religious.[31]

Although Kawai worked as a teacher, her travels through Europe, Canada, and the United States helped sharpen her determination to participate in the development of YWCA work in Japan. As the Y work became more of a priority, she reduced her teaching commitment to part-time. She insisted that her salary be raised within Japan: "for this would give the responsibility to the Japanese members, which

28. Harriet Taylor, "Report of Work in Japan," 1907, box 228–1791.

29. Miss Matthews, Report to the National Board of the U.S., 1917," box 228–1791.

30. Patessio, "Creation of Public Spaces by Women," 166.

31. Memorandum from Japan, May, 1918, box 228–1791.

is the only way to make the work become an indigenous, growing movement."[32] On her first day as National Secretary of the Japanese YWCA, she expressed a need to be an example to Japanese women. She realized that the work had to be led by a Japanese woman or it would be interpreted as "foreign work." She also shared Caroline Macdonald's concern that the movement foster national leaders but recognized that the foreign secretaries had been crucial in preparing her and others to take up this leadership.[33] Her friends advised her not to give up the security of teaching for a career with the Y, but she persisted. She justified her plans in a letter to Rouse: "Most of my friends are most kind in encouraging me in my new task but others are waiting to laugh at me. What ever it will be I am most sure that this work will never be a failure though I am."[34] Macdonald tried to convince her to become a full-time Y worker, but Michi declined. Macdonald threatened to some day pray her into it—an event that according to Michi finally happened in 1916. In 1911 the National Committee chose Michi as their representative on the Women's Subcommittee of the WSCF and she became chair of this committee in 1912. In addition she was a member of the World's Committee of the YWCA.

Michi was also pressed into service for the World Student Christian Federation (WSCF). Although she felt burdened by these multiple demands, there was much pressure on her to continue to represent the WSCF. Ruth Rouse, women's secretary of the WSCF, urged her to continue her work with that organization:

> The reasons which make you of such tremendous value to us as chairman and which makes us long to have you in America next year, are, I must admit, to a large extent sentimental reasons, but sentimental reasons in the very best sense of the word sentimental . . . We are standing for the unity of the Christian church throughout the world amongst all races and divisions of mankind. It is a striking lesson in unity when our offices are drawn very freely from different nations: and even if you and Mr. Wang did nothing—which is very far from being the case—the very fact of having your name on the letter head forces upon countless students one of the deepest and most important lessons that the Federation has to teach. I have seen the effect of this lesson again

32. Kawai, *ML*, 134–35.
33. Kawai to Rouse, 16 Sept, 1912, box 228–1785.
34. Ibid.

and again upon students of different nationalities. They do not think it is possible for men and women of all nations to work together for Jesus Christ. Our letter head shows them that this is so, and it is a witness moreover to them of the power of Jesus Christ in the Orient where they are always being told that Christianity has no message and no influence.[35]

Although in many cases Western women glamorized the exotic in Asian culture to promote an orientalism that marked women as "other," presumably Rouse's pressure on Michi to represent the WSCF was based on recognition of her skills in international work.

Michi felt that her nominal presence as chair was not essential and that Miss Tsuda was a better choice. In addition, as representative of the YWCA, Kawai believed that she should not hold two organizational leadership positions representing women's work. Ruth Rouse did not accept these reasons and argued that she had a unique point of view as an Asian woman with the additional perspective of knowing the Canadian, American, and European student work like no one else did. Rouse observed: "We feel that you will help interpret both Europe and East to America, and from your American experience help to interpret America in both Europe and the East."[36] Michi's ability to translate culture in both Eastern and Western contexts made her a desirable quantity for organizations who claimed that their field was global. Rouse reminded Kawai of the power of her presence during the war: "You made a deep mark on the women students of Europe who are members of our movements by your visit during the war, which was so much appreciated on both sides, and I believe in a particular way that you oriental women coming to us in Europe can do much to draw all sides together again and to help them look on their differences from a wider and deeper point of view. I think the best spirit of the East is need in the West right now."[37]

Mott's next visit to Japan took place in 1912 (the Emperor Meiji had died in July 1912). Since his first visit in 1898, Christianity had been recognized as a spiritual and moral force in society. He held a student meeting in Tokyo attended by 400 professors and students from seventy Y associations. During this visit Mott toured schools and visited Kobe Women's College. But the attempt to fulfill the evangelical purpose of his

35. Rouse to Kawai, 18 Oct, 1912, box 228–1784.
36. Kawai to Rouse, 1 May, 1913, box 228–1784.
37. Rouse to Kawai, 1 Jan, 1920, box 229–1784.

visit caused Mott insomnia; he struggled with the challenge of bringing in enough student secretaries to help convert the nation. Furthermore, by 1913, the student movement had a distinct social gospel emphasis rather than an evangelical one. He held lectures at Tokyo Imperial University. He was in Japan during the anti-Japanese agitation that produced the California Anti-Alien Land Act of 1913.

By 1913, Gwendolyne Watney, a British student movement worker, described the organization of nineteen Bible classes in Tokyo, two hospital nurses' associations, a monthly factory meeting, and a fundraising campaign for a foyer and small hotel. That the work was not without its difficulties is evident in her question, "Does Japan need more patience than England or is it that I have never realized the need for it so much before?"[38] Watney felt that the students were intensely hungry to know God. She taught three Bible classes in Japanese and one in English. In her estimation there was still inadequate knowledge about the facts of the Christian faith, but students were generally eager to discuss religious questions.

Although a large proportion of students had family connections to the Buddhist faith, their knowledge of Buddhism tended to be superficial and they had rarely made a systematic study of Buddhist teachings. Students were in poor physical condition as a result of too little exercise, recreation, or fresh air. Watney recommended that lectures should be given on fresh air and tuberculosis, as well as general health care, shorter study hours, and physical and mental recreation. Socializing with men provided a challenge to those who supervised the young women. Moral temptations were great and the "thoughtless or ignorant student only too often falls an easy victim to temptation." Such vulnerability, according to Watney, resulted from the lack of emphasis on Christian moral teaching or the moral aspect of the Christian life on the part of those who were in charge of student dormitories or who worked groups of students.

Christian student hostels, she believed, were not only important places where the Christian Student movement could lead students into the Christian life, but also provided a training ground where mature Christian students might learn to bear responsibility and develop their powers of leadership. Hostels provided close contact and fellowship with a deeper insight into daily Christian life; in order to model this Christian

---

38. G. Watney to Ruth Rouse, extracted for the members of the Women's Subcommittee of the WSCF, 13 March, 1913, box 228–1791.

life, the hostel would need to be overtly Christian with a strong *esprit de corps* between leaders and students and among students themselves. Student hostels could build Christian character, as she wrote: "Though the visible results seen in the lives of students in Christian Hostels are thought by some to be very inadequate and discouraging, yet one cannot but believe that the practical demonstration of the Living power of the Living Christ is the best apologetic for Christianity, and must have a deep and lasting influence."[39]

Japanese students came to Bible classes and attended religious instruction classes and churches to receive ethical teaching with a "desire to perfect themselves in the knowledge of Western thought or language, as far as any one can penetrate the motive of their asking for teaching now this seems to be prompted by nothing less than a great desire and thirst after God." Watney continued, "There is also a keen sense of lack of power in the personal life and a great longing for that Power which is seen working in the life of Christians."[40]

The denominational schools initially were less interested in student association work. These schools included Bible in the curriculum and had denominational clubs and voluntary groups such as the Kings Daughters Circles and Young Women's Christian Temperance Unions. However, missionaries increasingly requested the organization of voluntary work among students and sought affiliation with the worldwide student movement.[41]

Although Japan did not experience the chaos that European student movements endured during World War I, the YWCA was involved in extending refugee help to Armenian children and war relief for troops in Siberia. The Japanese economy was booming by the end of the war. The Emperor had died in 1912 and the subsequent Tashio Era witnessed the growth of citizens' movements including the suffrage movement. Women's University (Joshi Daigaku) was founded in 1918.

The notion of a public role for women was very limited, teaching being the prime example. Those single women who were of a class to participate in public life found that teaching and volunteering offered a world rich in fellowship. Kawai, national secretary of the Japanese YWCA, noted in 1919 that there was a narrow set of expectations

---

39. Watney, "Women Students of Japan, 1913," box 228–1791.
40. Ibid.
41. Taylor, "Report of Work in Japan, 1907," box 228–1791.

regarding women's work focused on the profession of teaching. A leadership role, such as secretary work for a voluntary organization, was largely unknown.[42] Women, she believed, needed training in order to take up leadership roles for the Japanese Y so that Y work could be seen as Japanese, rather than foreign work. Mission schools had suffered from a similar misconception. Kawai wrote: "We do not wish to fall into the same mistake; into which some of the mission schools fell some years ago. Though their efforts were sincere and good, their means were often criticized as unwise and so even today some of them cannot have the sympathy of the natives, as they think that the schools are foreign institutions."

One way to limit the association with Western control was to raise the support of Kawai's position from among Japanese women. The idea of a Japanese national secretary had increased interest in the work of the Y in small schools over the country and they were sending contributions to the national work.[43] Japanese graduates of Western universities took up leadership roles in Y camp work; one of the early camp conference committees was composed of women who had studied at Wellesley, Bryn Mawr, Smith, Cambridge, and Oxford.[44]

CONCLUSION

In a letter to Ruth Rouse, Michi Kawai observed that "where the Spirit of Christ is absent, you cannot have true internationalism."[45] Kawai's sense of internationalism had been shaped by her own Western and Christian-sponsored education and her experience in international voluntary organizations. Like many of the first generation of women who graduated from higher education, Kawai believed that her education was a privilege that she hoped to extend to women in Japan. She hoped that Japanese women could have a taste of the same friendship and fellowship that had been so much a part of her life and travels.

Friendship was not only a way to counter the isolation of individuals and of nations, but also offered a way to bridge the misunderstandings

42. Kawai to Rouse, 16 Sept, 1919, box 228–179.

43. Caroline Macdonald, "Report to World Missionary Conference, 1910, Commission III, Education in Relation to the Christianisation of National Life," box 228–178.

44. Mary G. Baker to Ruth Rouse, 22 Aug, 1913, box 228–179.

45. Kawai to Rouse, 25 July, 1921, box 228–1784.

that gave rise to conflict and war. Knowledge alone would not suffice to create the type of bonds Kawai imagined. She believed that a spirit of friendship could be rooted in Christian belief that would cement the bonds between individuals. Kawai's vision of friendship implicitly suggested that women think about their place in society.

Historian Renata Howe observes that the patronizing attitude of Michi Kawai toward Chinese delegates in her conference speech at a WSCF conference in Peking in 1920 noted that their facility in using the English language was a revelation to the Japanese. Her attitude added to the resentment of her brusque autocratic style."[46] Her attitude also reflected the deep-seated prejudices between Asian nations which would continue to be reflected on the world stage in wars and conflicts for domination between nations. Friendship and an active role in local, national and international politics would continue to suffer from blind spots as privileges were slow to extend to all women and those with power maintained blind spots about the causes of social problems well into the mid-twentieth century.[47]

Voluntary organizations, such as the YWCA and the WSCF, provided Japanese women with public space in which they could learn new skills and develop bonds with other women that built on and extended the space of participation beyond graduation. The increased desire to educate middle- and upper-class women in conjunction with expectations of their roles as wives and mothers provided a rationale for participation in education and leadership training. In addition, increased numbers of working women became the focus of philanthropy supported by upper- and middle-class women. In this sense, these voluntary movements had liberatory and emancipatory implications for members, whether these were explicitly or implicitly addressed and pursued. Such liberatory dimensions were conservative in intent, since the role of women in the family and by extension her mothering role in society relied on expectations based in Western and Protestant notions that were exported by women leaders such as Macdonald and Kawai. Women in Meiji era social reform were largely from privileged classes and sought to retain those privileges in an expanded role for themselves in society. Although women who worked in education and social reform were not interested in social reform of the root conditions that forced lower class women

---

46. Howe, "Australian SCM," 319.

47. Patessio, "Creation of Public Spaces by Women," 177.

to work in factories or prostitution, the fact that they sought to inform themselves and reach out to other social groups was in reality a radical step in the 1880s.

Western fascination with the East contributed to the establishment of a variety of mission and voluntary organizations that to some extent competed with each other. The YWCA developed programs in the schools in order to create a base of membership. Other organizations, such as the Women's Christian Temperance Union, that were not school-based experienced some difficulty in finding members since there were few other public venues. Participation of women in the public sphere was established in this era and facilitated to some extent by women's education and organizing experience in the federation and Y association activities. Japanese women were not passive recipients of Western teachings and social reform, but actively participated in creating new roles and freedoms for themselves that built on the ideology of wives and mothers but increased their ability to organize, speak, and participate in society as a whole. Despite those limitations, the processes that were begun in the late nineteenth and early twentieth century would transform education and voluntary movements in Japan, and through participation in the Federation, encourage indigenous leadership and participation on the world stage.

9

Sweden

SWEDISH STUDENT CHRISTIAN MOVEMENT 1897

The Scandinavian student movement owed its existence in part to Luther Wishard's cable to Northfield from Kyoto, relaying the message from the first student conference in Japan, "Make Jesus King." When student leader Karl Fries described this event to students gathered for a mission conference in Sweden, their immediate response was to organize. According to Rouse, the Swedish students were motivated by a desire to strengthen the spiritual power of the students of the Far East and by an awakening of devotion to John Mott. The Motts first visited Scandinavia in 1891. Prior to their visit, American J. B. Reynolds had toured the area under the auspices of the YMCA and invited students including the future ecumenical leader Nathan Söderblom (1866–1931) to attend the Northfield conference. After participating in events such as the Liverpool Conference, student leaders such as Norwegian Martin Eckhoff worked to organize Bible study circles among men and women students. Visits by Robert P. Wilder and Donald Fraser created interest in organizing Christian students.

Mott addressed students during the 1895 meetings and instructed them in the principles of student work, the need to broaden their scope, and the responsibility to engage in evangelism. He urged them to form an overall structure for the Scandinavian student movement with constituent national movements represented. They did so, with the result that Martin Eckhoff of Norway and Karl Fries of Sweden represented the Scandinavian student movement at the Vadstena Conference where the WSCF was formed. Although the Scandinavian student movement at that time functioned primarily as a loose network to organize confer-

ences, there was enough momentum to be considered a founding movement to the new federation.

Before 1897, Swedish students had been largely disinterested in either organized Christianity or missions. After Mott's visit in 1897, there
was a noticeable change in the student Christian movement. The circles
were reorganized with appointed leaders and the book *The Man Christ
Jesus* by Robert Speer became the focus.[1] Interest in missions grew and
a university settlement was established. The Christian student summer conference of 1899 was a success. Robert Wilder spent five weeks
among the students and many were convinced of the power and value
of prayer.[2]

There was also a Christian movement among women students.
Women had been admitted to Swedish universities in 1870, in Denmark in
1875, and in Norway in 1882. Finland, due to control by Russian authorities, was slower to admit women but after 1890, the numbers increased to
over seven hundred women by 1901. Early leaders in the Swedish wom-
en's movement—the novelist Frederika Bremer (1801–1865) and Ellen
Key (1849–1926), an essayist and feminist—helped bring about social
changes in Swedish society. Bremer's novels contributed to the passage
of a law in 1858 that gave legal independence to women over the age of
twenty-five. Women attained greater access to higher education due to
reforms in 1842, the opening of universities to women after 1870, and
the founding of teacher's colleges. Sonja Kovalevsky (1850–1891), the
first woman professor in a Scandinavian university appointed in 1889,
provided a powerful example for women students. New career options
such as medicine and teaching opened up with these academic opportunities. The numbers grew slowly in the first decades of women's higher
education. By 1897, Sweden had less than a hundred women students
dispersed between the two colleges in Gothenburg and Stockholm and
the two universities in Lund and Uppsala.[3]

Rouse was invited to visit Scandinavia by a woman named Fredda
Hammer who had founded a missionary society for women in 1894
in Sweden. In March 1897 she arrived in Copenhagen. One of her first

---

1. Speer, *Studies.*

2. Thorwall, "Report on the Women Student Christian Association," presented
at Zeist, The Netherlands, box 115–924, 4 pp. typescript, box 115–924, WSCF, YDS.
Subsequent references will refer to this collection unless noted otherwise.

3. Franzén, *Rouse,* 81.

contacts was with a Danish student, Thrya Möller, who she had met at Keswick the year before. There were only a handful of Danish women students at the time; by 1899 there were still only twenty.

When Rouse travelled next to Norway, she met again a small group of women students (three had been present at Vadstena for the founding of the WSCF) with whom she started a Bible circle. Rouse also spoke to mixed groups of men and women on topics such as missions.[4]

Rouse travelled by train to Sweden, where she stayed at the home of Karl Fries in Stockholm. Rouse spoke to groups of schoolgirls and teachers, as well as with the small group of university students who were largely skeptical about her aims. During her days in Stockholm, Rouse met with leaders of the YMCA and YWCA. According to historian Ruth Franzén, Sweden had experienced revivals in the nineteenth century that had Anglo-Saxon roots. Those associated with the Lutheran National Church regarded such revivals as a threat to their denomination and resisted anything associated with evangelical revivals. Women students in Uppsala, with a reputation for radical behaviour and rejection of conservative roles for women, regarded the religiosity of the YWCA with a great deal of hostility. Rouse was introduced to a number of key student leaders including Lydia Wahlstrom (1869–1954) who was a PhD student in 1897 and a leader of the Uppsala Women's Club. Although she initially resisted Rouse and the evangelical traditions she believed Rouse represented, she proved to be helpful in making links for Rouse to women students. Rouse held two meetings during her week in Uppsala and a small group of the women she had gathered continued to meet until Dr Mott returned in 1899.[5]

Upon their return to campus in the fall of 1899, women students worked with increased fervor in student Christian work. Despite this dedication, students continued to resist the idea of formal organization. When the president of the women's student association proposed the organization of a Woman's Student Christian Association on the basis of the belief statement required by the WSCF, she was voted down. The group then began a systematic study of missions. A new interest in social work led students to visit the poor and engage in Sunday School work and evening entertainments with magic lantern shows and lectures for street children. The students attempted to reach those with no religious

4. Ibid., 77–80.
5. Ibid., 88–89.

background through social gatherings that included Bible or missions study. Although there were separate student organizations for women and men, there were many joint activities. Women students were asked to lead daily prayer meetings along with the men. Monthly Christian Association meetings were coeducational with presentations of a student paper followed by discussion. Special communion services were held for both men and women students in different chapels belonging to the Swedish church.[6]

Mott's visit in 1899 to Scandinavia generated discussion among the students as to whether or not they professed to be Christian. Interest in his work varied with the greatest in Lund and the least in Copenhagen. Mott was invited to dine in the Danish royal palace and was entertained by royalty such as the Danish Count Joachim von Moltke (1860–1937). After a visit to Oslo, students waved him off at the train station singing the hymn, "All Hail the Power of Jesus' Name." In Stockholm, Mott was entertained by Prince Oscar Bernadotte. Although his visit did not create the tremendous interest of his campaign in the United Kingdom, some progress was made.

An advertisement in a Swedish newspaper in 1904 announced the impending return visit of Ruth Rouse. Because they resisted any influence by an English movement, students in Uppsala were upset when they heard of Rouse's proposed visit on behalf of the World Student Christian Federation. Lydia Wahlstrom cautioned Rouse that such advertising would not be effective. The women students of Stockholm were much more radical than in Uppsala and when they saw such an advertisement they suspected that it would involve conversions—a suspicion that would inhibit their willingness to attend.[7]

Student reaction reflected the history of Christianity in Sweden. The Reformation had resulted in the establishment of a state church. By the end of the nineteenth century about 85 percent of Swedes were officially Lutheran, with Catholicism as the second largest denomination. Thus, Swedish students, with their Lutheran heritage, did not have the Reformed zeal for missions and charity. In a letter to Rouse, Wahlstrom described those with religious inclinations as possessing a

6. Thorwall, "The Women Student Christian Association at Uppsala," typescript, 4 pp., box 115–921, n.d.

7. Lydia Wahlstrom to Ruth Rouse, 25 March, 1897, WSCF papers, RG 46, box 115, 921. All subsequent references will be to this collection.

certain haughtiness, a "contemplative mysticism that makes them spurn this zeal and regard it as a sort of religious puffings, a professing of the inner experience, an introducing of American business-like proceeding into Christian matters."[8]

Swedish students, according to Wahlstrom, also had a skeptical attitude toward the Bible that was rooted in German critical methodology. They felt that the Calvinist reverence for the letter of the Bible, especially the Old Testament, and for the keeping of the Sabbath, was extreme. Those most interested in the Christian student movement would likely be the students influenced by the German theologian Albrecht Ritschl (1822–1889). She predicted that students influenced by Ritschl would be troubled by the notion of Christ's divinity.[9] Some students were more open to the notion of a student movement because they had attended two Student Volunteer Mission Union events, in London in 1900 and in Edinburgh in 1904.

Hermaine Baart de la Faille, a Dutch student secretary who later served as a leader in Germany (1907–1922), accompanied Ruth Rouse on her visit to Sweden in 1905. Once they arrived in Sweden they separated in order to cover more ground; Rouse travelled to Lund and de La Faille went to Uppsala to visit the student movement there. In 1889 there had been only fifteen women students in Uppsala and they were fairly isolated socially.[10] In Uppsala she found twenty-five girls who attended Bible circles, of whom seventeen were actual members of the Christian Union. They had, in her estimation, a strong sense of their general sinfulness and confessed feeling that they were not good enough to call themselves Christians. Uppsala students, in her opinion, spent more time theorizing than actually doing. They were no longer as afraid of English or American student movement methods, but they spent a great deal of time discussing what they "ought" to think. She gave a series of lectures to the students and was pleased that the male students were also interested in hearing about the Dutch student movement. Reports of Dutch student social work in revival meetings and on the streets of Rotterdam fascinated them.[11]

8. Walhstrom to Rouse, 25 March, 1897, box 115–921.

9. Ibid.

10. Franzén, *Rouse,* 81.

11. Hermaine Baart de la Faille, "Report on a visit to Sweden," 22–30 Nov, 1905, typescript 8 pp., box 115–924.

The reorganization of the Swedish student work helped overcome some of the obstacles to growth. There were four secretaries with organizing capacities in specific areas: Bible circles, correspondence between the different universities in Sweden, mission Sunday, and librarian and treasurer. They also had a meeting in Stockholm with delegates from the four universities to discuss summer conferences. One evening Hermaine was invited to speak to thirty young women.[12]

Despite the initial resistance, after Rouse's visit student leader Lydia Wahlstrom organized the first Bible circle in the fall of 1897 with approximately fifteen members. The Swedish Women Student Christian Association grew out of these small Bible bands marked by a very loose organizational structure. Interest in this type of group could not, however, be sustained without a consistent leadership or curriculum. When the members did not feel confident enough to lead Bible study, they read sermons aloud to each other.

In addition to organizing local university Christian unions, by 1906 the committee of the Student Christian Movements (SCM) of Uppsala, Lund, and Stockholm was formed and this committee became the foundation of the SCM committee for Sweden. Some of the student organizers perceived a need to overcome divisions in the Scandinavian countries and to this end a group of representatives from Sweden, Norway, Finland, and Denmark met in 1908 to discuss their common interests in student organization.

Mott visited Sweden again in 1909, a decade after he had helped establish the Uppsala SCM in 1899. Mott's visit in 1909 was greeted warmly by students who met him at train stations singing their welcome. He spoke at the universities and was again received by royalty, including King Haakon VIII in Oslo. He travelled to Stockholm to give more speeches and to call on his friend from Northfield conferences, Professor and future Archbishop Nathan Söderblom. That winter student revivals occurred in both Sweden and Denmark, with renewed interest in Bible study, morning devotions, and personal evangelism. In Copenhagen Mott addressed audiences of 2000 students and in Finland the same. In response to his talks, Bible study groups were formed. In 1916, Mott made a quick trip to Copenhagen, Helsingborg, Malmo, Stockholm, and Uppsala. Dr. Fries, one of the original founders of the WSCF at the Vadstena conference in 1896, remained a leader in the SCM until 1921.

12. Ibid.

INGEBORG WIKANDER (1882–1942)

While a student at Uppsala University in 1902, Ingeborg Wikander became interested in Christian student work. She served as travelling secretary among women students in Sweden and as secretary for the Women's Board of Missions of the Church of Sweden. She wrote to Rouse that she was looking forward to reading her reports of the American student work but she did not like the student Y journal *The Intercollegian* very much. She associated the American student work with Salvation Army methods. In her opinion, religious movements were perplexing because it was the individual who had to be won for Christ, one soul at a time. She wondered, "Why do they always count and tell the number out, one, two, fifty converted! In America, they always seem to become Christians at once, and thus be quite sure of their position. You know that is a strange thing for us."[13] Her observations on the cross-cultural variations of religious expression would continue to intrigue her as she developed into a student leader and later a missionary to China.

Wikander expressed excitement at the prospect of attending the WSCF conference in Tokyo in 1907. It was an opportunity, she felt, to obtain "an insight into missionary things, which I could never get here at home."[14] This interest in "missionary things" would eventually grow into a calling to missions. As she moved toward making a commitment to a mission field, she worried about her own fitness for the field and she tried to anticipate the problems that might await her. She resisted the notion of dogma as a defining feature of mission work: "I think I have a very few of them, most are gone and I feel no want of getting new ones instead of the old. I don't believe dogmas belong to religion, they belong to philosophy . . . Christ never taught any dogmas at all." Dogma contributed to struggle and hatred between people. She wondered how missionaries in foreign fields worked when the differing teachings of churches and congregations resulted in doubts, something she thought must be more difficult among the "heathens" than at home. Her self-doubt at this point caused her to question her usefulness in a mission context. She felt that medical studies would have been a more useful preparation for

13. Wikander to Rouse, 26 March, 1905, box 115–922.
14. Wikander to Rouse, 20 March, 1906, box 115–922.

missions because then she could be more confident of her own role in the mission field.[15]

Wikander attended a conference in the summer of 1908 that brought together both women university students and *gymnasiasts* (students preparing to teach in elementary schools). She described the conference as a transformational experience: "It was such a wonder to me and I bowed in a feeling of both humiliation and gratitude because I felt that God was with us and He did the work himself."[16] During the same summer they had also had a conference with fifty or sixty representatives from Scandinavian countries. They made plans to meet in Denmark in 1910 to continue the student work together. Also during that summer, she met student secretary Kristen Möller. There was some debate at the conference about the rights of Scandinavian women to appoint a member to the WSCF executive. Because the Scandinavians refused to subscribe to the necessary confessional statement of belief, they were not allowed to do so. In 1909 Wikander served as a coach for Ruth Rouse prior to her visit to the student associations. She suggested to Rouse that she should spend her time getting to know students individually as opposed to having large meetings.

A meeting was arranged in 1911 for the *seminarists* (candidates for teaching in high schools) of the five higher normal training colleges in Sweden. At the meeting, fifty participants joined a Christian Union that would also co-operate with teacher's college students for the lower schools (*gymnasiasts*). The increased organizational structures created an increased demand for trained women leaders.[17]

In 1912 Rouse requested that the Swedish movement plan a conference in co-operation with the YWCA. Because the student movement had continued to include groups that would normally not interact socially or attend social clubs that included normal school students, gymnasia, and factory girls, Rouse hoped that the WSCF work would benefit from contact with the YWCA. She also requested that Wikander speak in different Scandinavian countries in preparation for the World's YWCA conference in 1914. The rationale Rouse provided was that YWCA leaders would be introduced to the leaders of the Student Christian Movement and would be helped to locate younger leaders for their own work. The speaking

15. Wikander to Rouse, 31 Oct, 1906, box 115–922.

16. Wikander to Rouse, 9 Nov, 1908, box 115–922.

17. Wikander to Rouse, 9 Nov, 1911, box 115–922.

tour would provide Wikander with an overview of YWCA activity in Scandinavia that could be used to plan the development of Christian student work. Apparently the link with the Y had already been established since Wikander was doing some work for the Goteborg YWCA.[18] During the summer of 1913, Wikander assisted with the new home for factory girls that housed about twenty residents and many guests.

In 1913, Wikander encouraged Rouse to make a return visit to Sweden. The visit generally boosted the profile of the movement and allowed for face-to-face discussions of pressing issues, such as the appointment of a Scandinavian representative to the World's committee. She hoped that the meetings with students would be evangelistic and promote a worldwide view of the student federation. Through small tea parties and gatherings, younger students would become acquainted with Rouse. Part of Rouse's proposed visit might also address the growing interest of students in social questions. She believed that such social questions, however, required a "religious grounding in the spirit that seeks its help in God."[19]

Wikander explained to Rouse that local student movements varied greatly; women students in Goteburg, for example, were quite reserved, especially in religious matters. The missionary spirit was not very strong, nor was their inner life reported to be sufficiently mature to support that interest. One student union in the higher training college (teacher training for girls' high schools) had discontinued its meetings due to lack of interest. The women students were subdivided into many special interest groups, including *gymnasiasts*, women students, *seminarists*, and school girls. In an effort to overcome this separation, they had combined women students, *gymnasiasts*, and young teachers, guided by a committee that arranged for summer conferences, work among factory girls, and guest speakers such as Rouse. A Bible study circle was organized and some of the girls also worked in the settlement movement.[20]

Wikander continued to encourage Rouse to visit, even though the impending war made that less likely. During World War I, Sweden, along with Norway and Denmark, attempted to preserve neutrality. As the war continued, however, tensions emerged. The government leaned toward the Germans because the king and elites identified with the German

18. Rouse to Wikander, 2 Dec, 1912, box 115–922.

19. Wikander to Rouse, 13 Feb, 1914, box 115–922.

20. Wikander to Rouse, 19 Feb, 1915, box 115–922.

monarchy, using the threat of Russia to attempt to maintain support. By contrast, the left saw Germany as the epitome of what was wrong with Sweden. The difference in allegiance increased after the February-March revolution in Russia. Thus, on the whole, the sympathies of Sweden were not aligned with England with the result that many women might boycott an event with a featured English speaker.

After Wikander's departure for China in 1915, student secretaries Ida Fischer and later Elsa Karlson replaced her in the Swedish movement that continued to grow. Karlson felt that the best method to increase interest and membership would be to try to engage young girls in the movement well before they went to university. The summer camp in 1918 had so many applicants that they had to turn students away. The economy and an outbreak of influenza that was ravaging the country complicated their work among students.

The student union had voted to support Ingeborg Wikander's missionary work with 1,000 crowns, the YWCA with 2,000, and the Swedish Women's Mission Association with 1,000. They were very happy to keep up contact with Wikander and circulate her reports. Karlson gave a lecture called "The Women in the New China," based on a synthesis of these reports. In this way, the national work supported the work overseas and directed students to the possibilities and challenges offered by missions work. The example of one of their "own" working overseas provided a powerful model for students considering missions work.

The movement in Sweden faced a particular set of obstacles, especially the skepticism and cynicism of students who viewed Christian student movements as both naïve and as associated with American ideas. This reluctance included the formal organization of a movement. With the help of local leadership, the women's and men's student movement gathered strength and participated in the Scandinavian Student Christian Movement as it federated with the WSCF at Vadstena in 1895. One of the Swedish students who used her student experience to move onto the international stage became a YWCA secretary in China. Wikander's experiences there are described in the following chapter, as she conquers her homesickness for Sweden and finds challenges in China that are rewarded by a love of the people there.

Swedish students were wary about Christian student organizing and resisted any application of movement "methods" to their student life. Feminist activism and reform led to the opening of universities and teacher's training to women. Swedish students were interested in social activism work and enthusiastically participated in charity projects directed toward the poor. The small groups dedicated to Bible study were reorganized with a more structured executive and concrete curriculum. Through the establishment of a Swedish student movement, an organizing committee was available to connect with the other Scandinavian partners. Mott's presence was warmly welcome in Sweden where his contacts included royalty and prominent citizens. The Swedish student movement supported Ingeborg Wikander's work in China and maintained a lively interest in missions there and elsewhere. The prominent leadership of Nathan Soderblom for more than two decades in the student movement was also a strong model to generations of Swedish students. Despite Lydia Wahlstrom's warnings to Rouse that the Swedish students would resist the organization of a movement, the SCM of Scandinavia was an important member of the WSCF and participated fully in these decades of growth.

10

China

IN 1893, JAMES ENDICOTT graduated from Wesley College at the University of Manitoba with the gold medal in philosophy. While at a student conference in Minneapolis in 1892, Endicott had heard John R. Mott speak and decided to serve as a missionary. He was chosen to represent his classmates at the newly opened mission field in Sichuan in the southwest of China.

He and his wife left in the summer of 1895 for Kiating. The city was already well served by missions; these included a French Jesuit mission, the British China Inland Mission, and the American Baptists. Anti-foreign riots flared up in the area, inspired by protest against the Treaty of Shimonoseki in which China ceded sovereignty over Taiwan to Japan and by increased taxes to cover war indemnities. Shortly after the Endicotts arrived, angry crowds were gathering in Kiating and other locations. Advised to leave, the Endicotts fled with only the clothes on their backs. As they made their way to their river transport, James brandished his Manitoba hunting rifle and shouted in Chinese for the crowd to stand back. They travelled two thousand miles to Shanghai where they spent the next year. Not to be deterred, however, they returned in the spring of 1896 carrying an order to the city from the Manchu provincial governor to reimburse them for the buildings that had been destroyed in the riots. With these Chinese funds, the missionaries set to work buying homes and land for a hospital, and building a church, dispensary, school, printing press, and bookroom.[1]

1. Endicott, *Rebel Out of China,* 8–12.

THE YMCA IN CHINA

While the Endicotts were busy building up the mission station, an American couple arrived via ship from Hong Kong to Canton in July 1896. John and Leila Mott were on a pioneering voyage on behalf of the student movement. Mott regarded the possibilities in China with optimism. As a result of defeat in the Sino-Japanese war of 1894–1895 the Chinese were more open to Western technological advances in order to rebuild their supremacy. Unrest was evident, however, in various anti-foreign riots which included the massacre of missionaries in Huashan in the province of Fukien. Just before Mott's arrival, riots had also occurred in the Shantung province—events that foreshadowed the Boxer Rebellion in 1900. Mott and the other missionaries hoped that Western education and beliefs would find their way into Chinese society, but they did not realize that the deep-seated contempt for the foreigner and the barbarian would create hostility to the gospel that would prove difficult to overcome. They focused on technique in this pioneering work, namely, to secure the students, develop the YMCA into an indigenous force, and later unite missions and denominations into an ecumenical endeavor. [2]

Mott visited several cities including Canton, Shanghai, and Chefoo in Shantung. While he addressed an August conference in Chefoo, Leila Mott spoke to women's groups. Another conference in Peking was attended by 600 delegates, including one hundred missionaries. The purpose of the conference was to organize local Y's and invite them into a national body that would affiliate with the WSCF. Everywhere Mott went, a new Y association was established. A conference in Shanghai with eight Chinese and twenty-four foreigners reported twenty-two new associations. The College YMCA of China was set up with a national committee composed of seven Chinese and seven foreign members. The national association was admitted to the WSCF and one Chinese delegate was appointed to attend the summer conference in Northfield. An SVM was organized as a part of the national YMCA and women volunteers were associated with this group.[3]

Missionaries had long been involved in the education and health care of the country. During the nineteenth century, Western science and literature had been spread by the missionaries. They established a

2. Hopkins, *Mott*, 176–79.
3. Ibid., 177.

printing press in Canton in 1833 as well as several colleges, such as Teng Chow College, St. John's College in Shanghai, and Methodist Episcopal University in Shanghai. Chinese students were also sent abroad for education; Yung Wing was sponsored by missionaries and graduated from Yale in 1854. In 1872 a group of students was sent to the United States, but in 1881 all students were recalled, reflecting another shift in educational policy.

Missionaries, whose work in education attracted eager audiences in the early part of the twentieth century, found their work suddenly restricted after the Boxer Rebellion of 1899–1900. Emperor Kuang Hsu had made an unsuccessful attempt in 1898 to change China into a modern constitutional society. There was widespread resistance and the Emporer was replaced by the Dowager Empress. In response to the attempt by European powers to carve up China's resources and railroads, the imperial court gave money to secret societies. Initially, these societies had been formed in opposition to the imperial government but in the face of rising anti-foreign sentiment, the Empress believed that they could be helpful in forcing out Europeans. In 1900 the Chinese gave foreigners an ultimatum to leave Peking and a siege against foreigners began. When Allied troops arrived in Peking to counter this threat, China declared war on them. The allied column relieved besieged foreigners from Peking and the Dowager Empress fled. The Boxer society was abolished in 1900.

In the aftermath of the Rebellion, European powers gained the right to maintain military forces in the capital, thereby placing the imperial government under house arrest. The Protocol also suspended the civil service examination and demanded repayment of the losses Europeans had suffered. In 1901 the education system was reformed to allow the admission of girls and the curriculum was changed to include Western mathematics, science, engineering, and geography. The civil service exam was revised in 1905.

The Dowager Empress died in 1908. The country was deeply divided. Sun Yat-sen was among a group of Cantonese radicals who argued for a constitutional government. When he attempted to set up a liberal regime in Canton, the coup failed and he fled China and became the expatriate leader of a revolutionary party. Yuan Shih-kai (1859–1916) was another leader who emerged. He was the governor of Shantung who had suppressed the anti-foreign Boxers and who consolidated his power by reorganizing the military along Western and Japanese lines. In 1905, when concessions related to the Russo-Japanese war increased the desire for reform in China, Yuan Shi-kai led the movement to repeal the state examinations.

Concessions and control by foreign powers caused China to look to Western ideas and education to increase its competitiveness on the world stage. The defeats suffered in the Sino-Japanese war (1904–1905) and the Sino-Russian conflict (1905) meant not only humiliation but also physical concessions in terms of railroads and sovereignty. When Russia refused to withdraw its troops from Manchuria after the Sino-Japanese war in 1905, Japan used its superior fleet to defeat the Russians and take over positions such as Port Arthur (Vladivostok). The czarist conscript troops were no match for the German-trained Japanese army. All three countries took note and revised their strategies accordingly. Germany had previously obtained Chinese concessions after the murder of two missionaries in Shantung in 1897, when they gained a ninety-year lease for railway and mining rights in the Shantung province. France, Great Britain, and Russia had also agreed on demands and leases as the economic potential of a largely undeveloped country became apparent to other empires.

When Mott arrived for his tour in 1901, the Boxer uprising had ended.[4] The anti-foreign and anti-Christian Boxer Rebellion had proved to be a blessing in disguise for the YMCA and its staff. The "hundred days of reform" were being swallowed in reaction, but the suppression of official exams gave an opportunity for missions-educated Chinese to enter the civil service and put a premium on Western-style education. The opening allowed room for the YMCA to play a far greater role in China's modernization than either Chinese or American secretaries had anticipated.

Although Mott had not planned to visit the North, there were many pleas that he do so, so he went to Peking. Of the 350 delegates attending the two-day conference there, almost all had been persecuted or had relatives who had been persecuted or killed. Back in Shanghai the Association staff conferred and, on board ship bound for Nanking, they prepared for a national convention at Nanking University. The convention brought together 170 delegates, of whom 131 were Chinese

4. See Esherick, *Origin of the Boxer Uprising*. See also Spence, *Gate of Heavenly Peace*; Linebarger, *China of Chian K'ai-Shek*.

representing thirty-three colleges, fifteen missionary societies, and eight provinces. Fourteen college presidents also attended. Student secretaries came from Japan, Korea, and Hong Kong. After the conference Mott held evangelistic meetings in Nanking, Shanghai, Canton, and Hong Kong that led to 196 conversions, a number he found remarkable because of the persecution and political opposition involved. As he left China in November 1901, he referred to that country as the Jericho of the student world because he could see the signs that the walls would someday fall. That day came in 1905 when the traditional examination system fell; the YMCA was ready to develop further into this open field.[5]

In the years between Mott's second (1901) and third (1912) visit, the Chinese Y continued to grow. As a non-denominational tool of outreach, the Y was ideally suited for pioneering in China as it offered Western-style advantages in leadership and education. Students who were sent overseas for education during this period could connect with similar organizations in their new country, whether it was the United States or Japan. The Tokyo WSCF conference in 1907 noted the presence of large numbers of foreign students, particularly Chinese, who had been sent to study in the country. Rouse estimates that there were 8,000 Chinese students, not including Koreans, in Tokyo at the time of the WSCF conference, but that total had earlier been as high as 14,000. At the conference-related evangelistic meetings, Sherwood Eddy (1871–1963) observed that the Chinese were far more responsive than the Japanese. When he eventually responded to Brockman's invitation to speak in China, he found himself speaking to 4,000 students a day. In 1912–1913, Mott and Brockman would receive an unprecedented response in their joint campaigns in China.[6]

On his third visit in 1913, Mott found a new China. The Manchu dynasty, under the weak successor to the Empress, the last Emporer Pu Yi, was dismantled by 1912 and replaced by a national, democratically elected Assembly. When Sun Yat-Sen resigned his acting presidency in favour of Yuan Shih-Kai in February 1912, he relied on Yuan to take on the cause of the revolution and the new republic. Yuan stayed in Peking and attempted to hold the country by governing from the north. The parliamentary elections of 1913 gave the Revolutionary Party, now called the Kuomintang, a majority of seats; however, bribery and terror

5. Hopkins, *Mott*, 259.
6. Ibid., 317.

characterized this regime. Yuan ruled through military mandarins until he died in 1916. When he died, he left a divided country, a weak parliament, and a series of local armed groups headed by their own generals. China entered a phase of internal chaos that lasted from 1916 to the late 1920s.

Historian Alvyn Austin notes that in 1900 there were 2,000 Protestant missionaries; in 1905, 3,300 missionaries; and in the 1920s, approximately 8,300 missionaries. Before World War I, most of these were British, but by 1919, 50 percent were Americans, 33 percent British, and 17 percent were European.[7] The YMCA—and the WSCF with which it was linked—was meeting its goals and employed twenty-eight Western secretaries. The YMCA's platforms, because they were associated with both gradual change and social reform, found an eager audience. The pro-democracy revolution was approaching, and the Y was in touch. The revolutionary attitude was a key factor in the success of the conferences and Mott's evangelistic missions. Yuan had given the movement assurance of religious liberty. Sun was a professing Christian. Officials attended church services, supported the YMCA, and endorsed certain mission programs. Public addresses thanked the Christian church for the introduction of reforms.

In Mott's twenty-five day tour, he visited all the major centers including Hong Kong, Canton, Shanghai, Soochow, Nanking, Hankow, Peking, and Tientsin where he held evangelistic meetings with eager audiences of approximately 1,000 young men. Mott met with leading government officials and educators. Part of his task was to work with the secretaries in China to establish a budget for building and secretaries. By 1910 the budget had grown to $425,000 and in 1912, there would be seventy-five International Secretaries in China. After attending the National Conference of the YMCA of China, Korea, and Hong Kong in Shanghai, Mott was convinced that the Y had to be led by Chinese nationals. The first Chinese general secretary of the YMCA was C. T. Wang in 1915.

The attitude toward Western influence in China was once again altered, however. Between 1915 and 1920, intellectuals became increasingly more politicized. The centre of this activity was Peking University. After the decisions of the Paris Peace Treaty in 1919 appeared to betray China's trust and interest in favour of the Japanese, student unrest

---

7. Austin, *Saving China*, 86.

reached a peak and spread among other groups, especially laborers. China had declared war against Germany in 1917 and had made a substantial contribution to the Entente victory. Chinese laborers had dug trenches in France at great cost to lives. The May 4th movement in 1919 resulted in demonstrations against the Treaty of Versailles and Japanese concessions of German land in Shantung. The protest spread to other cities and resulted in boycott of Japanese goods.

A new sense of nationalism gathered the country together in protest against the imperialists taking over the nation. With the reorganization of the Kuomintang and the founding of the Communist Party (CCP), anti-imperialism became not only an ideology but a political choice. Influenced by the success of the Russian Revolution, the attraction of Marxism-Leninism was felt in China. As the Russian example appeared to indicate, a country did not need to reach a high level of industrialization and capitalism before it could have a socialist revolution. A valid alternative to Western models presented itself at a time when the West had lost it credibility among the Chinese for diplomatic betrayal. Thus in 1921 the Communist Party was founded in Shanghai with the active help and encouragement of Russian agents.

WOMEN'S WORK WITH THE YWCA

In 1890 the YWCA of China was started as a student association in Hung Tao School in Hanzhou by Mrs. Stewart. She was the wife of Leighton Stewart who founded Yenching University and was later US Ambassador to China. The first city YWCA was founded in Shanghai in 1908. In 1923 the first national convention of city YWCAs took place in Hanzou where the national council of the Chinese YWCA was established. The World YWCA in 1894 extended an invitation to the U.S., Great Britain, Sweden, and Norway as well as India and China.

Women volunteers, teachers, and missionaries set off for the Far East motivated by the search for adventure combined with a desire to apply their education and to share with other women the privilege they had experienced in the early decades of women's higher education. Thus, the religious call and perceived need of "sisters" abroad inspired women to leave family and friends for short- or long-term missions.[8] Life in a

---

8. The motivations of missionaries have been explored in such works as Ruth Compton Brower and Rosemary Gagan. See also, Robert, *Gospel Bearers*; Robert, *American Women in Mission*; Semple, *Missionary Women*.

foreign setting offered different constraints from life at home, but also opened up new possibilities.[9]

Women missionaries sent out by a variety of denominations and countries found themselves part of a community of expatriate women. Most China missions required two years of language study before a candidate could find her own work. Vacations at summer resorts such as Kuling, Chikungshan, Mount Omei, and Douglas Heights brought women together for a few weeks of fellowship and fun.[10]

Prospective women missionaries arrived with university education or professional preparation in teaching or medicine and relevant work experience. Some women had served in student volunteer contexts such as Y work among students in universities—Nebraska (Grace Coppock), Sweden (Ingeborg Wikander), Mount Holyoke and New England (Matilda Thurston). Prior to meeting her husband, Matilda Thurston had worked as travelling secretary for the Student Volunteer Movement in the eastern colleges of the United States during 1904–1906 and in her travels visited forty colleges east of the Mississippi. She was a graduate of Mount Holyoke and had years of teaching experience in the U.S.; two years in a junior college in Marash, Turkey; and five years in the Yale School at Changsha. After her husband's death, she returned to China determined to carry on their educational mission.

YWCA workers in China kept in touch with their supporters back home. A Miss A. E. Paddock, National Secretary of the YWCA in Shanghai, appealed to the organizing committee for the Student Volunteer Movement conference to be held in Liverpool. She asked the West to send YWCA workers to China who understood the challenges of dealing with poverty. Poverty, she argued, was oppressive; it kept people from developing skills and from being eligible for evangelization. Paddock cited the work of Red Cross engineers investigating flooding along the Yangtze River as one of the best models for development work. Such development work would facilitate the acceptance of the doctrine of Jesus. Paddock wrote: "Poverty has stunted the souls of millions of those made in the image of God—until now notably in the famine sections men sit idly awaiting the possibility of famine relief, or death." Equally essential, she believed, were students who would be interested in

9. Eder, "Constructing Opportunity."

10. Austin, *Saving China*, 136.

working among Muslims in China since there were very few Christians working among the thirty million Muslims.[11]

Although women workers in China were acutely aware of the unrest and threats posed to them as foreigners in an increasingly hostile environment, they often chose to stay in dangerous situations, armed with a sense of duty to those they served and to their call. Minnie Vautrin was one. An American from Secor, Illinois, Vautrin graduated from Illinois State Normal and the University of Illinois. She taught at a high school and then spent two years in Chinese language school from 1912 to 1914. She established a girls' school in Luchow (Sichaun). During a furlough she completed an MA at Columbia Teachers' College and then joined the faculty at Nanking College. She later joined the faculty of Ginling College and became its vice-president. During the Nanking massacre of 1937–1938, she harboured, fed, and educated thousands of refugees in her school. Her despair in the end over those she could not help or save led to her eventual suicide.[12]

Education in China underwent a restructuring that affected the mission of women educators in this period. Girls' schools initiated by missionaries had been planted as early as the 1840s and were not subject to the same government regulations as those applied to the boys' curriculum. The traditional Confucian-based exam system had been abolished in 1905. Subjects targeted as a high priority for development included English and science. Education for girls had to be built from the kindergarten level up. Although there was some education at the primary and high school level, there were no possibilities for higher education for women. One group of sixty-three students was sent abroad in 1919 to complete their post-secondary education.[13]

Other options for women's higher education in China at this time included the Bridgman Academy in Peking—a school that later helped form the North China Union College for Women in 1908. North China Union became part of Yenching University in 1920, one component of which was the Yenching College for Women. In Nanking, the Methodist Girls' School Hwei Wen offered post-secondary courses. Some girls

11. A. E. Paddock to R. Rouse, 28 Nov, 1911, RG 46, 221–1195, YDS Special Collections.

12. See website for her story. Online: http://history.alliancelibrarysystem.com/IllinoisAlive/files/ep/htm2/ep000033.cfm.

13. Thurston, *Ginling College*, 1.

were allowed to study with their brothers at the male Canton Christian College. In 1914, a freshman class entered the Women's College of South China (Hwan Nan) in Foochow, but by 1917 only two years of college were offered there.[14] Prior to the establishment of Ginling College, Mrs. Thurston visited schools in Peking and Shanghai to survey the field.

The WSCF in China worked closely with the YWCA. As with the student work in Japan, there could be no student federation until women's higher education had been solidly established. As an initial step, Y associations were established in schools and later with factory women. The Y offered fellowship and organized Bible and Christian knowledge classes, as well as training in a range of skills, hygiene, physical culture, and discussion of social questions. Not only were the notions of association a novel idea for the Chinese, but the doctrines of Christianity were almost completely foreign.

Voluntary movements like the YWCA valued the development of indigenous leadership and to this end supported Chinese women who travelled to the United States for education and helped them find placements on return. Education was both the central attraction for Chinese women and the method that North American missionaries used to disseminate their organizational methods. For women such as Wu Yi-fang, graduate of the University of Michigan, this training and support eventually resulted in her installation as first president of Ginling College (1928–1952). The educational structures established by missionary and voluntary groups thus provided an infrastructure for the application of the skills of foreign-trained Chinese women, as well as ongoing support. In return, the values of Western Protestantism were carefully woven into a powerful educational force of indigenous women who provided models for generations of schoolgirls and women.

Teachers in the early years at Ginling College came from a number of notable American schools including Smith, Oberlin, Vassar, and University of Michigan. One student had a BA from Vassar as well as a BD from Hartford Seminary. The principal hoped to offer special courses in pre-medicine, education, and religion to fit students in the three fields of ministry related to the needs of body, mind, and spirit.[15] Students' physical health was followed quite closely and records were kept of their medical histories. By 1918, the college had its own doctor; Dr Merrow, a

14. Ibid., 12.
15. Ibid., 16.

graduate of the University of Michigan, had practiced for ten years in the United States prior to serving in China.

The YWCA was an integral part of college life from its earliest inception. The Y served the neighborhood by starting a Sunday school and a day school. When the school had a resident physician, the Y also supported a local clinic. Colleges like Smith developed a relationship with Ginling that helped its graduates find placement in graduate programs in the United States. Twenty of the forty-three graduates of the first four classes gained higher degrees from American institutions including University of Michigan, Boston University, DePauw, Columbia Teachers' College, University of Iowa, University of Minnesota, and Smith. In the next two generations of Chinese women students, graduates attended Oberlin, Hartford Seminary, Clark University, University of Chicago, Northwestern University, Colorado Teacher's College, Wellesley, Pomona, Mount Holyoke, as well as Oxford, University of Paris, and University of Geneva.[16]

Many mission agencies representing a variety of denominations ran a school in association with the Shansi Mission in the 1880s. The Carleton Project, involving Carleton College, Smith, Wellesley, and others, supported Chinese education in the early 1900s.[17] Students also travelled to Canada in search of higher education, such as that provided by the Lillian Massey School of Household Science at the University of Toronto.

Returning missionaries, Y leaders, student secretaries, and faculty generated new interest, activity, fundraising, and support for work in China. In addition, Asian studies were promoted in Western universities and a rationale provided for North American departments of Oriental languages and literature and art as well as political studies, comparative religion, and international relations.

It would be misleading to regard the women's educational effort in China as completely separate from education and voluntary organizations for men. As noted earlier, Matilda Thurston was married to Yale graduate Lawrence Thurston. Thurston was a representative of the movement to "muscular Christianity" that glorified sports and Christian service. Thurston and his associates founded the Yale-China Association

16. Ibid., 22.

17. See The American Context of China's Christian Colleges and Schools. Online: http://www.library.yale.edu/div/colleges/about.html.

after involvement with the Student Volunteer Movement for Foreign Missions.[18] On arrival in China, the couple settled into the expatriate community with a social life centered in the club, food, and friends that recreated life "at home." After researching the field, Thurston suggested that the Yale mission focus on education. The couple travelled first into the interior to investigate an abandoned mission compound in Shanxi province, but decided in favour of an inland mission in Changsha, Hunan. The province had been considered desirable by a variety of mission groups.

After the Boxer Rebellion of 1900, treaties opened Changsha and other Hunan cities to foreign settlement and thus by 1903 more than fifty missionaries from the United Kingdom, United States, Canada, Finland, Germany, Scotland, and Australia had established missions there. A commission of missionaries met to decide how to divide the territory in Hunan and awarded the commission of higher education to the Yale mission. Unfortunately, before he could begin the task, Thurston returned to the US due to illness and died of tuberculosis. The Yale mission would develop without him and eventually his widow would return to establish higher education for women.[19] Her vision for education was no doubt shaped by her own education at Smith and her experience in Turkey, but no less by the influence of her husband's vision for the Yale mission and the experience of being expatriates in a mission community in China. The mission for higher education for women can never be considered entirely separate from the work for men and the missionary enterprise as a whole, which was sometimes driven by church and denominational interests, and sometimes by collegiate-based organizations that were broadly Christian but inter-denominational. In addition, the educational front was integrated with a religious vision and a social service mandate that developed both the work of the Y and a student movement that could be federated into the larger aims of the WSCF.

What kinds of educational backgrounds did Western student secretaries who served in China bring to their work? Some were trained and experienced teachers in science, arts, physical education, and other languages. American Frederica Mead Hiltner prepared for missionary work at Ginling College by studying at Teachers' College, Columbia, and at Union Theological Seminary taking Master's Degrees in English and

18. Chapman and Plumb, *Yale-China Association*.
19. Ibid., ch. 1.

Religious Education. In 1918 she departed for China to spend four years at Ginling. Religious pedagogy or Christian Education allowed women to gain expertise in such areas as Bible teaching—an area of teaching that was most appropriate to the educational mission of women, particularly as it was not to be confused with preaching or proclamation. Grace Coppock became a student volunteer in 1905 while studying at the State University of Nebraska. She went to China under the foreign division of the National Board (circa 1911). She took a leading role in developing the YWCA of China as a Chinese movement with indigenous leadership, similar to the work of Canadian Caroline Macdonald in Japan. Her early death in 1921 was a great blow to the YWCA in China.[20] In her annual report to the World's YWCA in 1913, Coppock observed that the rising numbers of women in education meant that within ten years, fifteen million women students would be enrolled in China's government and private schools. The Y hoped to bring the ideals of Christian womanhood to these women, but such a task required many more workers.

Coppock reported that one new secretary had been hired, Yung Hai Chun of Wellesley (class of 1913), who worked in the dept of Physical Education with a Miss Mayhew. Another worker, a Miss Thomson, was on loan from the Presbyterian Mission for two years. Thomson was placed in Canton in order to allow Mayhew two years for language study. In Foochow, many women students wanted to study the Bible and there were not enough Bible teachers. To meet this need, a Miss Wells and a Miss Helen Bond Crane were transferred to Foochow. The Tientsin association became a full-fledged association with a Miss Saxelby as general secretary.

In 1913, Shanghai was the site of the second Y secretaries' conference with twelve foreign and two Chinese secretaries in attendance. Student conferences were also held in other sites throughout China in 1913. Other centers with no Y movement, such as the Wu-Han cities, were sending urgent appeals for workers. Chengtu in the province of Sichuan was asking for workers. Y associations were even springing up with no leaders.[21] This period of growth demonstrates that Chinese

20. Rouse noted that it was a tragedy that the WSCF and the YWCA have no collection of Grace Coppock's letters and thoughts because she felt that she had been as significant as Caroline Macdonald in her contributions to overseas work.

21. Grace L. Coppock, extracted for the Women's Subcommittee of the WSCF, 30 Sept, 1915, box 221–1695.

women found the concept of a student association attractive. The Y could not, however, keep up with the demand despite desperate appeals for leaders made to affiliates in Europe and North America.

Summer conferences like the 1915 summer conference in Foochow were new events for Chinese students. The one hundred and thirteen delegates who assembled on the first night far exceeded the organizers' expectations. They were eager to learn. The group represented thirteen cities, twenty-three schools, and four denominations.[22] That same summer, a conference was also held in Nanking at the Methodist Girls School building, with 186 registered delegates. The day started with a quiet hour at 6:30, followed by breakfast, Bible class, and "Method Hour" that studied ways to promote the Association work. The morning meetings were set aside for talks about Christian service for women in the home, as teachers, doctors, evangelists, and in social service. By contrast, the evening meetings provided inspirational work on Christian discipleship. Many of the delegates had never attended such an event and arrived with no idea what to expect.

One woman, Christiana Tsai, suffered the displeasure of her upper-class family at her conversion to Christianity. She had devoted herself to evangelistic work through the Presbyterian mission, hosting home-based small group events for Chinese women. She spoke at a summer conference on the topic "Every Woman a Soul Winner." Another organization, the "8 Weeks Club," required members to read the Bible and pray every day during the holidays and do one or more forms of social service. [23]

At the Tientsen Conference that same summer, eleven schools were represented, of which seven or eight were Chinese schools. Fifty-one women attended who were either very new Christians or non-Christians. The program was similar to other conferences with the exception of the class on methods, which was omitted. One of the speakers was Pastor Cheng Ching, the Chinese Secretary of the Chinese Continuation Committee, who gave two addresses on the death and resurrection of Jesus Christ. Another speaker was C. T. Wong, former Minister of Foreign Affairs in Peking, who spoke about his experience as a YMCA leader. He lectured on the proper place of women in the home and their role in the

22. Extract of a letter of Miss Helen Bond Crane, Women's Subcommittee of the WSCF, 1915, box 221–1695.

23. Extract of a letter from Winnifred Jacob, Women's Subcommittee of the WSCF, 11 July, 1915, box 221–1695.

training of children. A Chinese woman taught three daily Bible classes. In the afternoon the delegates played games. Dolls were distributed to the great delight of the participants. A total of six conferences were completed during the summer of 1915.

Another Y worker, Ruth Paxson, recounted giving a dizzying round of speeches in 1916 in schools that were often followed by "decisions for Christ." In the midst of these conversions and enthusiastic reception of activities by the Y workers, there was a hint of imminent political unrest. Three years previous Coppock had described unsettled conditions in the country that led to the cancellation of several conferences.

INGEBORG WIKANDER IN CHINA 1915–1923

Ruth Rouse wrote to Grace Coppock in 1915, recommending the services of Swedish student secretary Ingeborg Wikander. The support for her work would be undertaken by the Swedish YWCA and perhaps by the British or American Foreign Department. Her experience included time as a travelling secretary for the Swedish YWCA and a placement in the World's Y office in London. She was a gifted teacher and her English skills were fairly good. Her travels had taken her to China and Japan twice; she had visited missions in India and America; and she had attended two or three WSCF conferences. According to Rouse, Wikander exhibited a deepening spiritual life that would enable her to withstand the hardships of life in China. Although she had suffered from typhoid fever after the Tokyo WSCF conference, she had recovered fully.[24]

Rouse's recommendation carried weight; Wikander was sent to China. In 1916, Rouse mentioned that she felt that Wikander was rather depressed and discouraged but Rouse believed it was a case of "the inevitable depression that comes to every new missionary." Wikander went to language school in Nanking and took her language exam in Shanghai. She left for Ginling College in the autumn of 1915. There were fifteen girls at the college that was located in a former Chinese palace.[25]

24. 2 April, 1915, box 221–1695.

25. The house had been a palace belonging to the fifth son of Li Hung-chang, who had risen to power by suppressing the T'aip'ing rebellion. It was described as the house of a hundred rooms, but in reality it consisted of two large rambling Chinese mansions set side by side, each containing four paved courts. The mansion was adapted for college purposes. The name Ginling was given in 1914 and replaced the name The Union College for Women. Eight mission boards had participated in the establishment. Five mission boards including Northern Baptists, Disciples of Christ, Northern and

Her tasks included taking assigned chapel service once a week and teaching physical culture. Her correspondence notes that the principal, Mrs. Thurston, was "fine" and all the teachers, Americans, were fine as well.[26] Some discussion took place as to where to find a more permanent assignment. As one possible site, Chengtu had the advantage of being the site of a large missionary centre and a Mrs. Edward Wallace (formerly Rose Cullen, a Victoria College graduate) was located there as well.[27]

Wikander made a trip to the United States in January 1916 and then returned to China. In the summer she went to Foochow to spend three months and then to Kuliang in the mountains above Foochow. She had been living with Grace Coppock in Shanghai for several months. Her placement continued to be discussed—an uncertainty that may have been the result of political change. After one of the secretaries in Foochow, a Miss Crane, had a serious breakdown, Wikander was suggested as her replacement.

In the summer of 1916, Wikander confessed to feeling overwhelmed; she had not realized what it would mean to join an international movement where one was the only representative of one's country. She felt very tied to the Swedish student movement; hearing about conferences and camps at home made her heart ache. The scale of work in China made her potential contribution seem insignificant. Success seemed more attainable in Sweden where so many workers were available to help. She realized that "by the time I have learnt something, it will be time for me to go home."[28] Yet, she conceded, the voice of Christ was calling her and perhaps she needed to come to China to see that in Sweden things seemed to just grow on their own.

Her sense of loneliness increased that summer in a foreign landscape, with no lakes, no flowers, no stillness of woods, just bare mountains and a burning hot sun. The Chinese landscape was her desert experience. Her American companions seemed young and satisfied with their own company. "Just to have one person, that spoke your language and knew your world, what a comfort that would be," she wrote nostalgically. She acknowledged that God was present there, even in the desert,

---

Southern Methodists, and Northern Presbyterians each gave about 10,000 U.S. dollars to help support the college and staff. See Thurston, *Ginling College*, 5.

26. Wikander to Rouse, 8 Oct, 1915, box 221–1700.

27. Rouse to Wikander, 19 Oct, 1915, box 221–1700.

28. Wikander to Ruth Rouse, 29 Aug, 1916, box 221–1700.

allowing her to know Christ better there through both his sacrifice and his love. She wished she could thank him for giving her "just a very little share in His sufferings." She had a growing conviction that those at home in Sweden need to share in the China work and that the YWCA had a very big and wonderful piece of work to do, but it needed to get more workers from Europe, from England, and from Scandinavian countries. The American workers, she argued, had much to learn but also had gifts to give. She conceded that Grace Coppock had a broad understanding of the field and that was a comfort to her.

In Wikander's opinion, if a Scandinavian woman secretary could be persuaded to come to China, she should be big, tall, nice looking, sporting, and ladylike. "The look" meant a lot in mission work, she felt, and as for her own look, among the Chinese she could do all right, but among the Americans she felt that she would always be taken for someone just out of school.

She admitted that she felt as if Ruth Rouse were present, loving and good and big as always, and she could "get free of herself by talking it freely out to her."[29] She studied Mandarin with a teacher four hours a day. When she met Chinese women, she liked them very much and longed to find her own proper work. But the necessary preparation meant that it took a long time before secretaries could be assigned. After days of twisting her tongue to pronounce Chinese and then speaking English the rest of the time, she longed to speak her own language.[30]

The new Y Association headquarters opened in Shanghai—three new houses in Chinese style and a big yard with a tennis court. One building was intended for the national work, another for local work, and the third for the new program in physical training. The opening was only briefly overshadowed by political events; Wikander believed that the situation called for the departure of Yuan Shi-kai.

In 1917, a place had been found for her in Changsha, the capital of Hunan, where she would be the first YWCA secretary. Her sense of vocation had intensified: "I begin to feel how in me is growing a deep love for this people." Two potential co-workers at the college provided her with hope. One was a Chinese girl who had been brought up in a Swedish

29. Ibid.

30. Wikander to Rouse, 8 April, 1916, box 221–1700.

Mission School; she had witnessed an attack wherein two Swedish missionaries had been murdered but her family had escaped.[31]

Another Swedish worker named Miss Nothorst, who had been sent out by the Swedish state church to work with the YWCA, joined Wikander. The latter wrote again with cheerful optimism about her a growing sense of deep love for the Chinese people: "There is so much to do out of the fine material they are. And there is so much warmth and love hidden in their souls that often has little opportunity of growing and coming in blossom."[32] Her optimism continued through the summer of 1917 in Kuiling where she was living in a Swedish home in an expatriate community of about sixty. Although she was still pursuing language study, she would be allowed to start some work that fall. They planned an evangelistic campaign for Changsha in the fall and invited a Mr. Brickman, followed by Yale graduate and Y leader Sherwood Eddy, and then Miss Paxson. Other planned activities included a Bible institute for women, special meetings, visitation work, and Bible classes. Wikander served as secretary of the committee and shared accommodation with a Miss Morton, president of the only high school for girls in Hunan.

This enthusiasm at finding her place had diminished somewhat when she confided to Rouse by the end of 1917, "More and more I begin to feel as if there was no place for me out here Ruth. I have none of the gifts that are needed here. And I probably was too old to come out, I mean too fixed in my own ideas and too deeply rooted in my work and surroundings at home." If she were a nurse, or a physical director or if she could sing or play or be domestic, she could be useful. To add to her misery, she was still not fluent enough in Chinese to lead Bible classes. She did not feel she could work together with American secretaries because there were so many differences in methods and in beliefs. There were two small YWCA associations in Changsha, one group of high school girls who were so young she hardly knew what to do with them, and one among the nurses in the Yale Hospital.[33]

31. Wikander to Rouse, 1 May, 1917, box 221–1700.

32. Wikander to Rouse, 11 March, 1917, box 221–1700.

33. The Yale-China Association, created in 1901, is a private, non-profit organization based on the Yale campus that is dedicated to promoting an understanding between Chinese and American people through the medium of education. Yale-China helped to introduce Western medicine to China in the early 20th century by establishing a teaching hospital in Changsha that bore its name, Hsiang-Ya (Hunan-Yale) Hospital. The Hsiang-Ya Medical College and Nursing School were founded a few years later. Now

Hunan became the location of political conflicts in 1918 between the north and south, with instability reflected in the fact that the governors had changed three times in six months. Refugees crowded missionary compounds; during Easter there were 300 refugees. The consuls urged foreign women to leave, but they refused. Wikander agreed with speaker Sherwood Eddy that it was the darkest hour for China, but conversely the brightest hour for the Church in China. The trials had brought her very close to the Chinese.

Increased support in Sweden for foreign missions was a positive sign that pleased Wikander. A conference in Uppsala drew 300 delegates from the university. Archbishop Söderblom and the crown prince of Sweden both offered increased support for China missions. In central China, seventeen Swedish or Swedish-American agencies worked together demonstrating an increased spirit of cooperation.

Wikander experienced growing friendships with Chinese women, among them her landlady and a young women, Ugao, who she hoped would be their first Chinese Y secretary. The young woman had attended a foreign school in Shanghai and spoke English well. She had lived in the YWCA hostel in Shanghai while she taught at the "suffragette" school from which she had also graduated. Since she was the only one in her class who had not become a Christian, Wikander hoped that she too would soon convert. In 1919, Wikander realized her hope as she observed the baptism of Ugao, who had been functioning as her language teacher and helper. Ugao's mother came, accompanied by a dozen other Tso family members, none of whom had ever been in a church. Ugao had been in Shanghai from her sixteenth until her twenty-sixth year when her mother requested her return to Changsha the same summer Wikander arrived. Ugao had refused to be considered for the post of YWCA secretary, but she wanted to be a volunteer and to continue giving language lessons to Wikander. In Changsha they planned to set up a committee of Chinese women, most of whom were untrained in Association work but were very interested in learning. One committee was hoping to open a hostel in the Chinese house they used for classrooms. The official opening of their buildings was attended by leading foreign missionary women, Chinese students, and teachers from

---

known as the Xiangya School of Medicine, these institutions are part of Central South University in Changsha and continue close collaboration with Yale-China.

mission and non-Christian institutions. The women of Hunan were very progressive and very capable.[34]

Wikander invited her hostess, a Madame Tso, to a private Bible study. Tso's high social position allowed her to extend her influence so that their Y opened even earlier than expected. Wikander wrote about her happiness working with such women and claimed that she had "found her new world in China and a blessed place it was God led me to after some hard years of loneliness and restlessness."[35] In retrospect, Wikander realized that she had written unhappy letters in her first years in China and she thought at the time that she would never be happy again—but to her surprise she had found happiness. The Y was opened in November 1919 with approximately ninety members and a board of Chinese women; this was significant because they were the first Association in China to commence without any foreigners on the board.

Wikander left China for a Swedish furlough in April 1920. In December, 1921, she wrote Rouse that she was sorry she was missing the preparations for the Peking conference by being in Sweden. However, she attended the twentieth anniversary of the student movement in Sweden. She concluded that the outlook for the student movement was not very bright since the Free Church students were forming a movement of their own and the split had weakened the work. She hoped to be able to organize a school for handwork in Changsha. She believed that Swedish workers could help with such a project whereas the Americans had no tradition of embroidery similar to Sweden's. In her view, the school would enable the women in Changsha to earn money and would preserve cultural traditions like embroidery. In addition, this training could be combined with exposure to Christian life and thought.[36]

Swedish students by 1921 were not drawn to the student movement: "We are mostly old hands there. I don't see the new ones."[37] A summer conference for women was planned to try to attract new students. Wikander's work included travelling for both the Y and the student movement visiting schools and other sites. She found it easier to reach new students at the conferences than at the universities. Despite the low

34. Wikander to Rouse, 22 May, 1918, box 221–1700.

35. Wikander to Rouse, 20 April, 1919, box 221–1700.

36. Wikander to Rouse, 17 Dec, 1921, box 221–1700.

37. Ibid.

interest among students, Wikander remained optimistic because she felt that there was a general movement back to religion and to Christianity.

In 1922 Wikander wrote from Sweden that she had been very busy writing a large book on China for the Student Movement Missionary Series and helping a little in the work for gymnasiasts and factory women. The summer program was about to begin and she planned to attend five different events, in addition to the Swedish Student Christian Movement Conference and the YWCA general conference.[38]

Her next letter to Rouse was written on a ship in China in 1922 while travelling up river from Nanking to Hankow. She arrived in time for a conference of all the student secretaries of the YWCA who were assembled to consider the student question in response to a request by students at the Peking conference asking for the establishment of a coeducational National Christian Student Movement of China. Although the prospective association wanted some connection with the Y in America, they hoped for self-government and a constitution to be worked out by them. Wikander was asked to consult with the women students on this constitution that would be connected with the Y and with the men's movement. In 1923 they hoped to have the first general convention for all China with elected representatives for all the student and city Y's.

Wikander had been asked to do travelling work in colleges and schools with emphasis on religious education. This request came from increased questioning of the role of Western thought and literature. She had been asked to explore the idea of what Christianity stood for both individually and socially. This work meant she would leave Changsha to work with Annie Seesholtz and other student workers at headquarters. She hoped to spend a month at Ginling College, where she had spent her first year in China, in the company of an old friend, Principal Thurston. The college had increased its student body to eighty students from the eighteen who were in attendance when she visited in 1917.

By the summer of 1923 Wikander prepared for vacation in the mountains in Kuiling. She had decided on return that she could not leave her work to become a travelling secretary since she felt that Changsha still needed her and furthermore, travelling work needed a younger person since the students were "rustical and wild" and she felt she would be too conservative to deal with them.

38. Wikander to Rouse, 7 June, 1922, box 221–1700.

Some unrest was evident in a strike at Changsha against the Japanese because they were "so successful in travel and everything and are gaining ground every day in China while the Chinese fight between themselves—and go on strikes and parades."[39] The students in the girls' high school had marched in the streets in defiance of the school's administration and many would likely be suspended. Their zeal, she felt, was both childish and foolish. An air of mischief and rebellion was in the streets as people disrobed anyone who wore clothing made of Japanese cloth. They tore trousers from people and sometimes hurt the poor or elderly.

Although a few sincere patriotic souls held steadfast among these rebellious citizens, most "seemed to be beset of a fierce mob spirit and I very often think we are going the same way in China as Russia went the last ten or twenty years!"[40] The upper class, in her view, was degenerate and weak, sinful and lazy, but hope rested with the farming class and the women. They had some moral backbone still and kept to their duties and their work while the rest ran after selfish gains or new fashions, but a restless spirit was pervasive.

Writing from South India as she was preparing for the next leg of her final return home, she observed, "it seems I have come to an end of these years of work in China." The missionaries had been ordered out by consular command. It seemed better to leave before communications were cut off and hostilities escalated. The political climate was painful to witness as she observed: "I just could not stand to see the Chinese turn in anger and fury against us—as I do love them and wanted to have these years of friendship in my memory without the dark shadows of acts of hatred that the best kind of Chinese regret as keenly as we do and feel ashamed of."[41] She felt that the Chinese secretaries were well trained and able to do the work on their own as they had been doing. She had prepared for that in the past years. Her friend Ugao had taken up the post of General Secretary in Changsha and she could take comfort in knowing the work was continuing.

Wikander had been asked to become National General Secretary of the YWCA in Sweden in the fall. She felt that the old order had to give way to the new and her job was to help usher in the new. She was pleased

39. Wikander to Rouse, 5 June, 1923, box 221–1700.

40. Ibid.

41. Wikander to Rouse, 26 April, 1922, box 221–1700.

that there was full unity about calling her home to the task, even among the younger staffers.

In retrospect, she felt that she had grown through her experiences in China. Although the first period had been tough and she was forced to continue with God's help, she believed that her tasks had been finished. Although joy and inner peace accompanied the completion of her task, she reflected on her own failures and suffering.

On her way home, she visited the Indian cities where the Church of Sweden mission was working. She spoke to YMCA and YWCA groups, and met with WSCF secretaries in Madras. She called for a closer union between the churches of India and China with the hope that some of the best Indian workers would go to China to preach messages of sympathy and love in the days of suffering in China. She wrote: "I feel that in these days when the missionaries from the West have to leave China, it would mean more than ever before if the ties of love and cooperation were strengthened between the Church here in the East specially India and China who have so much to give to each other and so very much to learn from each other." Those countries complemented each other, whereas the countries of the West often irritated them to the breaking point by being so similar—"being equally proud, equally blinded by race pride, equally materialistic in our outlook and ways of working." She enquired after Rouse's new position with the International Student Service and noted that "it was part of a sad feeling to know you officially have left the Student Movement but I am sure you are there all the same like so many of us who have had to leave it for one reason or another."[42]

Her correspondence does not comment on the Peking conference of 1922 that she missed or the student unrest which followed it. According to historian Alvyn Austin, the Christian student movement trained a generation of radicalized leaders who "equated true Christianity with the destruction of imperialism." Students formed an Anti-Christian Student Federation in 1922 to express their own sense of nationalism: "it is us who will save China."[43] As Wikander turned her gaze to the forests and woodlands of her beloved Sweden, and the task of building the Swedish student movement, she presumably tried to take stock of what had accomplished, and what had been left undone.

42. Wikander to Rouse, 5 June, 1923, box 221–1700.

43. Austin, *Saving China*, 102.

When Mott next visited China in 1922 it was for the purpose of attending the WSCF conference in Peking. Mott neither chaired nor organized the conference—he was more than happy to let indigenous leaders such as C. Y. Cheng take charge. The war had not devastated student work as it had in Europe. An Anti-Christian Student Federation had emerged in reaction to the coming of the WSCF and in response to a mission atlas that assigned the entire country to mission boards. Although the publicity was not harmful for the conference, the disruption of the post-conference deputations was considerable. The Chinese leaders of the WSCF conference were concerned with internationalism and interracial positions that had emerged at Beatenberg. There was disagreement, however, about support of a WSCF position for pacifism. Not all delegates were convinced that force was essentially evil. Other issues raised included German war guilt by Dr. Georg Michaelis, chair of the German SCM. These issues did not die out, but "in the next few years the Federation came to see that opposing viewpoints were integral to the universal inclusiveness that was its genius."[44] Mott left on one of the last trains before the rail line was cut by the civil war.

The China Continuation Committee Conference was also held in Shanghai in 1922. One thousand delegates attended and more than half were Chinese. The Committee produced a national body, the national Christian Council, which became a member of the International Missionary Council. National Christian Councils were also formed in Korea, Japan, and India.

The Marxist movement would eventually move Chinese students leftward, leaving the Y to appear conservative. Still in 1922, the Y had a lot of prestige and Sun Yat-sen proposed that the Y join the Kuomintang to save China. When the Y decided this could not be done, Russia was invited instead. Before Mott's next visit in 1925, the Y was being severely criticized and an era of Western-inspired student organizing had come to an end.

CONCLUSION

China caught the Western imagination as a field for student and mission work. Western interests were also involved in the economic opening up of the nation. In both commerce and missions, the welcome of foreigners

---

44. Hopkins, *Mott*, 609.

gradually wore out. Internal politics saw the end of traditional rule and the beginning of attempts to bring China into a modern constitutional government. Although strong leaders emerged, none was able to bring about the changes in military, government, and social reform that would have allowed China to resemble a democratic nation.

The work of the YMCA, YWCA, and WSCF gathered momentum as compulsory education became established and women's education became accepted. Chinese students educated in the student movement brought their leadership skills to the movement and provided the indigenous leadership to help the movement take root.

Internal and external politics could not, however, be ignored. Attempts to impose Western-style democracy on China in the period between 1910 and 1920 failed due to the lack of the necessary skills and attitudes that would support that type of political reform. Nor was there sufficiently strong leadership to gain control of the military and the warlords. Western leaders perceived the outcome of the peace talks following World War I as the ultimate betrayal of China. Russia, by contrast, provided the support and leadership China sought as it moved into nationhood. The gathering Marxist revolt would not be silenced; and the student movement's voice would gradually lose momentum and place in the face of revolutionary politics that had no room for foreign religion.

Conclusion

THIS STUDY OF WOMEN'S role in the WSCF ends in 1925, a year when the organization had faced major challenges to its survival and had managed to adapt successfully. Many changes in the basis and organization of the federation had taken place, resulting in the creation of a related but separate organization to address the needs of student relief. In the decades from founding to 1925, the WSCF had shifted from an overt evangelical focus to a more inclusive and interfaith perspective. The travels of such leaders as Mott and Rouse ensured that the perspectives of a worldwide movement would be brought from the margins to the center of the student movement.

The history of the WSCF provides an important insight into the history of higher education particularly since in many regions, the notion of affiliation with national and an international network was so new. The federation provided a link between students in different countries and enabled the sharing of communications and publications around the world. Such sharing did not mean, however, conformity in local contexts. Indeed, the federation's resilience can partly be attributed to the flexibility of structure that allowed national movements to preserve their identity while federating with the world movement.

Organizationally, the WSCF modeled itself on precursors from the student world and early student clubs. Societies on the exclusively male campuses gathered for the purpose of supporting an issue or a cause and later diversified to include athletics and social functions. Early student clubs were generally met with approval by university authorities, as the aims appeared to support the overall purposes of the college or university. The YMCA provided an important model and training ground for leaders who were involved in student movement work as well. Indeed, it is difficult to separate the history of the YMCA and its supporters from the federation, since its personnel and purposes were so enmeshed in the early decades. The story of the male student movement must include the leadership training that targeted talented young students and mentored them for life long careers in the student movement. The work of the YMCA, the SVM, and the WSCF depended on the charismatic and indefatigable leadership of men such as Reynolds, Wishard, Speer, Mott, and Wilder, who travelled incessantly to promote the vision of Christian internationalism among students. Essential to this formation was the participation in student camps and conferences. For students from Europe who travelled to North America for such events, or Americans who were present at key student conferences in England and Europe, these experiences were not only memorable, but they were formative in shaping life long vocation and vision.

As women moved into higher education in a variety of countries in Europe, the United Kingdom, Australia, and North America, student clubs and organizations were part of the extracurricular menu. Such clubs provided an opportunity for women to gain skills in leadership and public speaking. In certain women's colleges of the northeastern United States, the missionary agenda also provided rationale for professions such as medicine and teaching overseas.

Missions oriented curriculum and social clubs supported those who chose to work overseas and supported a variety of educational missions and individual exchanges. Some women were more comfortable in organizations that were less directly linked to churches or missionary organizations and these found a home in such work as the Missionary Settlement for University Women in India.

In coeducational universities, the YMCA remained a single sex movement with the women engaged in the YWCA. Missions oriented clubs were often from the onset a coeducational enterprise. Regardless of the preferences of the organizers, women who were filling universities in growing numbers around the world, demanded to be included in the student movement and by 1905 had a representative in the WSCF to address their concerns. The women's work would not have thrived without the financial support of several wealthy women such as Grace Dodge and Mrs. C. McCormick, who supported the work of the women's department and the WSCF with their vast family fortunes. The focus of the women's work shifted from a focus on personal conversion and spiritual formation to the reform of society. The shift of concern was reflected in the movement of women into professions such as social investigation and social work in the early twentieth century.

Ruth Rouse, while still a student at Girton, became involved in the Student Volunteer movement and attended conferences such as Keswick in 1894. Her preparation for the unique position as women's secretary in the WSCF was partly due to her presence in the developing student movement at key junctures, and partly due to experience gained in a variety of contexts with student work. Rouse travelled to Scandinavia to greet a fairly uninterested audience of women students, followed by placements with the YWCA in North America. Very few women could have gained such a broad perspective of the conditions of women students at the time. Part of her work involved visits to colleges and universities in North America, where she met students and faculty who supported the international goals that were developing from within the Y and the student volunteer work. Her goal to serve as missionary in India was cut shot by illness—life had another plan for her talents and energy.

Rouse's talents included both a synthetic ability to gather information from diverse individuals and student groups and share such information with members of the women's department. She also extended personal friendship to many women's secretaries around the world who poured out their hearts and concerns to her in correspondence. Her ability to keep up with the care of her siblings and her mother, international friendships, travel, writing, and speaking is remarkable. Her ability as well to collaborate with John Mott and the male leadership of the WSCF seems to suggest her own diplomatic abilities, no doubt learned as an early graduate of the women's education movement, whose members learned to balance their commitments with a degree of caution about overt conflict or unfeminine behaviour. Her role in editing the papers of the WSCF suggests that she had some control in shaping the official record, including her personal thoughts or reflections on the individuals with whom she worked. Her own historiographic work on the WSCF has provided a helpful synthesis of the themes, as well as an insider's view of the major contributions of the federation.

North American and British influences largely shaped the federation. However, when the federation moved into countries with no preexisting national student movement, it faced new challenges. Students in Russia were disenchanted with state religion and saw the clergy as collaborators with repressive regimes. Protestant groups had attempted to make inroads into Russian culture, such as the Pashkovites, but their dedication was generally met with persecution. Mott attempted to reassure the Orthodox clergy that the student movement would respect the Orthodox affiliation of students. They remained unconvinced and banished Mott from Russia. Such resistance only increased Mott's determination to find other ways to organize students.

Neither Rouse nor Mott might have predicted the events that led to the Russian Revolution. Baron Nicholay, however, warned already in the early 1900s that a disaster similar to the French Revolution was heading for Russia. The work among men and women took small steps forward, organized in small study groups that would not attract official attention under local leaders who risked much to fulfill the purposes of the movement. The Russian Revolution almost defeated this fledging movement. Student leaders were imprisoned and student members tried to survive in the disastrous conditions that characterized post-revolution Russia. Russian students studying outside of the country became a focus of WSCF relief efforts in Switzerland as their desperate physical and emotional state required a variety of interventions.

Student relief became a priority in the early 1920s and Rouse's knowledge of the situation was helpful in the response through the newly organized European Student Relief. Even student relief proved impossible to organize in this decade. By 1924 the relief efforts were withdrawn and contact between the student movement and the rest of the world was cut off.

The federation's involvement in Russia provided an important training ground for leaders on the complexity of planting a student movement in inhospitable ground. Successes were achieved as the SCM of Russia was formally acknowledged as a member of the federation in 1913. At that time, few would have predicted the difficult times that lay ahead for the Russian student movement in Russia and the diasporic student movement in Europe. Despite the difficulties in sustaining this national movement in the years after its formation, the interaction with Orthodox members pushed forward an ecumenical vision that might have remained latent much longer without the contact with Russian students.

For both Mott and Rouse, as well as other student leaders, this valuable experience not only reshaped the membership requirements in the federation, but opened the field to Orthodox participation in other parts of the world. The fruits of this experience resulted in the complex planning and pre-conference work that resulted in the participation of

Orthodox leaders and students in the Constantinople Conference—an event that foreshadowed later ecumenical assemblies and organizations such as the World Council of Churches. This participation shaped a generation of leaders who were sympathetic and sensitive to inter-religious and inter-cultural dialogue and generated the creative development of liturgy and practice that found its way into worship of student groups and churches in the following decades. The Russian chapter was in many ways a turning point for the federation that opened up a path of resilience and adaptation to the present day.

The federation work in Switzerland combined elements of the pioneering work with Russian students with the work with disenchanted Protestant students in Scandinavia. Swiss students included large numbers of foreign students who were often politically engaged and religiously skeptical of such student organizing. Their own religious affiliations included Orthodox, Jewish, Catholic faiths, as well as a variety of Protestant denominations. The large numbers of women students demanded the attention of the women's desk as the American, Elizabeth Clark, was chosen to develop student work in this complex environment. Clark's work was complicated by a mixed reception by the male leaders of the Swiss national student movement. Her own funding derived from American sources—a support that may have increased resentment towards her at the local level. The challenge was enormous, partly due to diverse language, ethnic, religious, theological, and gender differences that threatened to split the movement rather than create a unified purpose. To further complicate the matter, the rise of conflict generated by WWI meant that the country was further split into language and ethnic groups that affiliated with different sides of the war. Political neutrality could not overcome the harsh divisions within the country and within the student movement.

Despite such adversity, the federation's secretaries developed creative programs that provided concrete assistance to desperate students. Indeed, programs of self-help and retraining developed in Switzerland formed models of adult education that continue to this day in development and adult education. Hospitality and friendship proved a winning combination through the outreach of community kitchens and foyers. The European Student Relief took such methods into other countries and into work with refugee and displaced students. The transformation of the ESR into an organization called the International Student Services provided a non-judgmental, non-denominational organization that supports international friendship, refugee relief, and student exchange to the current day. It is unfortunate that the organizations that developed from the early beginnings of the WSCF have generally forgotten or distanced themselves from the history of the WSCF. The current revival of the North American branch of the WSCF demonstrates a continuity of purpose with the aims of international friendship and relief that were developed in the Swiss national student movement through workers such as Elizabeth Clark.

Student work in France had origins in the YMCA and the work of James Reynolds who spent several years working in Europe to promote that organization. France was the site of inter-country collaborations through the organization of student hostels and foyers under the auspices of the Y and funded by philanthropic support from the United States. Mixed methods were required to meet the needs of foreign students from diverse countries, as well as French students who resisted the notion of Christian clubs and outreach. The challenges of this work were met by some gifted leaders who were able to reach out to the women students in a variety of ways that did not threaten their beliefs but challenged them on a moral and ethical basis. Jeanne Pannier extended hospitality to women through her home. Natalie Orgewsky, a veteran of the Russian student movement, brought essential experience to the movement in its attempt to reach out to Russian students in Paris.

The French movement used a variety of methods to reach out to reluctant students. Reading clubs, Bible study groups, and mission focused events found acceptance among different groups of students. In the universities of the south of France, there were students from Orthodox and Jewish faiths that required a different type of outreach. Student secretaries Suzanne de Dietrich and Suzanne Bidgrain provided a wise and accepting space for these diverse student groups. Indeed, the women's work during the war years and after shaped an ecumenical stance that was at odds with the men, particularly when they returned from the war and found the movement significantly altered through the leadership of women. De Dietrich also contributed to the French and the federation as a whole by her development of new methods of Bible study that helped provide a unifying focus for student events in camps and study circles. Although the social aspects of student movement involvement were a consistent draw for students, the educational and formational aspects of the federation must also be acknowledged. Not only Bible studies, but also a vast number of publications were distributed through the SCM networks and discussed in relevant journals. Although each movement had a preference for different study topics and methods, there were best-sellers that shaped student thinking on a variety of Biblical, theological, ethical and political issues.

In Japan, the opening by the Meiji government to Christian churches fueled a sense of optimism that the nation would be converted. Missionary outreach organized schools and study groups and provided support for Japanese women who were engaged in educational projects. The YMCA found a niche in Japanese society that was further expanded by foreign workers and programs to teach English. The Y structure was more acceptable than missions organizations and took root in a variety of cities and towns. Visits by John Mott provided evangelistic meetings to educational institutions and students.

Women's work in Japan was also channeled through the YWCA. The goal of such work was from its beginning to develop indigenous leadership. One such leader was Michi Kawai, who had been educated in the United States at a women's college in Pennsylvania. Kawai sampled the possibilities of student work in the United States and in Europe and dared to dream that Japanese women might enjoy the same advantages. Supported by American and Canadian secretaries, the Y gathered members and organized summer camps for women. Kawai served the YWCA, the WSCF, and promoted her own school for women. Her presence at the WSCF Conference in Japan modeled indigenous leadership in the international movement that was institutionalized in her eventual position in the WSCF as chair of the Women's Sub Committee in 1912 and as vice-chair of the federation from 1920–1922.

National student movements in Europe sponsored student secretaries to work in overseas contexts, such as Ingeborg Wikander, who worked in China. Such sponsorship was a radical departure from the apathetic student groups who resisted student organization in the late nineteenth century. Women students in Sweden enjoyed access to higher education by the late nineteenth century. They were, however, highly skeptical of the outreach by Ruth Rouse, who visited groups of school girls, teacher's college students and university students to promote the ideal of a Christian student movement. Swedish students, bored by the traditions they associated with their largely Lutheran origins, were also hostile to evangelical piety and American or British methods. Social causes however engaged students in work in the inner city and in orphanages and settlements. Small groups meeting for Bible study slowly gained acceptance, supported by visits by Mott and Rouse.

Despite their resistance, the Swedish Student Christian Movement grew and participated in the larger Scandinavian student movement. Ingeborg Wikander was herself a student at Uppsala in the first decade of the twentieth century. She had experience working with women students and with a missionary board. Her travels to attend the WSCF conference in Japan presumably inspired her to consider international work herself, a goal that was supported by her acquaintance with Rouse. By 1915, Wikander had sailed for China, supported partly by the student union and partly by the Women's Mission Association.

Wikander joined missionaries in China from a variety of countries who saw China as a vast frontier for conversion and development. Among students, the YMCA had been active since the late nineteenth century travels of Y organizers such as Luther Wishard. Missionaries were at times chased out of the country and at other times were welcomed as representatives of Western progress and knowledge. The Y offered the advantages of Western education and leadership without the burden of too much association with Christianity or missions. Mott extended a great deal of energy and effort in visiting China several times, holding large meetings in cities and universities.

Women's work in China also developed along YWCA lines. Girl's schools allowed for further expansion of Y initiatives until post secondary options were available. The WSCF worked closely with the YWCA in order to build the beginnings of student movement work. Education provided a valuable tool of outreach as Chinese women took advantage of mission schools or opportunities to study abroad.

Wikander worked with the YWCA in China developing Bible study and camp work for women. Not a career missionary, Wikander returned to Sweden to continue work with the Y after less than a decade in China. She left before political conditions forced the departure of missionaries. Her experience had changed her views of China and indeed of the world, and she presumably influenced Swedish students with her insights after her return to her homeland.

The optimism which had been an intrinsic part of the organizational culture and mission of the WSCF was tempered by events in

Russia and China and by events of World War I. Progress occurred in the form of the expansion of Western culture and Protestant religion to both unchurched and resistant students of the universities in Europe, Asia, and India. Such setbacks might have defeated a less resilient organization. The WSCF, however, with its energetic ambassadors of friendship, gathered in the post war period for a process of reconciliation that foreshadowed such processes in this century.

The notion of Christian internationalism expanded to include Orthodox and Roman Catholic participants. Ultimately, the aspects of the WSCF that proved most effective in hostile situations also provided the key to survival over time. The WSCF was a leader in creating a fairly simple but efficient structure that federated national student movements together.

It is difficult now to imagine a time before national and international organizations were commonplace. The WSCF was a leader in creating a fairly simple structure that provided a world federation. Supported by the incessant travel of a handful of leaders, the Federation created a global presence through publications, speakers, telegraphy, and letters. Conferences in strategic locations created and supported student movements in countries where such an idea had never before been tried. The eager and increasing numbers of women students helped create a women's department with a dedicated woman leader. Ruth Rouse had a remarkable ability to keep in touch with women leaders, inspire and model leadership, and maintain a demanding schedule, as well as care for family members. Rouse was trained on the job as she pioneered and investigated the conditions of women students in countries such as Russia or worked with existing student movements in North America.

The WSCF, perhaps due to its relatively simple structure, proved to be resilient and was able to adapt to the context in various countries. Unlike the SVM with its more unified focus, the WSCF adapted its mission and vision to move from a trans-denominational to an ecumenical organization, early recognizing the need for strong indigenous leadership and the needs for students who belonged to other faiths or who professed no religious faith.

Mott served other organizations in the 1920s including the World's Alliance of YMCA's, the International Missionary Council, and European Student Relief. By 1928 Mott was to surrender the American YMCA and the WSCF, but he would continue to serve the World's Alliance of YMCA's.

Although the work of the WSCF was groundbreaking, there were occasions when the movement misread the international situation—in the Middle East, China, and Russia. Yet the misinterpretation of some of these international situations was not confined to the organization but shared by the Western governments with whom the movement and Mott's friendship were closely affiliated. In fact, the boundaries between organization and diplomacy were less rigid than one might believe; Mott himself served as a member of the Root diplomatic mission charged by the President to investigate conditions in Russia. Indeed, women secretaries in India, China, Japan, Russia, and Western Europe sometimes found themselves with the language skills and contacts necessary to gain significant understanding of political situations. Their distance from the head office in New York also allowed them to function with some independence and to develop and act on their own best judgment. Women found different ways to respond to the social problems and political conflict of the time.

The WSCF was a lay movement in which students with an ever more diverse background and experience could find possibilities for work. Because the student movement was not identified with a church or denomination, it was able to function more creatively and to work in settings where the church would not have been welcome. In China this contributed to rapid growth in the early twentieth century allowing the Y to move into communities as a representative of modern Western ideas that were for a time welcome there.

Education was a key element of the success of the Federation. This educational strategy built on the experiences of college students. SCM and WSCF publications distributed Bible study outlines, studies of social problems, missionary history, studies of geographic regions and religions. New Bible study publications such as those pioneered by Suzanne de Dietrich and Henry Sharman caught on with students and graduates and became part of the methodology in adult education and small group work. Dialogic education allowed for rapid training of leaders and experts who could then equip other groups of individuals. The lay nature of the movement and Mott's insistence on indigenous leadership meant that the movement slowly reinterpreted the margins and allowed for representation of movements with more recent development such as Japan and India. Two of the first four chairs of the Women's Subcommittee were Asians—Lilavati Singh (from 1907 to 1908) and

Michi Kawai (from 1911 to 1920). Asian male leaders such as Honda, Azariah, and C. Y. Cheng quickly rose to prominence in their national movements and in the Federation.

The period covered by this book witnessed the rapid growth of the WSCF while it also witnessed an increase in the processes of globalization, technological change, population movement, economic, and political change. These changes affected the WSCF and interrupted its claim to speak for the student population of the world to the Christian Church. As World War I and revolutions in a number of member countries affected the work and mandate of the student movement, the WSCF would continue to reinvent itself by means of negotiations and exchanges with member countries and individuals. A lasting place for the Federation was negotiated in the work of student refugee relief as the twentieth century brought an unending number of natural and human disasters that disrupted the life of students in a variety of countries. Although the mandate has changed and evolved into its current manifestation, it is in the creation of a worldwide vision that the founders of the WSCF would find common ground with today's Federation.

Appendix

List of Federation Conferences or General Committee Meetings, 1895–1925

1895	Vadstena Castle, Sweden
1897	Williamstown, Massachusetts
1898	Eisenach, Germany
1900	Versailles, France
1902	Soro, Denmark
1905	Zeist, The Netherlands
1907	Tokyo, Japan
1909	Oxford, England
1911	Constantinople, Turkey
1913	Lake Mohonk, New York
1915	Prague, Czechoslovakia
1920	St. Beatenberg, Switzerland
1922	Peking, China

Bibliography

MANUSCRIPT SOURCES

Yale Divinity School Library Special Collections

Student Volunteer Movement Papers, Record Group 42 (RG 42)
John R. Mott Papers, Record Group 45 (RG 45)
World Student Christian Federation Papers, Record Group 46 (RG 46)

United Church Archives/Victoria University Archives

Emma R. Kaufmann Personal Papers
Margaret Addison Personal Papers

JOURNALS

The Student Volunteer [1893–1898]. Chicago: Student Volunteer Movement for Foreign Missions.
The Student World [1908–1969]. New York: World's Student Christian Federation.

BOOKS AND PAMPHLETS

The Foreign Mission School at Cornwall, Connecticut 7.3 (1929). Online: http://digital.library.okstate.edu/Chronicles/v007p242.html (accessed on 17 Nov 2007).
Proceedings of the ISMA 1882. Online: http://hdlhandle.net/10118/6 (accessed on 17 Nov 2007).
Proceedings of the ISMA 1886. Online: http://hdlhandle.net/10118/6 (accessed on 17 Nov 2007).
Adler, Elisabeth, editor. *Memoirs and Diaries: The World Student Christian Federation (1895–1990)*. Geneva: World Student Christian Federation, 1994.
Albisetti, James. *Schooling German Girls and Women: Secondary and Higher Education in the Nineteenth Century*. Princeton: Princeton University Press, 1988.
Allen, Richard. *A Social Passion*. Toronto: University of Toronto Press, 1971.
Anderson, Betsy. "A Canadian perspective on the W.S.C.F. North American Region." *Journal of Ecumenical Studies* 32 (1995) 402–6.
Austin, Alvyn, and Jamie Scott, editors. *Canadian Missionaries, Indigenous Peoples*. Toronto: University of Toronto Press, 2005.
Axelrod, Paul, and John G. Reid. *Youth, University, and Canadian Society*. Montreal: McGill-Queen's University Press, 1989.

Baerwalk, Reuben C. "Visions in Conflict." *Journal of Ecumenical Studies* 32 (1995) 339–403.

Barker, Verlyn A., and Thurber, L. Newton. "World Student Christian Federation Centennial: U.S. Historical Biography." *Journal of Ecumenical Studies* 32 (1995) 657–62.

Beaseley, W. G. *The Modern History of Japan*. London: Weidenfeld and Nicholson, 1963.

Beaver, R. Pierce. *American Protestant Women in World Mission*. Grand Rapids: Eerdmans, 1968.

Bebbington, David. *Evangelicalism in Modern Britain. A History from the 1730s to the 1980s*. Grand Rapids: Baker, 1992.

Bevans, Stephan B. *Models of Contextual Theology*. Maryknoll, NY: Orbis, 1997.

Birkett, Dea. *Spinsters Abroad: Victorian Lady Explorers*. Oxford: Oxford University Press, 1989.

Blackett, R. J. M. *Building an Antislavery Wall: Black Americans in the Atlantic Abolitionist Movement, 1830–1860*. Baton Rouge: Louisiana State University Press, 1983.

Boonstra, John. "A Brief Research Sketch on the Goals and Objectives of the W.S.C.F. in North America: 1969–1978." *Journal of Ecumenical Studies* 32 (1995) 384–99.

Bowie, Fiona, Deborah Kirkwood, and Shirley Ardener. *Women and Missions: Past and Present: Anthropological and Historical Perceptions*. Oxford: Berg, 1993.

Boyd, Nancy. *Emissaries: The Overseas Work of the American Y.W.C.A. 1895–1970*. New York: Woman's, 1986.

Brackney, William H. *Christian Voluntarism: Theology and Praxis*. Grand Rapids: Eerdmans, 1997.

———. "The Legacy of Helen B. Montgomery and Lucy W. Peabody." *International Bulletin of Missionary Research* 15 (1991) 174–79.

Braisted, Ruth Wilder. *In This Generation. The Story of Robert P. Wilder*. New York: Friendship, 1941.

Brauer, Kinley, editor. *Paths to Power. The Historiography of American Foreign Relations to 1941*. Edited by Michael Hogan. Cambridge: Cambridge University Press, 2001.

Brouwer, Ruth. *New Women for God*. Toronto: University of Toronto Press, 1990.

Brower, Ruth. *Modern Women, Modernizing Men*. Vancouver: University of British Columbia Press, 2003.

Brueggeman, Walter, and George W. Stroup, eds. *Many Voices, One God*. Louisville: Westminster John Knox, 1998.

Burke, Sara V. *Seeking the Highest Good: Social Service and Gender at the University of Toronto, 1888–1937*. Toronto: University of Toronto Press, 1996.

Burton, Margaret. *Mabel Cratty: Leader in the Art of Leadership*. New York: Woman's Press, 1929.

Burwash, Nathanel. *The History of Victoria College*. Toronto: Victoria College, 1921.

Carey, Clifford M., editor. *Between Two Centuries: Report of the Centennial International Y.M.C.A. Convention*. New York: Association, 1951.

Chapman, Nancy, and Jessica Plumb. *The Yale-China Association: A Centennial History*. Hong Kong: Chinese University Press, 2001.

Christie, Nancy, and Michael Gauvreau. *A Full-Orbed Christianity: The Protestant Churches and Social Welfare in Canada, 1900–1940*. Montreal: McGill-Queen's University Press, 1996.

Clements, Keith. *Faith on a Frontier: A Life of J. H. Oldham*. Geneva: WCC, 1999.

Cook, Sharon Anne. *"Through Sunshine and Shadow": The Woman's Christian Temperance Union, Evangelicalism and Reform in Ontario 1874–1930.* Montreal: McGill-Queen's University Press, 1995.

Corrado, Sharyl. *Early Russian Evangelicals: Ministry Lessons for Today.* The Global Center, 2000. Online: http://www.samford.edu/groups/blobal/ewcmreport/articles/ew08410.html (accessed on 20 October 2004).

"Inventory of the William Alphaeus Hunton Papers, 1926–1970." Schomberg Center for Research in Black Culture. New York Public Library, New York.

Curti, Merle E. *American Philanthropy Abroad.* New Brunswick, NJ: Rutgers University Press, 1963.

Davenport, Thomas, and Laurence Prusak. *Working Knowledge. How Organizations Manage What They Know.* Boston: Harvard University Press, 2000.

Davis, Donald E., and Eugene P. Trani. "The American YMCA and the Russian Revolution." *Slavic Review* 33 (1974) 469–91.

De Dietrich, Suzanne. *Cinquante ans d'histoire de la Féderation universelle des associations chrétiennes d'étudiants 1895–1945.* Paris: Semeur, 1947.

———. *Rediscovering the Bible: Bible Study in the World's Student Christian Federation.* Geneva: WSCF, 1942.

de Mayer, Jenny. *Adventures with God in Freedom and in Bond.* Toronto: Evangelical Publishers, 1948.

Dodge, Grace. *A Bundle of Letters to Busy Girls on Practical Matters.* New York: Funk and Wagnalls, 1887. Reprint edition, New York: Arno, 1974.

Douglas, Ann. *The Feminization of American Culture.* New York: Knopf, 1977.

Dunn, Margaret. *The Dauntless Bunch: The Story of the Y.W.C.A. in Australia.* Clifton Hill, Victoria: YWCA of Australia, 1991.

Eder, Elizabeth. "Constructing Opportunity: American Women Educators in Early Japan." College Park, MD: University of Maryland, 2001.

Eisenmann, Linda. "Reclaiming Religion: New Historiographic Challenges in the Relationship of Religion and American Higher Education." *History of Higher Education Quarterly* 3 (1999) 295–306.

Elliot, Mark. "Russian Evangelical Roots." *East-West Church & Ministry Report* 4.3 (1996) 12.

Endicott, Stephen. *James G. Endicott: Rebel Out of China.* Toronto: University of Toronto Press, 1980.

English, Leona. "Third-Space Practitioners: Women Educating for Justice in the Global South." *Adult Education Quarterly* 55 (2005) 85–100.

Esherick, Joseph W. *The Origins of the Boxer Uprising.* Berkeley: University of California Press, 1987.

Everist, Norma Cook. *The Church as Learning Community.* Nashville: Abingdon, 2002.

Fenn, Eric. *Learning Wisdom: Fifty Years of the Student Christian Movement.* London: SCM, 1939.

Flory, Margaret. "Reports on Ecumenical Events Held in Conjunction with the World Student Christian Federation Centennial Celebrations in 1995." *Journal of Ecumenical Studies* 32 (1995) 662–68.

Franzen, Ruth. "The Legacy of Ruth Rouse." *International Bulletin of Missionary Research* 17 (1993) 154–58.

———. "Rivals or Allies? Gender Interaction in the Finnish Student Christian Federation 1897–1914." *Scandinavian Journal of History* 19 (1994) 117–41.

————. "Ruth Rouse (1872–1956). The Unsurpassed Grand Old Lady." In *Towards a Women's History in the World Student Christian Federation*, edited by C. Balan-Sycip, 64–69. Geneva: WSCF, 1995.

————. *Ruth Rouse among Students*. Uppsala: Swedish Institute of Mission Research, 2008.

Fraser, Agnes Renton Robson. *Donald Fraser of Livingstonia*. London: Hodder & Stoughton, 1934.

Fraser, Donald. *African Idylls: Portraits and Impressions of a Life on a Central African Mission Station*. 4th ed. London: Seeley, Service, 1925.

————. "The Legacy of Donald Fraser." *International Bulletin of Missionary Research* 18 (1994) 32–37.

Gagan, Rosemary. *A Sensitive Independence. Canadian Methodist Missionaries in Canada and the Orient, 1881–1925*. Montreal: McGill-Queen's University Press, 1992.

Garner, Karen. *Global Feminism and Postwar Reconstruction: The World YWCA Visitation to Occupied Japan, 1947*. Online: http://www.historycooperative.org/journals/jwh/15.2/garner.html (accessed on 6 July 2005).

Gauvreau, Michael. *The Evangelical Century*. Montreal: McGill-Queen's University Press, 1991.

Gidney, Catherine. "A Long Eclipse. The Liberal Protestant Establishment and the Canadian University, 1920–1970." Montreal: McGill-Queen's University Press, 2004.

Gidney, R. D., and W. P. J. Millar. *Professional Gentleman. The Professions in Nineteenth-Century Ontario*. Toronto: University of Toronto Press, 1994.

Graham, Abbie. *Grace H. Dodge. Merchant of Dreams*. New York: Woman's, 1926.

Graham, Gael. *Gender, Culture, Christianity: American Protestant Schools in China, 1880–1930*. New York: Lang, 1995.

Griesinger, Jan. "World Student Christian Federation—North America Region Women's Project." *Journal of Ecumenical Studies* 32 (1995) 592–98.

Haggis, Jane. "White Women and Colonialism: Towards a Non-Recuperative History." In *Feminist Postcolonial Theory: A Reader*, edited by Reina and Sara Mills Lewis, 161–89. New York: Routledge, 2003.

Hall, M. R., and H. F. Sweet. *Women in the Y.W.C.A. Record*. New York: Association, 1947.

Hare, Jan, and Jean Barman. *Good Intentions Gone Awry: Emma Crosby and the Methodist Mission on the Northwest Coast*. Vancouver: University of British Columbia Press, 2006.

Harris, Ruth M. "Gender Equality in the W.S.C.F.: Inter-regional Encounters." *Journal of Ecumenical Studies* 32 (1995) 574–93.

————. "Student Ministries and Global Mission Involvement from the Perspective of a U.S. Denomination." *Journal of Ecumenical Studies* 32 (1995) 620–36.

Hawkins, Thomas R. *The Learning Congregation*. Louisville: Westminster John Knox, 1997.

Hedlund, Roger. *Roots of the Great Debate in Mission: Mission in Historical and Theological Perspective*. Bangalore: Theological Book Trust, 1997.

Henkin, David M. *The Postal Age: The Emergence of Modern Communications in Nineteenth-century America*. Chicago: University of Chicago Press, 2007.

Hill, Patricia. *The World Their Household: The American Women's Foreign Missionary Movement and Cultural Transformation, 1870–1920.* Ann Arbor: University of Michigan Press, 1985.

Holmes, Madelyn. *Forgotten Migrants: Foreign Workers in Switzerland.* Rutherford, NJ: Fairleigh Dickinson University Press, 1988.

Hopkins, C. Howard. *History of the Y.M.C.A. in North America.* New York: Association, 1951.

———. *John R. Mott, 1865–1955.* Grand Rapids: Eerdmans, 1979.

Horowitz, Helen Lefkowitz. *Alma Mater.* Boston: Beacon, 1984.

Howe, Renata. "The Australian Student Christian Movement and Women's Activism in the Asia-Pacific Region, 1890s–1920s." *Australian Feminist Studies* 16.36 (2001) 311–23.

Hunt, Felicity. *Lessons for Life: The Schooling of Girls and Women, 1850–1950.* Oxford: Blackwell, 1987.

Hunter, Jane. *The Gospel of Gentility: American Women Missionaries in Turn-of-the-century China.* New Haven: Yale University Press, 1984.

Hunton, Addie W. *William Alphaeus Hunton: A Pioneer Prophet of Young Men.* New York: Association, 1938.

Hutchinson, William. *Errand to the World: American Protestant Thought and Foreign Missions.* Chicago: University of Chicago Press, 1987.

Hutson, Jean Blackwell. "Addie Waites Hunton." In *Notable American Women, 1607–1950,* edited by Edward T. James, 240–41. Cambridge: Harvard University Press, 1996.

James, Cathy. "Practical Diversions and Educational Amusements: Evangelia House and the Advent of Canada's Settlement Movement, 1902–09." *Historical Studies in Education* 10.1–2 (1998) 48–66.

———. "Reforming Reform: Toronto's Settlement House Movement, 1900–1920." *Canadian Historical Review* 82 (2001) 55–90.

James, Janet Wilson, editor. *Women in American Religion.* Philadelphia: University of Pennsylvania Press, 1980.

Jenks, Jeremiah Whipple. *The Political and Social Significance of the Life and Teachings of Jesus.* New York: YMCA Press, 1908.

Johanson, Christine. "Autocratic Politics, Public Opinion, and Women's Medical Education During the Reign of Alexander II, 1855–1881." *Slavic Review* (1979) 426–43.

Kawai, Michi. *Japanese Women Speak.* Boston: Central Committee of United Study of Foreign Missions, 1934.

———. *My Lantern.* Tokyo, Japan: Privately published, 1939.

———. *Sliding Doors.* Tokyo, Japan: Keisen-Jo-Gaku-en, 1950.

Kemeny, Paul Charles. *Princeton in the Nation's Service.* Oxford: Oxford University Press, 1998.

Kenez, Peter. *History of the Soviet Union from the Beginning to the End.* Cambridge: Cambridge University Press, 1999.

Kinnaird, Emily. *Reminiscences.* London: Murray, 1925.

Kinsler, Ross, and Gloria Kinsler. *The Biblical Jubilee and the Struggle for Life.* Maryknoll: Orbis, 1999.

Lagenskjold, Greta. *Baron Philip Nicholay.* Translated by Ruth E. Wilder. London: SCM, 1924.

Lapierre, Alexandra. *Women Travellers: A Century of Trailblazing Adventures, 1850–1900*. Paris: Flammarion, 2007.

Latourette, Kenneth Scott. *World Service: A History of the Foreign Work and World Service of the YMCA Associations of the United States and Canada*. New York: Association, 1957.

Lindsay, Jessie B. "The History of the Missionary Settlement for University Women." *The Student Movement* 17,4 (1916) 10–12.

Linebarger, Paul. *The China of Chian K'ai-Shek: A Political Study*. Boston: World Peace Foundation, 1943.

MacMillan, Margaret. *Paris 1919*. New York: Random, 2001.

"Make Jesus King." Report of the International Students' Missionary Conference, Liverpool, January 1–5, 1896. New York: Revell. 1896.

Marsden, George. *The Soul of the American University*. New York: Oxford University Press, 1994.

Marshall, Megan. *The Peabody Sisters: Three Women Who Ignited American Romanticism*. New York: Mifflin, 2005.

Mathews, Basil. *John R. Mott, World Citizen*. New York: Harper, 1934.

McClintock, Anne. *Imperial Leather: Race, Gender, and Sexuality in the Colonial Conquest*. New York: Routledge, 1995.

McCue, Theresa. "Meiji Maiden: Umeko Tsuda and the Founding of Higher Education for Women in Japan." PhD thesis, University of Massachusetts Amherst, 2005.

McFadden, Margaret. *Golden Cables of Sympathy: The Transatlantic Sources of Nineteenth-century Feminism*. Kentucky: University of Kentucky Press, 1999.

Meijer, J. M. *The Russian Colony in Zurich (1870–1873)*. Assen, The Netherlands: Van Gorcum, 1956.

Mobley, Kendal P. *Helen Barrett Montgomery: The Global Mission of Domestic Feminism*. Dallas: Baylor University Press, 2009.

Montgomery, Helen Barrett. *Helen Barrett Montgomery: From Campus to World Citizenship*. New York: Revell, 1940.

———, editor. *Western Women in Eastern Lands*. New York: Garland, 1987 [1911].

Moor, Lucy M. *Girls of Yesterday and Today*. London: Partridge, 1911.

Morse, Rebecca. *Young Women: A History of the YWCA*. Chicago: American Committee of the YWCA, 1901.

Mott, John R. *The Decisive Hour of Christian Missions*. New York: Student Volunteer Movement for Foreign Missions, 1910.

———. *The World's Student Christian Federation*. n.p., 1920.

Mott, John R. "The Volunteer as a Force." *The Student Volunteer* 1–2 (1893). Mott Papers, Record Group 45, Series V, box 132–2343, YDS, New Haven, CT.

Myers, Bryant L. *Walking With the Poor*. Maryknoll, NY: Orbis, 2004.

Nidiffer, Jane. "Poor Historiography: The 'Poorest' in American Higher Education." *History of Higher Education Quarterly* 39 (1999) 321–36.

Ober, C. K. *The Association Secretaryship*. New York: Association, 1918.

———. *Exploring a Continent*. New York: Association, 1929.

Ogren, Christine. *The American State Normal School*. New York: Palgrave MacMillan, 2005.

Parker, Michael. *The Kingdom of Character. The Student Volunteer Movement for Foreign Missions (1886–1926)*. Lanham, MD: University Press of America, 1998.

Patessio, Mara. "The Creation of Public Spaces by Women in the Early Meiji Period and the Tokyo Fujin Kyofukai." *International Journal of Asian Studies* 3 (2006) 155–82.

Pederson, Diana. "'Keeping Our Good Girls Good': The YWCA and the 'Girl Problem' 1870–1930." *Canadian Women's Studies* 4 (1986) 20–4.

Peterson, Derek, and Jean Allman. "Introduction: New Directions in the History of Missions in Africa." *Journal of Religious History* 23 (1999) 1–7.

Pierard, Richard. "John R. Mott and the Rift in the Ecumenical Movement During World War I." *Journal of Ecumenical Studies* 23 (1986) 604–18.

Pierson, Delavan Leonard. *Arthur T. Pierson.* New York: Revell, 1912.

Piper, John F. *Robert E. Speer.* Louisville: Geneva, 2000.

Porter, Andrew. *Religion Versus Empire? British Protestant Missionaries and Overseas Expansion, 1700–1914.* Manchester: Manchester University Press, 2004.

Porterfield, Amanda. *Mary Lyon and the Mount Holyoke Missionaries.* New York: Oxford University Press, 1997.

Potter, P., and T. Wieser. *Seeking and Serving the Truth: The First Hundred Years of the World Student Christian Federation.* Geneva: WCC, 1997.

Prang, Margaret. *A heart at Leisure from Itself: Caroline Macdonald of Japan.* Vancouver: University of British Columbia Press, 1995.

Prentice, Alison. "Scholarly Passion: Two Persons Who Caught It." In *Women Who Taught: Perspectives on the History of Women and Teaching,* edited by Alison Prentice and Marjorie Theobald, 258–84. Toronto: University of Toronto Press, 1991.

Pui-Lan, Kwok. *Postcolonial Imagination and Feminist Theology.* Louisville: Westminster John Knox, 2005.

Putman, J. Harold. *Egerton Ryerson and Education in Upper Canada.* Toronto: Briggs, 1912.

Rauschenbusch, Walter. *The Social Principles of Jesus.* New York: Association, 1918.

Reeves-Ellington, Barbara, ed. *Competing Kingdoms.* Chapel Hill, NC: Duke University Press, 2010.

Reynolds, J. B., S. Fisher, and H. B. Wright, editors. *Two Centuries of Christian Activity at Yale.* New York: Putnam, 1901.

Rice, Anna V. *A History of the World's Young Women's Christian Association.* New York: Women's, 1947.

Richard, Gaston. *La Vie et l'oeuvre de Raoul Allier 1862–1939.* Paris: Berger-Levrault, 1948.

Robert, Dana. *American Women in Mission: A Social History of Their Thought and Practice.* Macon, GA: Mercer University Press, 1996.

———. *Gospel Bearers, Gender Barriers: Missionary Women in the Twentieth Century.* Maryknoll, NY: Orbis, 2002.

———. "The Origin of the Student Volunteer Watchword: 'The Evangelization of the World in This Generation.'" *International Bulletin of Missionary Research* 10 (1986) 146–49.

Romero, Patricia, editor. *Women's Voices on Africa: A Century of Travel Writings.* Princeton: Princeton University Press, 1992.

Rouse, Ruth. *God Has a Purpose: An Outline of the History of Missions and of Missionary Method.* London: SCM, 1935.

———. *John R. Mott: An Appreciation.* Geneva: World's Student Christian Federation, 1929.

————. *Rebuilding Europe: The Student Chapter in Post-War Reconstruction*. London: SCM, 1925.

————. *World of Today and the Gospel, Missionary Tracts for the Times; no. 3*. London: SPCK, 1915.

————. *The Worlds' Student Christian Federation*. London: SCM, 1948.

Rouse, Ruth, and Stephen C. Neil, editors. *A History of the Ecumenical Movement, 1517–1948*. 3rd ed. London: SPCK, 1954.

Rouse, Ruth, and H. Crichton Miller. *Christian Experience and Psychological Processes*. London: SCM, 1917.

Rowland, Wilmina. "The Contribution of Ruth Rouse to the World's Student Christian Federation." MA thesis, Yale University, 1937.

Sanecki, Kim. "Protestant Christian Missions and Empire: The World Missionary Conference of 1910, Edinburgh, Scotland." MA thesis, Georgia State University, 2006.

Sanneh, Lamin. *Whose Religion Is Christianity? The Gospel beyond the West*. Grand Rapids: Eerdmans, 2003.

Saunders, Una. *Mary Dobson, Musician, Writer and Missionary*. London: Black, 1926.

Seat, Karen. *"Providence Has Freed Our Hands." Women's Missions and the American Encounter with Japan*. Syracuse, NY: Syracuse University Press, 2008.

Selles, Johanna M. "The Role of Women in the Formation of the World Student Christian Federation." *International Bulletin of Missionary Research* 30 (2006) 189–91.

————. *Methodists and Women's Education in Ontario, 1836–1925*. Montreal: McGill-Queen's University Press, 1996.

————. *Women's Role in the History of the World Student Christian Federation*. Vol. 6, *Y.D.S. Occasional Publication*. New Haven: Yale Divinity School Library, 1995.

Semple, Neil. *Faithful Intellect. Samuel S. Nelles and Victoria University*. Montreal and Kingston: McGill-Queen's University Press, 2005.

Semple, Rhonda Anne. *Missionary Women: Gender, Professionalization, and the Victorian Ideal of Christian Women*. Suffolk, UK: Boydell, 2003.

Service, Robert. *The Russian Revolution 1900–1927*. New York: St. Martin's, 1999.

Setran, David P. *The College "Y": Student Religion in the Era of Secularization*. New York: Palgrave MacMillan, 2007.

Seymour-Jones, Carole. *Journey of Faith: The History of the World YWCA 1945–1994*. London: Allison & Busby, 1994.

Shedd, Clarence. "Some Early Student Religious Societies and Intercollegiate Beginnings of the SCM 1858–1900." PhD thesis, Yale University, 1932.

————. *Two Centuries of Student Christian Movements*. New York: Association, 1934.

Shore, Marlene. *The Science of Social Redemption*. Toronto: University of Toronto Press, 1987.

Showalter, Nathan. *The End of a Crusade: The Student Volunteer Movement for Foreign Missions and the Great War*. Lanham, MD: Scarecrow, 1998.

Sims, Mary S. *The Natural History of a Social Institution. The Young Women's Christian Association*. New York: Woman's Press, 1935.

————. *The Y.W.C.A. An Unfolding Purpose*. New York: Woman's Press, 1950.

Sissons, Charles. *A History of Victoria University*. Toronto: University of Toronto Press, 1951.

Smalley, Martha. *The Legacy of John R. Mott, Yale Divinity School Library Occasional Publication*. New Haven: Yale Divinity School Library, 1993.

Smith, Harry. "Review of 'W.S.C.F.: A Community of Memory and Hope.'" *Journal of Ecumenical Studies* 32 (1995) 461–63.

Smyth, Elizabeth, Sandra Acker, Paula Bourne, Alison Prentice. *Challenging Professions: Historical and Contemporary Perspectives on Women's Professional Work.* Toronto: University of Toronto Press, 1999.

Speer, Robert. *Studies of the Man Christ.* New York: Revell, 1896.

Spence, Jonathan. *The Gate of Heavenly Peace. The Chinese and their Revolution 1895–1980.* New York: Penguin, 1981.

Stewart, James Brewer. *Holy Warriors: The Abolitionists and American Slavery.* New York: Hill & Wang, 1976.

Stone, Daniel. *The Polish Memoirs of Daniel Rose.* Toronto: University of Toronto Press, 1975.

Swain, David L. "Review of 'Memories and Diaries: The World Student Christian Federation (1895–1990).'" *Journal of Ecumenical Studies* 32 (1995) 463–65.

Tatlow, Tissington. *The Story of the Student Christian Movement of Great Britain and Ireland.* London: SCM, 1933.

Theobald, Marjorie. *Knowing Women: Origins of Women's Education in 19th Century Australia.* Cambridge: Cambridge University Press, 1996.

Thompson, T. Jack. *Christianity in Northern Malawi: Donald Fraser's Missionary Methods and Ngoni Culture.* Studies in Christian Mission 15. Leiden: Brill, 1995.

———. "The Legacy of Donald Fraser." *International Bulletin of Missionary Research* 18 (1994) 32–37.

Thompson, Terry. "The History and Archives Project of the World Student Christian Federation." *Journal of Ecumenical Studies* 32 (1995) 451–59.

Thurber, Newton L. "Guide to W.S.C.F. / S.C.M. Centennial Historical Resources and Archives in the U.S.A." *Journal of Ecumenical Studies* 32 (1995) 459–71.

———. "The World Student Christian Federation Centennial." *Journal of Ecumenical Studies* 32 (1995) 315–19.

Thurston, Mathilda. *Ginling College.* New York: United Board for Christian Colleges, 1955.

Tikhonov, Natalia. *Student Migrations and Feminization of European Universities*, 2004. Online: http://barthes.ens.fr/clio/revuews/AHI/english/tiko.html (accessed 5 Feb. 2008).

Tucker, Ruth. *Guardians of the Great Commission: The Story of Women in Modern Missions.* Grand Rapids: Academie, 1988.

Valverde, Mariana. *The Age of Light, Soap, and Water: Moral Reform in English Canada, 1885–1925.* Toronto: McClelland & Stewart, 1991.

Van Die, Marguerite. *An Evangelical Mind: Nathanael Burwash and the Methodist Tradition in Canada, 1839–1918.* Montreal: McGill-Queen's University Press, 1989.

Vicinus, Martha. *Independent Women: Work and Community for Single Women, 1850–1920.* Chicago: University of Chicago Press, 1985.

Voelkel, Jack. "Great Cloud of Witnesses." Online: *http://www.urbana.org/articles.dfm?RecordId=899* (accessed 17 Nov. 2008).

Wahlstrom, Timothy. *The Creation of a Student Movement to Evangelize the World.* Pasadena, CA: William Carey International University Press, 1980.

Weatherford, Willis Duke. *Negro Life in the South, Present Conditions and Needs.* New York: YMCA, 1910.

Weber, Hans Ruedi. *Asia and the Ecumenical Movement 1895–1961.* London: SCM, 1966.

————. *The Courage to Live: A Biography of Suzanne de Dietrich*. Geneva: WCC, 1995.

Weisenfeld, Judith. *African American Women and Christian Activism*. Cambridge: Harvard University Press, 1997.

Westfall, William. *The Founding Moment*. Montreal: McGill-Queen's University Press, 2002.

Wheeler, W. Reginald. *A Man Sent from God: A Biography of Robert E. Speer*. Westwood, NJ: Revell, 1956.

Whipper, Francis A. Rollin. *Life and Public Services of Martin R. Delaney*. Boston: Lee & Shephard, 1883.

Williams, Penny. "Pioneer Women Students at Cambridge." In *Lessons for Life*, edited by Felicity Hunt, 171–91. Oxford: Blackwell, 1987.

Wilson, Elizabeth. *Fifty Years of Association Work among Young Women, 1866–1916*. New York: YWCA, 1916.

Winks, Robin. *The Blacks in Canada: A History*. Montreal: McGill-Queen's University Press, 1997.

Wishard, Luther. *A New Programme of Missions*. New York: Revell, 1895.

————. *The Students' Challenge to the Churches*. New York: Revell, 1895.

Workman, E. Clark. *The Silver Bay Story, 1902–52*. Lake George, NY: Silver Bay Association, 1952.

Wright, Robert. *A World Mission: Canadian Protestantism and the Quest for a New International Order, 1918–1939*. Montreal: McGill-Queen's University Press, 1991.

Wrong, Margaret. *Ideas and Realities in Europe*. London: SCM, 1925.

Yasutake, Rumi. "Men, Women, and Temperance in Meiji Japan: Engendering WCTU Activism from a Transnational Perspective." *Japanese Journal of American Studies* 17 (2006) 91–111.

Subject and Name Index*

---

* Numbers in italics indicate figures.